GREENING EUROPE

Greening Europe

2022 European Public Investment Outlook

Edited by
Floriana Cerniglia and Francesco Saraceno

OpenBook
Publishers

https://www.openbookpublishers.com

ISBN Paperback: 9781800649057
ISBN Hardback: 9781800649064
ISBN Digital (PDF): 9781800649071
ISBN Digital ebook (epub): 9781800649088
ISBN Digital ebook (azw3): 9781800649095
ISBN XML: 9781800649101
ISBN HTML: 9781800649118
DOI: 10.11647/OBP.0328

Cover image: Photo by Dylan Leagh on Unsplash
Cover design: Jeevan Nagpal

Contents

Part II: Challenges   **85**

The *Outlook* is the result of a joint effort by several economists belonging to a wide range of academic institutions and policy institutes; they all wrote in their personal capacity.

The work was coordinated by Floriana Cerniglia and Francesco Saraceno with logistical and financial support by CRANEC—Centro di ricerche in analisi economica e sviluppo economico internazionale, Università Cattolica del Sacro Cuore—Milan; Fondazione Astrid, Rome; and OFCE-SciencesPo Paris.

The authors are affiliated to the following institutions:

- Agora Energiewende (Germany)
- Astrid (Italy)
- Bruegel (Belgium)
- Cabinet Belgian Minister of Social Affairs and Health
- CRANEC, Centro di ricerche in analisi economica e sviluppo economico Internazionale, Università Cattolica del Sacro Cuore, Milan (Italy)
- Center for European Political Studies—CEPS, Brussels (Belgium)
- European Commission, DG Energy, Brussels (Belgium)
- European Investment Bank, EIB
- Fondazione Astrid—Rome (Italy)
- German Council of Foreign Relations
- International Monetary Fund, IMF
- Istituto Regionale Programmazione Economica della Toscana—IRPET (Italy)
- Katholieke Universiteit Leuven (Belgium)
- La Sapienza University, Rome (Italy)
- Luiss School of European Political Economy, Università Luiss Guido Carli, Rome (Italy)
- Macroeconomic Policy Institute—IMK (Germany)
- Netherlands Economic Observatory, Rotterdam—NEO (Netherlands)
- Netherlands Organization for Applied Scientific Research—TNO (Netherlands)
- Observatoire français des conjonctures économiques, OFCE-SciencesPo, Paris (France)
- Solvay School of Université Libre de Bruxelles—ULB, Brussels (Belgium)
- Universidad de Cantabria (Spain)
- Universidad de Castilla-La Mancha (Spain)
- Universidad Loyola Andalucía, Seville (Spain)

Acknowledgements

As this European Public Investment Outlook goes to print, we want to express our gratitude to those who made our work possible: first and foremost, to all the chapter authors who enthusiastically provided this instalment with high-quality contributions; they also simplified our job as editors by (generally!) respecting the deadlines, responding to our queries, and addressing the referees' concerns. The result is a collective volume that has a consistent message throughout.

We also sincerely thank Alberto Quadrio Curzio, President of CRANEC, Franco Bassanini, President of Fondazione Astrid, Xavier Ragot, President of OFCE-Sciences Po for their constant support and encouragement. Their help was essential in securing financial and logistical support and, even more importantly, in putting the issue of public investment at the centre of their respective institutions' scientific projects even when it was not a fashionable theme in the public debate.

Our thanks also go to Giovanni Barbieri from CRANEC for his efficient and painstaking and patient editing of the third instalment of European Public Investment Outlook. Thanks are also due to Micaela Tavasani from CRANEC for her proofreading. Last but not least, our gratitude goes to Alessandra Tosi, of Open Book Publishers, who smoothly managed the refereeing process, and who believed in and supported our project since it began in 2020. The editorial team at Open Book Publishers once again moved swiftly and efficiently in turning a somewhat messy manuscript into a polished and published book.

Floriana Cerniglia
Francesco Saraceno

Preface

Franco Bassanini, Alberto Quadrio Curzio,

and Xavier Ragot

This *European Public Investment Outlook*, like its two precursors, is written in a time of great uncertainty and turmoil. Europe continues to grapple with the cascading after-effects of the COVID-19 pandemic, which now have been further aggravated by the war in Ukraine, the upheavals in the energy supply and price market, and the looming risk of an impending cycle of global stagflation.

European policymakers seem to have learnt the lessons of the mismanaged sovereign debt crisis and have tackled the challenge of economic recovery through the adoption of mostly unprecedented fiscal policies like the activation of the Stability and Growth Pact general escape clause, a temporary easing of the rules on state aid, the launch of a large investment plan financed with grants and loans funded through the issuance of European sovereign debt and economic stimulus packages. Now they must take a solid step forward and provide effective and sustainable responses to the challenges to Europe's security and strategic autonomy and to a potentially devastating energy crisis that has engulfed Europe. The national resilience and recovery plans must be used not only to achieve the original objectives set forth (recovery from the pandemic, social cohesion, structural reforms and investment in strategic sectors to enhance potential growth and to ensure a green and digital transition); but it must be used also—in our view—to ensure that the transition to a greener Europe and faster achievement of energy independence (or at least a lower energy dependence on supplies from politically unreliable countries) will not come at too high a cost for Europe's economy and future.

To achieve the climate goals and steer EU economies towards a more sustainable path, significant economies of scale can be exploited. The EU budget provides a crucial contribution toward fighting climate change and reaching its climate objectives. With the 2014–2020 multiannual financial framework, the EU reached its goal of spending 20% (221 billion euros) of available funds on climate-related measures. For the 2021–2027 period, the target is to allocate 30% (557 billion euros) of the available resources provided by the EU budget and Next Generation EU to climate spending.[1]

---

1   https://ec.europa.eu/info/strategy/eu-budget/performance-and-reporting/mainstreaming/climate-mainstreaming_en.

    https://doi.org/10.11647/OBP.0328.14

However, the plans and projections for reaching carbon neutrality and transitioning to a greener economy were drawn when Europe was under the illusion of having only peaceful neighbours and the energy sector was subject to what could be considered a normal historical cycle of market contractions and expansions. The recent uncontrolled flux in energy prices due to scarcity and volatility has provided a glimpse of what a transition to a low-carbon economy can become if not properly managed, and how recurrent market crunches can hinder a decarbonisation trajectory. The current energy crisis has put the axis for greening Europe security-affordability-sustainability under unprecedented strain, putting the EU economic recovery at risk; moreover, they make it harder to reach environmental targets notwithstanding the significant budget allocations.

The 2022 European Public Investment Outlook (*Greening Europe*) has as its core focus the successful ecological transition of EU countries to a greener Europe. Like the previous European Public Investment Outlooks,[2] this work brings together research from European institutions, university departments and think tanks to explore related issues from a wide range of viewpoints and to continue building a network of economists and policymakers that share an interest in the topic of public investment. The format remains the same as the 2020 and 2021 Outlooks: Part One identifies public investment trends and needs in Europe and in a select group of countries, addressing the initiatives taken to ensure a successful ecological transition. Part Two shines a spotlight on a series of specific topics related to energy and to green transition.

There are a few themes that emerge consistently through the different editions of the Outlook. The first is the need to protect public investment through an appropriate fiscal governance framework. The second is a broad definition of investment, encompassing tangible as well as intangible capital accumulation.

As a reminder to the reader, the 2020 Outlook, *A European Public Investment Outlook*, went to the very heart of public investment by focusing on intangible capital and the epochal turn away from the "fiscal austerity plus national reforms" to a "European public capital spending plus national reforms" approach, embedded in the ambitious Next Generation EU programme and the issuance of "Eurobonds" by the European Commission; the 2021 Outlook, *The Great Reset*, focused on post-pandemic recovery, the National Resilience and Recovery Plans (NRRP), and the new financing facilities.

The crucial issue discussed in the previous two European Public Investment Outlooks remains unsolved: despite a growing focus on sustainability objectives, international financial rules and the behaviour of global investors continue to penalise long-term investments in infrastructure and the ecological transition; the new European policies that support public (and private) investment (and the related instruments) are, for now, exceptional and temporary. Yet, the recurring tempestuous crises that have engulfed not only Europe but the entire world, demonstrate that some

---

2   See   https://www.openbookpublishers.com/books/10.11647/obp.0222;   https://www.openbook publishers.com/books/10.11647/obp.0280.

form of permanence should be grafted into them. The questions of if and how are still underlying in the debates on how to make the NGEU programme permanent in order to face new emergencies and ensure the creation of essential European public goods, how to develop a common EU central fiscal capacity and a truly common energy policy, how to reform the Stability and Growth Pact, how to reach and maintain climate goals, and how to support sustainable growth and European competitiveness in a scenario of global stagflation and the central banks' drifting towards less accommodating, if not restrictive, monetary policies.

Greening Europe was coordinated by Floriana Cerniglia (Cranec—Università Cattolica) and Francesco Saraceno (OFCE—Sciences Po) in an increasingly complex environment. The authors of the different chapters come from various institutional backgrounds and have collaborated admirably, enriching the work with their unique perspectives. These "diversities" have contributed valuably to the quality of this Public Investment Outlook and made the message that has emerged even more substantial.

Introduction

Floriana Cerniglia and Francesco Saraceno

Ever since the Global Financial Crisis of 2008 macroeconomic theory has been in a state of flux. The crisis challenged the central tenet of the consensus that dominated since the 1980s, namely that markets are capable of absorbing macroeconomic shocks and converge back to the natural equilibrium with little or no help from macroeconomic policy (for details see Saraceno 2017, 2022). Rediscovering the old Keynesian recipes, the meltdown of the financial sector and the collapse of private aggregate demand were met by a timely and bold policy response, with central banks providing liquidity and governments stimulus plans to sustain demand and economic activity.

The success of the pragmatic policy response to the crisis inevitably triggered soul-searching among academics and policymakers. This "rethinking macroeconomics" (Blanchard 2016) is ongoing and wide-ranging, from the reconsideration of the merits of capital controls to the reassessment of the timing and nature of structural reforms, the interaction of monetary and fiscal policy (especially at the zero lower bound), the relationship between cycle and trend, the impact of income distribution on economic performance, and more. While a new paradigm has not yet emerged from this debate, we may safely assume that the cursor between markets and governments has swung back towards the centre and that macroeconomic policy will have a more important role than in the past.

Specifically, the pre-2008 consensus had sidelined fiscal policy: within a framework of a limited role for macroeconomic policy at large, monetary policy was to be preferred because it was less subject to biases (such as appropriation by vested interests and political cycles) and implementation lags. This consensus was the backdrop for the European fiscal framework, more specifically the Stability and Growth Pact strongly limiting discretionary fiscal policy. Determining the role of government expenditures and revenues, therefore, is pivotal in the current reassessment. Experience from the past decade has shown that fiscal policy strongly affects growth and convergence: for the better when in 2008 (and again in 2020) it kept the EU economy afloat through widespread stimulus packages; and for the worse when, during the sovereign debt crisis, it turned procyclical deepening the woes of Eurozone's peripheral countries.

 https://doi.org/10.11647/OBP.0328.15

Following the 2008 crisis, the debate on fiscal policy effectiveness mostly dealt with the issue of how to use countercyclical fiscal policy to stabilise the economy during a financial crisis with features that were quite well known since the 1930s: the collapse of private sector demand that required Keynesian fiscal stimuli. This explains why the debate on the size of multipliers was particularly lively during that period (for an account, see Gechert and Rannenberg 2018).

In a second phase, attention shifted to fiscal policy for the long-term. On the one hand, it became evident that short run policies, through their impact on the depth and duration of the cycle, could have a strong impact on long term potential growth through the destruction of human and physical capital (Blanchard et al. 2015; Fatás and Summers 2018). On the other hand, public investment and industrial policy took centre stage as tools to foster potential growth (and incidentally contribute to the sustainability of public finances). Decades of subdued public capital accumulation, low levels of interest rates (IMF 2014) and complementary public and private investments (Durand et al. 2021) all called for a public investment push. The first *European Public Investment Outlook* (Cerniglia and Saraceno 2020) took stock of this new awareness, drew a gloomy picture of the state of public capital in *all* of the EU countries, and emphasised the need to adopt a broad definition of capital, comprising both tangible and intangible assets to boost human capital (such as social capital).

The emphasis of the *2020 European Public Investment Outlook* on intangible capital proved prescient when, with the COVID-19 pandemic, we entered a third phase of the debate on fiscal and industrial policy: starting from the spring of 2020, policymakers increasingly focused on public investment as a means for providing not only physical and human capital, but also global public goods such as health care and education. Meanwhile, the pandemics acted as a powerful reminder that the efforts for economic recovery needed to be framed within the broader long-term goals of ecological and digital transitions (and the not-emphasised-enough social transition). The pandemics proved that, for most of these public goods, the appropriate scale for an efficient provision and cost-effective financing, is the European one. This was the justification for the flagship programme Next Generation EU (NGEU). Since the European Union lacks a central fiscal policy, NGEU is coordinating the national recovery plans by means of strict conditionalities on the scope and timing of public investments and reforms (European Commission 2020). This was done to ensure the attainment of common goals of recovery from the pandemic, cohesion, and investment in strategic sectors to ensure a green and digital transition.

Next Generation EU is probably the most innovative instrument introduced by the EU in decades. It was therefore a somewhat obvious choice to devote the 2021 instalment of the European Public Investment Outlook (*The Great Reset*, Cerniglia et al. 2021) to issues focusing on post-pandemic recovery, NGEU, and the National Resilience and Recovery Plans. The common thread emerging from the chapters that compose *The Great Reset* is once again the gap in tangible as well as intangible public infrastructures and the potential for the NGEU programme to act as a game changer for public investment not only through the 750 billion euros that it will mobilise, but also through crowding-in private investments and the multiplicative effect on the private economy. As this manuscript goes to press (December 2022), the European Commission has disbursed the second instalment of NGEU funds and most National Recovery and Resilience Plans are broadly on track to meet their milestones and deadlines.

The long-term dimension of the debate on fiscal policy since 2020 has highlighted its role in ensuring a successful ecological transition; this is the topic of *Greening Europe*, the 2022 European Public Investment Outlook. Like the previous Outlooks, *Greening Europe* brings together research from European institutions, university departments, think tanks, and other institutions. In doing so, we not only have the objective of exploring a wide range of points of views, but also to keep building a network of economists and policymakers sharing their interest in the topic of public investment. Investment for a Green transition is tackled from a wide range of perspectives, from its financing to the value of green multipliers, the regulatory issues that arise, the need to redefine industrial policy, the investment needs in the field of energy (this specific subject has of course become central in the course of 2022 due to the war in Ukraine), the debate on the governance of the Eurozone, and more. As with the other Outlooks, two themes have emerged from the uncoordinated work of the chapters' authors:

The first is the need to protect public investment through an appropriate fiscal governance framework. As we write this introduction (November 2022), the Commission has just unveiled its proposal for a reform of the Stability and Growth Pact. Unfortunately, there is little ground for optimism. The energy crisis, recent political developments in Italy and, above all, the German government's minimalist approach to the rewriting of the rule (contrary to what seemed to be the case during the pandemics, see Saraceno 2021), have yielded a proposal that, while significantly improving on the current Stability and Growth Pact,[1] clearly does not go far enough to protect public investment. If the new rule will resemble the proposal, it will become of paramount importance to create a fiscal space for public investment at the European level. A mild reform of the Stability and Growth Pact should push those interested in effective fiscal governance to urgently table a proposal for creating central fiscal capacity for the EU (Buti and Messori 2022).

The second theme that emerges from *Greening Europe* is the challenge to ensure a constant flow of investment, appropriately coordinated at different levels of government. Multilevel governance (at the EU and national levels) is a pivotal aspect

---

1   The Commission proposal scraps controversial variables such as the structural balance (in favour of an expenditure rule) and foresees a country-specific debt reduction path, based on Debt Sustainability Analysis. These are welcome changes to a rule that was cumbersome and pernicious; but there is no explicit recognition of the importance of public investment. See https://ec.europa.eu/commission/presscorner/detail/en/ip_22_6562.

for ensuring, in the coming decades, a comprehensive yet detailed investment plan that addresses the needs that arise beyond those of the single states. Moreover, a system with fragmented competences, among levels of government, would require much stronger coordination mechanisms to: a) quickly respond to exogeneous shocks and b) implement strategic projects/missions that require coordination between different levels of governments during the various implementation phases.

Greening Europe (like the previous instalments) is divided in two parts: an overview of public investment in Europe and in a select group of countries, (France, Germany, Italy, Spain) and a spotlight on a series of specific topics related to green transition.

Part One provides an assessment of the state of public investment in Europe as a whole (Chapter 1) and then focuses on the four largest EU economies. The common thread running through these chapters is understanding Europe's Green transition by assessing the roles of energy policy, energy security and climate transition. These chapters also update, where relevant, the data presented in the two previous editions and provide a description of the impact and policy response of the respective economic recovery plans as part of NGEU to the economic crisis caused by the COVID-19 pandemic and now further exacerbated by the war in Ukraine.

Chapter 1 by K. Atanas, D. Revoltella, A. Brasili, and J. Schanz describes how the war in Ukraine poses new challenges for public investment in the EU. It has worsened the macroeconomic environment by increasing uncertainty and raising energy and other input costs. Concerns over public debt and increases in current expenditure, to contain the impact of higher energy costs, might decrease government spending on investment. That said, large EU-wide programmes will be supporting governments' investments over the coming years, in particular through the Recovery and Resilience Fund and RePowerEU. RePowerEU is designed to rapidly reduce dependence on Russian fossil fuels—a challenge that can be addressed only with coordinated policies and efforts both at the national and EU levels. While the cost may not be overwhelming, it comes on top of the large investment needs related to transitioning to a net-zero carbon economy. The solidarity within the European Union will need to be a key ingredient for successfully overcoming these challenges.

In **Chapter 2**, M. Hamdi-Cherif, P. Malliet, F. Reynes, M. Plane, F. Saraceno, and A. Tourbah argue that public investment in France has been on a downward trend since 2009, rebounding only in the wake of the COVID-19 crisis, with the objective of supporting global demand and spurring economic growth. The increase in investment, however, is less pronounced than during the global financial crisis. Orienting investment towards low-carbon capital within the framework of a long-term emission reduction goal, despite being unprecedented in history, is also insufficient, especially if its level is not maintained over the coming decades. The type of low-carbon transition strategy chosen—either relying more on technological progress or reaching a significant reduction in energy consumption (a Sobriety scenario)—will noticeably impact the composition and amount of investment needed to meet the targets.

In **Chapter 3**, K. Rietzler and A. Watt emphasise that against the backdrop of an increasingly broad consensus that Germany has substantially underinvested in public goods for an extended period, the new Traffic Light Coalition Agreement sets out ambitious spending plans that go beyond the modernisation of Germany's infrastructure and speeding up decarbonisation. At the same time, it has also committed to the debt brake and to avoiding tax hikes. Moreover, since the establishment of this new government, other fiscal challenges have arisen because of the war in Ukraine and a sharp rise in energy and food prices. By exploiting the scope of short-run flexibility (the debt brake is currently still suspended) and new off-budget measures, the government is seeking to square this circle by allowing greater investments in the face of competing demands. The national plan under the Recovery and Resilience Facility (RRF) complements national initiatives; but in Germany's case, it is of limited macroeconomic relevance. The latest developments in RRF projects are sketched out in the chapter.

In **Chapter 4**, G. Barbieri, F. Cerniglia, G. F. Gori, and P. Lattarulo provide a general overview of the Italian National Recovery and Resilience Plan (NRRP) with a focus on the investment needs to ensure an ecological transition. The NRRP contains six missions, of which Mission 2 is specifically dedicated to the ecological transition (approximately 59.5 billion euros); however further resources for the transition are also available in other Missions under climate objectives. In total, the available resources are around 71.7 billion euros. This means that out of the total funding allocated to the NRRP (191 billion euros), 37.5% is dedicated to green investment, which is slightly above the minimum threshold set by the EU. In absolute terms, because of the size of the Italian NRRP, this is by far the most significant investment out of all the EU countries. The NRRP is a huge gamble for the future of Italy due to the sheer number of resources involved, the deep structural lags that must be overcome, and the major political consensus needed on the overall objectives and/or missions.

Chapter 5 by J. Villaverde, L. Ibáñez Luzon, D. Balsalobre-Lorente, and A. Maza summarises the different public initiatives in the Spanish energy market in recent decades, always within the European Union framework. At the same time, it portrays the current turbulent situation, marked by the crisis unleashed by the COVID-19 pandemic and Russia's invasion of Ukraine. The chapter reviews the historical evolution of the energy mix in Spain, with a focus on the effect that the different energy packages approved by the EC and their implementations have had on it. The chapter concentrates on the Spanish government's policies and plans, within the guidelines set by the EU, especially Next GenerationEU and REPowerEU, in support of a green transition over the 2020–2030 period.

Part Two of the *2022 European Public Investment Outlook* focuses on a selection of themes related to the extremely ambitious and optimistic European Green Deal, which aims to provide a roadmap towards sustainable economies and ensure a just and inclusive transition. The chapters on green spending multipliers (Chapter 6) and green investment requirements (Chapter 7) focus on the positive impact of green expenditure on economic activity. The chapters on public spending needed to reach the EU's climate targets (Chapter 8) and the EU plan to reduce dependence on Russian fossil fuels (Chapter 9) provide preliminary snapshots of the fiscal implications and the energy investments required for an effective green transition. The chapter on public spending for future generations (Chapter 10) proposes an innovative expenditure aggregate to better capture the public sector's contribution to economic and social development and environmental protection, while the chapter on Green Finance Standards (Chapter 11) discusses the effectiveness of green bonds and maximising the effectiveness of climate investments and finance. The chapter on the Do No Significant Harm principle (Chapter 12) presents a case in favour of a broader approach to the principle, thereby transforming it into an effective lever for investments within a sustainable development strategy and for rapidly achieving European energy security. The last chapter, which focuses on a socially just green transition (Chapter 13), argues that achieving such an objective requires an integrated approach.

In **Chapter 6**, N. Batini, M. Di Serio, M. Fragetta, G. Melina, and A. Waldron argue that fixing the twin climate and biodiversity crises is still possible, but it requires stewarding the global economy within limits set by nature. The chapter addresses the question of whether there is "a trade-off between spending on the green economy and an economy's strength," and two key results are discussed. First, every dollar spent on green activities can generate more than a dollar's worth of economic activity, whereas non-green spending returns less than a dollar. Second, for spending categories that are comparable, like renewable versus fossil fuel energy, multipliers on green spending are about double their non-green counterparts. The findings suggest that investments in energy and land/sea use transitions may be economically superior to those offered by supporting economic activities that involve unsustainable ways of producing energy and food.

The EU countries' priorities on climate and environmental spending, as reflected in the allocations of the Recovery and Resilience funds, are assessed in **Chapter 7** by K. Lenaerts, S. Tagliapietra, and G. B. Wolff. The results suggest that the priorities differ significantly. Also, broader estimates of the required investments are provided, and these indicate that annual investments in energy and green tech must increase by 2 percentage points of GDP to reach climate neutrality by 2050, both globally and in Europe. Policies, therefore, must focus on boosting private investment and creating a viable green tech sector.

In **Chapter 8**, C. Baccianti argues that the 2020s are a crucial decade for steering the European Union towards climate neutrality and decreasing dependence on imported fossil fuels. In the period from 2021–2030, public expenditure on climate investment across the EU should increase by 1.8% of GDP (1.1% excluding investment in public transport) compared to the previous decade. The bottom-up analysis of the chapter reveals that almost three quarters of that spending will go to the construction and transport sectors. Filling such a significant public green investment gap will be challenging for EU countries with little fiscal space, especially once the Recovery and Resilience Facility comes to an end.

Chapter 9 by M. G. Tertr and B. Saveyn provides an estimate of the investment needs and additional costs of bringing the EU's dependence on fossil fuels from Russia to zero by 2027, with a specific focus on natural gas. This analysis was used to prepare the REPowerEU plan presented by the Commission on the 18th of May 2022. Decoupling the EU from Russian fossil fuel imports has already begun and will pass through various stages affecting both demand and supply. From this perspective, the analysis indicates that implementing the full potential to reach zero-dependence could require 300 billion euros cumulative from now to 2030—which is beyond the Fit for 55 proposal. By the end of 2027, this transition could correspond to approximately 210 billion euros in investment. These REPowerEU investments correspond to about 5% of the total Fit for 55 investments up to 2030 and would come in addition to them. The Commission analysis estimates that the Fit for 55 and REPowerEU measures combined could save the EU 80 billion euros annually on gas imports, 12 billion euros on oil imports, and 1.7 billion euros on coal imports.

L. Ferrari and V. Meliciani in **Chapter 10** propose a new "quality" of public spending (public spending for future generations) measure which goes beyond the traditional distinction made between public gross fixed capital formation and public current expenditure. The proposed aggregate is more in line with the objectives and policies introduced at the European level such as NextGenerationEU, which requires EU countries to spend a certain percentage of their resources on projects aimed at promoting digital and green transition, scientific research, and social cohesion. Highly indebted countries have significantly decreased the share of GDP for public spending for future generations, especially since the financial and sovereign debt crises. However, countries have not reduced their share of total public expenditure of GDP. It is suggested that national governments and the EU fiscal rules should focus more on the composition of public spending, not only public gross fixed capital formation, but also current expenditures that have long-run effects on sustainable development such as education, R&D and environmental protection.

X. Liang and Z. Gao in **Chapter 11** argue that climate change is one of the greatest challenges that humans are facing in this century. Mobilising investment and finance in addressing climate issues is key to unlocking actions on climate change across countries. The estimated investment required to achieve the climate mitigation goal established in the Paris Agreement ranges from US$1.6 trillion to US$3.8 trillion annually from 2016 to 2050, while the tracked annual flow of climate finance is US$579 billion on average. Despite significant growth in climate finance flows, the gap remains substantial. In response to the gap, an issue that must be urgently addressed is maximising the effectiveness of climate investment and finance. Developing Green Finance, such as green bonds, green funds, or green loans, has provided hope for a potential solution to bridge the climate change funding gap. Since the first green bonds were issued in 2007 by the European Investment Bank (EIB), the green financial market has grown rapidly in both scale and market coverage. Green bonds remain the dominant asset in terms of market share. In 2021, green, social, sustainability, sustainability-linked, and transition-themed debt reached US\$1 trillion with growth spearheaded by green bond issuance. This represents a twenty-fold increase from 2015, and accounts for 10% of the global debt markets.

In **Chapter 12**, C. De Vincenti argues that the concrete implementation of the Next Generation EU strategy and the recent aggravation of the energy security question have brought a crucial issue to the fore: what is really meant by the Do No Significant Harm (DNSH) principle. Up to now, EU documents have adopted an extremely restrictive interpretation of the principle that hinders essential investments for the green transition and the diversification of energy supplies. In this chapter an alternative interpretation of the DNSH principle is proposed, which could transform it into an effective lever for the required fundamental investments.

Chapter 13 by C. Alcidi, F. Corti, D. Gros, and A. Liscai builds on the issue that finding a balance between the objectives of economic growth, environmental sustainability and social fairness has been one of the key priorities of the EU agenda in the last years. While the link between economic growth and social and ecological objectives has historically received much attention, the socio-environmental nexus has received much less. Some scholars recently attempted to identify the possible functions that the welfare state could perform to accompany the green transition. Based on this recent literature, the authors identify two main functions (activating and buffering) that are not mutually exclusive. An important distinction is made in the logic under which the welfare intervention is carried out. Two different types of logic can underpin eco-social policies: compensatory or integrated. They show that an integrated approach to social and environmental policies seems to be the most suitable solution to achieve green and positive social outcomes.

Overall, the contributions in *Greening Europe* depict a mixed picture. On the one hand, the issue of ecological transition is now steadily among the top priorities of policymakers; this is all the more clear in the current energy crisis, when difficult decisions such as the reopening of coal plants to meet short-term needs are clearly seen as temporary. Luckily, most policymakers do not seem ready to sacrifice long-term sustainability goals to face short-term shocks. On the other hand, nevertheless, the contributions of this European Public Investment Outlook highlight the colossal financing needs, the regulatory hurdles, and the institutional shortcomings that will need to be tackled for a successful transition. We hope that *Greening Europe* will contribute to a debate that will remain central for years to come.

References

Blanchard, O.J. (2016) "Rethinking Macro Policy: Progress or Confusion?", in Blanchard, O.J. et al. (eds), *Progress and Confusion: The State of Macroeconomic Policy*, Boston: MIT Press, http://www.jstor.org/stable/j.ctt1c2crr6.30.

Blanchard, O.J., E. Cerutti, and L.H. Summers (2015) "Inflation and Activity: Two Explorations and their Monetary Policy Implications", *IMF Working Papers* 15/230 (November).

Buti, M. and M. Messori (2022) "Reconciling the EU's domestic and global agendas", *VoxEU* 11 April; https://cepr.org/voxeu/columns/reconciling-eus-domestic-and-global-agendas.

Cerniglia, F. and F. Saraceno (eds) (2020) *A European Public Investment Outlook*. Cambridge: Open Book Publishers, https://doi.org/10.11647/obp.0222.

Cerniglia, F., F. Saraceno, and A. Watt (eds) (2021) *The Great Reset: 2021 European Public Investment Outlook*. Cambridge: Open Book Publishers, https://doi.org/10.11647/OBP.0280.

Durand, L., R. Espinoza, W. Gbohoui, and M. Sy (2021) "Crowding In-Out of Public Investment", in Cerniglia F. and Saraceno F. (eds), *The Great Reset: 2021 European Public Investment Outlook*. Cambridge: Open Book Publishers, https://doi.org/10.11647/OBP.0280.07.

European Commission (2020) "Guidance to Member States Recovery and Resilience Plans", *Commission Staff Working Document* (September 17): SWD (2020) 205 final.

Fatás, A. and L.H. Summers (2018) "The Permanent Effects of Fiscal Consolidations", *Journal of International Economics* 112 (November): 238–50.

Gechert, S. and A. Rannenberg (2018) "Which Fiscal Multipliers Are Regime-Dependent? A Meta-Regression Analysis", *Journal of Economic Surveys* 32(4): 1160–82.

IMF (2014) "Legacies, Clouds, Uncertainties", *World Economic Outlook* (October). https://www.imf.org/en/Publications/WEO/Issues/2016/12/31/Legacies-Clouds-Uncertainties.

Saraceno, F. (2017) "Rethinking Fiscal Policy: Lessons from the European Economic and Monetary Union", *ILO Employment Working Paper* 219 (August). https://ideas.repec.org/p/ilo/ilowps/994964091602676.html.

Saraceno, F. (2021) "Europe After COVID-19: A New Role for German Leadership?", *Intereconomics* 59 (March/April): 65–69. https://ideas.repec.org/a/spr/intere/v56y2021i2d10.1007_s10272-021-0955-z.html.

Saraceno, F. (2022) "The Return of Fiscal Policy. The New EU Macroeconomic Activism and Lessons for Future", *ILO Working Paper* 59 (April): 1–31. https://www.ilo.org/global/publications/working-papers/WCMS_843672/lang--en/index.htm

PART I
OUTLOOK

1. Challenges for Public Investment in the EU

The Role of Policy, Energy Security and Climate Transition

Andrea Brasili, Atanas Kolev, Debora Revoltella, and Jochen Schanz

Introduction

The war in Ukraine poses new challenges for public investment in the EU. We describe these challenges and the expected evolution of public investment in the first section of this chapter. By raising uncertainty and increasing energy and other input costs, the war depresses the macroeconomic environment. Concerns about high levels of public debt have re-emerged for some countries and tightened financial conditions in particular in Southern Europe. New demands arise for current expenditure, such as to contain the impact of higher energy costs. This might detract governments from investment spending. Public investment itself is forced to move away from investments that increase average growth, and towards those that primarily increase resilience to future shocks, such as investments in energy security and military equipment. Despite these challenges, public investment is to continue to increase over the coming years, supported by substantial EU funds. The challenge remains the effective deployment of those funds.

A key area for public investment since the start of the war in Ukraine is improving the security of energy supply. In the second part of this chapter, we describe the challenges that member states face and the EU-level response, the REPowerEU programme. Rapidly reducing the dependence on Russian fossil fuels is a tall order that can be addressed only with co-ordinated policies and efforts both at the national and EU-wide levels. The cost may not be overwhelming, but it comes on top of large investment needs related to the transition to a net-zero carbon economy. Solidarity within the European Union is a key ingredient for successfully overcoming these challenges.

The current challenges for public investment may well persist for some time. They should not distract from the long-term goal of setting the EU economy on a greener,

https://doi.org/10.11647/OBP.0328.01

more sustainable path. On the contrary, they should be taken as an opportunity to increase the coherence of the design of a more secure, greener, and more integrated EU energy market and should accelerate its implementation.

1.1 Public Investment in the EU: Trends and Outlook

1.1.1 Public Investment Is Facing New Challenges

In the late 2010s, public investment had picked up after a range of policy reforms. The long decline in public investment that followed the global financial crisis (GFC) and the European sovereign-debt crisis had created large investment needs. The EU fiscal framework appeared to have the unintended consequence of encouraging member states to reduce public investment spending relative to other expenditures during fiscal consolidations. Reforms made the EU fiscal framework more flexible. More emphasis was placed on stepping up public investment in particular in R&D, digital technologies, and mitigating climate change. The European Fund for Strategic Investments (EFSI) provided a new source of funding.

The support for public investment became clearly visible when COVID-19 hit the global economy in 2020. EU fiscal policy responded[1] in two phases, addressing short- and longer-term needs. The activation of the general escape clause of the Maastricht Treaty and the relaxation of state aid rules enabled national authorities to provide debt-financed emergency support. In turn, the Recovery and Resilience Fund (RRF) was designed to strengthen the EU's growth potential in the longer term by steering public expenditure towards investment.

Now a new adverse shock has hit the European economy: the war in Ukraine. The war will make the implementation of existing investment plans more difficult and risks to absorb resources for current spending and for investments in resilience. Inflation and, in some EU member states, higher wage growth are driving up the costs of investments in infrastructure and energy efficiency. A sharp increase in demand and persistent supply chain disruptions delay the delivery in particular of green and digital investments. Governments throughout the EU are increasing current expenditure to reduce the pressure of higher energy prices on households' and firms' budgets. Large investments in resilience, such as in military capacity and diversification of gas supplies, would have been unnecessary had the geopolitical situation not changed. A new EU programme, RePowerEU, is providing some support (see the section on the security of energy supply and the climate transition).

---

1   See the EIB Investment Report 2021/2022 "Recovery as a Springboard for Change" and last year's 2021 European Public Investment Outlook.

1.1.2 Despite these Challenges, Public Investment Will Continue to Increase

Against this background, member states forecast that their public investment will grow just above GDP over the coming years (Figure 1.1 and Figure 1.2).[2] For Central and Eastern European countries (CEE), this means that the ratio of investment to GDP will remain just below its historical high of 5%, whilst it will remain stable at around 3.5% in Northern and Western European countries (NW), and will almost reach that level in Southern European countries (SE).

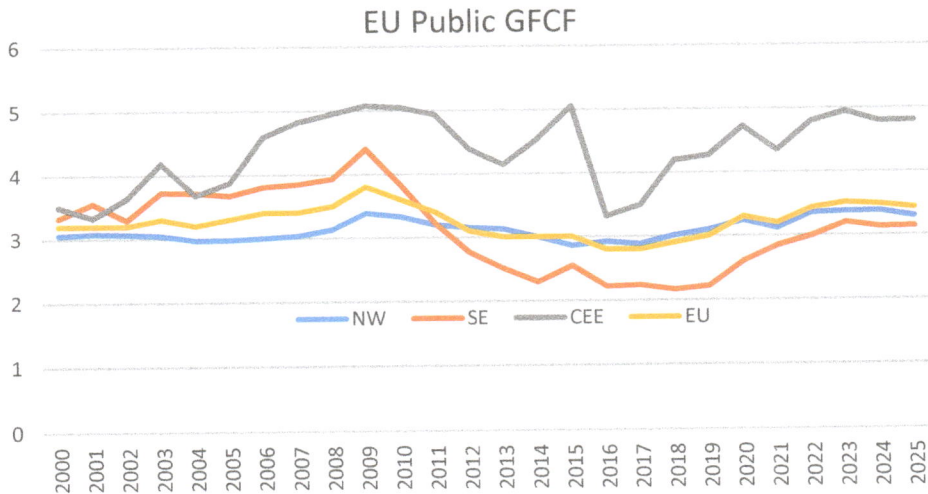

Fig. 1.1 Public investment, % GDP.
Source: AMECO online, EIB calculation based on MS Stability and Convergence plans

Public investment spending is set to rise in particular in Central and Southern Europe. Most of these countries expect to receive large allocations from EU Structural Funds and the RRF relative to their GDP. The boost to investment is likely to be large, particularly in the short run because funds from the 2014–2020 budget period need to be spent by the end of 2023, and RRF resources by the end of 2026. For some countries in Eastern Europe, grants from the RRF and the cohesion funds add up to over 25% of their 2021 GDP (Figure 1.3). Additional support will be available in the form of loans under the

---

2   See the 2022 European Semester National Reform Programmes and Stability/Convergence Programmes, https://ec.europa.eu/info/business-economy-euro/economic-and-fiscal-policy-coordination/eu-economic-governance-monitoring-prevention-correction/european-semester/european-semester-timeline/national-reform-programmes-and-stability-or-convergence-programmes/2022-european_en.

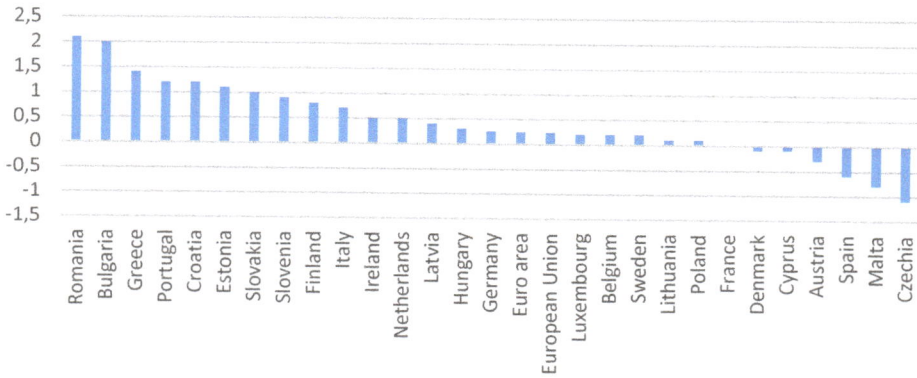

Fig. 1.2 Change in the ratio of public investment / GDP between 2025 and 2021.
Source: AMECO online, EIB calculation based on MS Stability and Convergence plans.

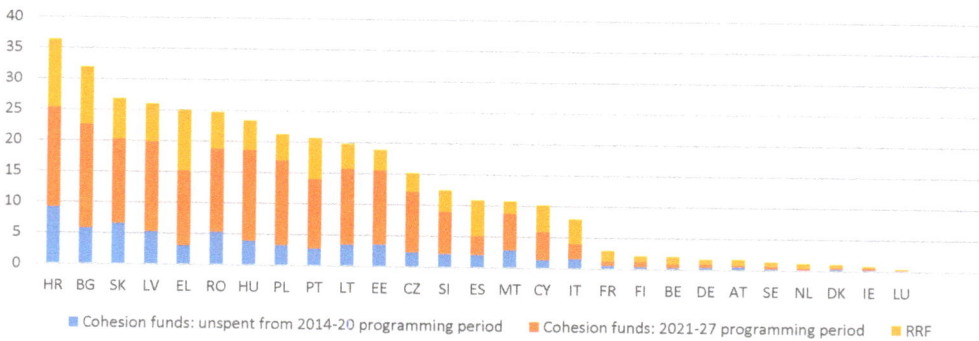

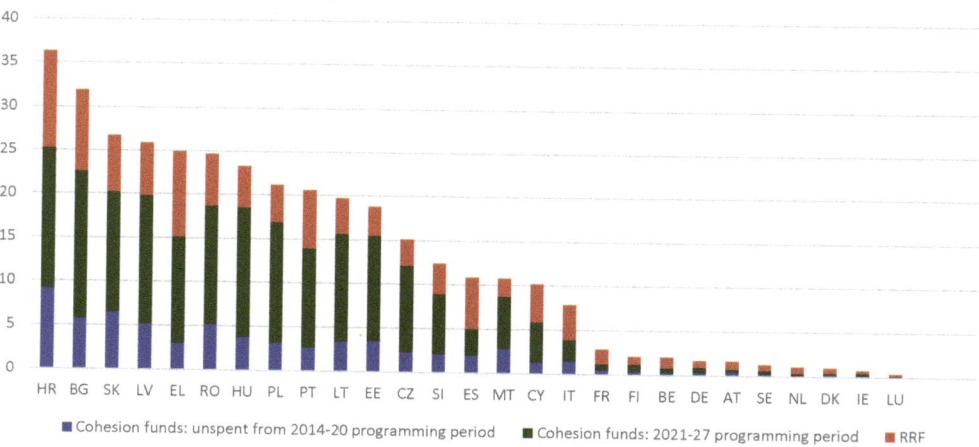

Fig. 1.3 Key EU grant programmes to support investment, % of 2021 GDP.
Source: European Commission and EIB. Data as of 31 August 2022.

RRF. In Italy, grants and loans from the RRF will cover half of the expenditures on public investment for 2024–2025 (Table 1.1).[3]

Table 1.1 General Government Investment, as a % of GDP

		2021	2022	2023	2024	2025
Bulgaria	GFCF	3.3	4.8	5.4	5.3	5.3
	of which RRF	0.0	0.5	1.3	1.1	1.0
Estonia	GFCF	5.7	7.5	7.6	7.4	6.8
	of which RRF	0.0	0.1	0.4	0.3	0.1
Greece	GFCF	3.6	5.5	4.9	5.1	5.0
	of which RRF	0.1	0.9	0.9	1.0	0.8
Italy	GFCF	2.9	3.1	3.6	3.5	3.6
	of which RRF	0.1	0.9	1.2	1.7	1.7
Portugal	GFCF	2.5	3.2	3.6	3.7	3.7
	of which RRF	0.0	0.6	0.8	0.7	0.6
Slovenia	GFCF	4.7	6.4	6.6	5.8	5.6
	of which RRF	0.2	0.3	0.6	0.8	0.7

Source: AMECO online, MS Stability and Convergence plans

Most member states have already received some of their RRF funding. At the end of August 2022, all but six member states had received 13% of their allocation as pre-funding following the European Commission's approval of their Recovery Plans (Figure 1.4). The four large Southern European states plus Slovakia, Croatia and France, had also received additional funds whose disbursement depended on the achievement of milestones and targets from their Recovery Plan. Relative to their GDP, payouts were particularly large in Greece, followed by Croatia, Spain, and Italy.

The timely implementation of the RRF still faces substantial hurdles. First, even though all RRF-funded investments have to be implemented by 2026, across the EU only 5% of the milestones (for policy reforms) and targets (for investments) in member states' Recovery Plans had been met by the end of August. Second, some projects may be delayed by persistent supply chain disruptions, such as for renewable energy, and by shortages of labour, such as for investments in construction. Finally, some investments may require additional funding because the price of the investment goods has increased since the plans were finalised. This is the case in particular for investments related to the green transition. That said, the awards of investments linked to the RRF in the EU's central procurement database appears to be picking up, suggesting that the implementation of investment projects is starting to gain speed (see Figure 1.9 below).

---

3   We included in this table those countries from East Europe and South Europe that specified in their Stability and Convergence plan the share of public investment that is financed thanks to the RRF; those not included did not provide this information.

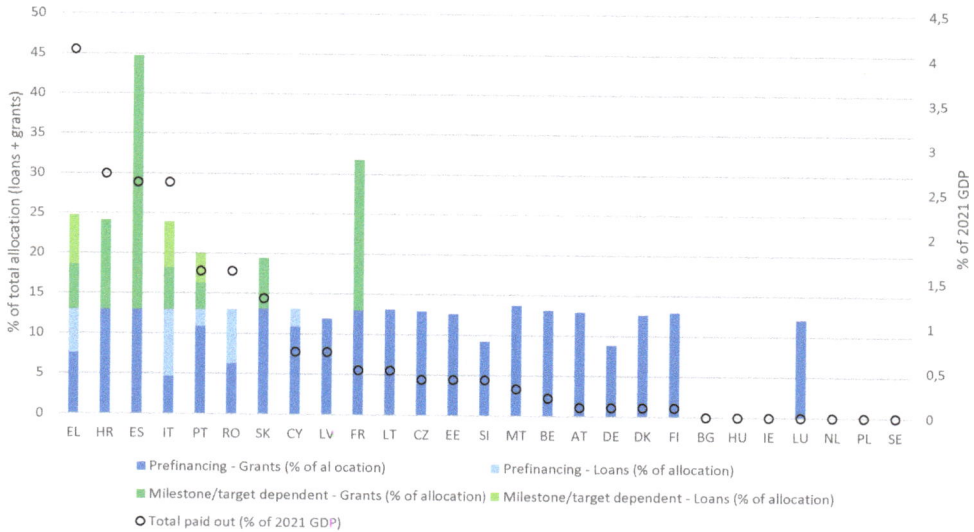

Fig. 1.4 Payouts from the Recovery and Resilience Fund.
Source: European Commission and EIB. Data as of 31 August 2022.

1.2 Local Government Investment Is Catching up

Considering the challenges of public investment, it is crucial to understand what is happening to public investment according to the different levels of government at which it is decided. Eurostat publishes data on public investment for central, state and local governments. Because state governments only exist in federal government systems (Austria, Belgium, Germany, and Spain), we collapse state and local governments into one category. Figure 1.5 shows the evolution of the share of GDP for the two categories of investment, normalising it at 100 in the year 2005. It is well known, particularly in the SE countries, that the decline in public investment in the aftermath of the twin crises of the GFC and the European sovereign-debt crisis was particularly severe at the local level.

The decline in local government investment was longer and steeper. It remains to be seen to what degree the RRF promotes an increase of capital stock of regions and territories. It may well be the case that the impacts of public investment on growth and potentially on private investment depends on the level of government that invests. Using Eurostat data for the twenty-seven EU countries, the aggregate multiplier of local investment appears to be larger and seems to have a more persistent impact on growth (Figure 1.6).[4]

---

4   The multipliers have been estimated using local projections in a panel dataset of EU countries. Details are available from the authors.

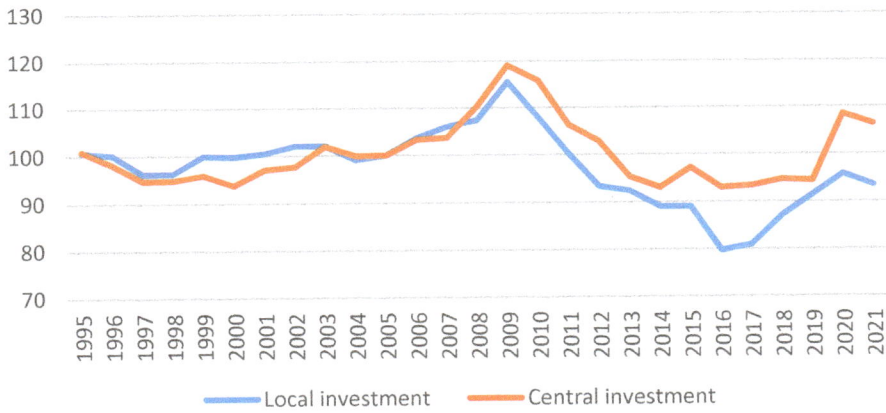

Fig. 1.5 Local and central government investment (2005=100).

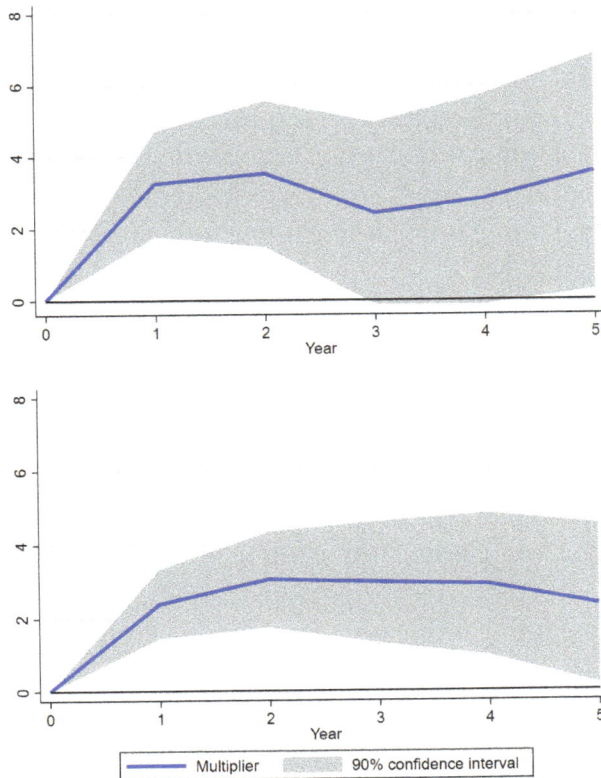

Fig. 1.6 Multiplier of GDP in response to public investment at different level of Government. *Source*: Brasili et al. (forthcoming).

While it is difficult to quantify the distribution of the RRF by government level, the contribution of the measures to social and territorial cohesion, one of the six policy pillars that the EC suggested for RRF, is a reasonable proxy. According to the EC scoreboard,[5] 10% of the measures have social and territorial cohesion as the main pillar, and for 35%, it is the secondary pillar.

The EC scoreboard also includes a detailed list of the measures that have already satisfied certain milestones or targets. Meeting these milestones and targets is a condition for further disbursements from the RRF. As per 1 September 2022, the scoreboard includes 282 measures, 88 of which are classified as investment measures, while the other 194 are reforms. Considering the whole set of measures, 12 include social and territorial cohesion as their only pillar, and 106 other measures include it as one among a range of pillars.

1.3 Public Investment on Digital Services Is on the Rise

Government procurement notices provide an interesting snapshot of the composition of investment-related public sector spending across the EU. (Because of restricted coverage and data quality issues, they should only be regarded as indicative of public spending.[6]) One noticeable development, to some degree driven by the pandemic, is that the share of procurement for digital goods and services has increased. Over the past few years, awards related to construction investments comprised around two thirds of public authorities' investment-related procurement awards (Figure 1.7). About 15% were awarded for digitalisation projects (mostly IT services) and 10% for transport equipment. Since the pandemic, however, the share of awards for digitalisation has increased substantially, driven by an expansion of IT services procurement (Figure 1.8). With its focus on digital investment, the RRF has also incentivised additional spending on digitalisation.[7] By 2022Q2, out of around €21bn contract awards linked to the RRF, €15bn were for digital goods or services (Figure 1.9).

---

5   Updated on the 25 plans endorsed by the EC as of 30/06/2022.
6   Because procurement award notices are classified according to criteria different from Eurostat national accounts, expert judgement was used to identify awards related to public investment. Procurement notices only have to be published above certain thresholds and the practice of voluntary publishing depends on the member state. Award notices suffer from errors and omissions and reporting practices differ across time and member states. Not all procurement notices for goods, services, or works partly funded by the RRF may have been designated as such by the tenderer. The information on procurement awards should therefore only be treated as indicative of trends in public investment.
7   See, for example, European Commission (2022d).

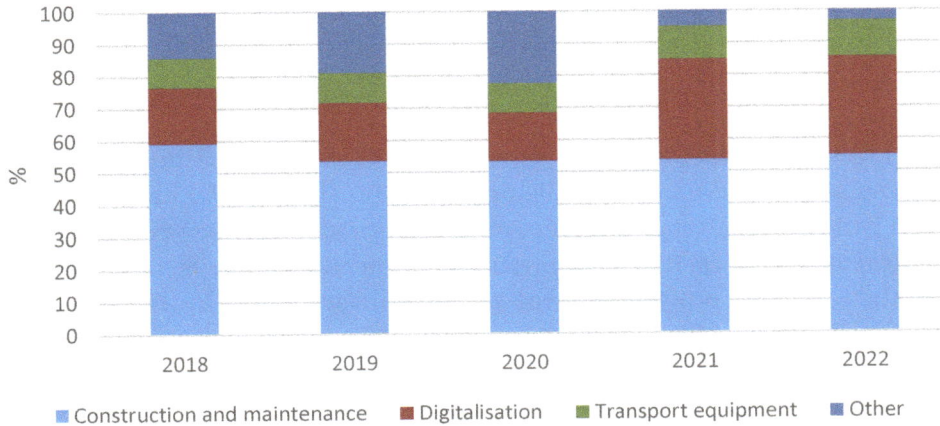

Fig. 1.7 Contract awards for public investment.
Source: EIB estimates based on TED Public Procurement Database. 2022 awards included up to the end of June.

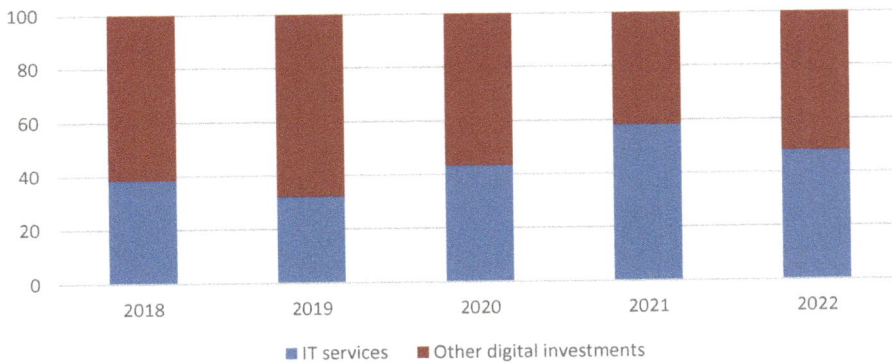

Fig. 1.8 Contract award for digital public investment.
Source: EIB estimates based on TED Public Procurement Database. 2022 awards included up to the end of June.

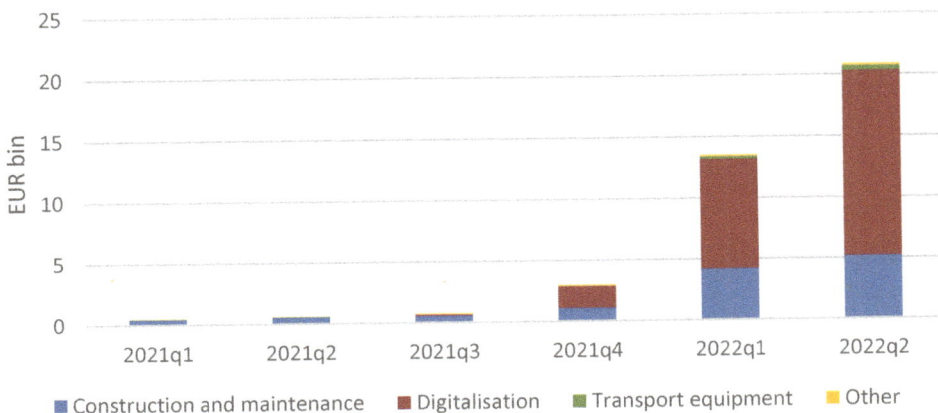

Fig. 1.9 Cumulative value of contract awards for public investment linked to the RRF.
Source: EIB estimates based on TED Public Procurement Database.

1.4 Capital Transfers Are Set to Remain above Average

Public investment does not only involve gross fixed capital formation in the public sector, but also capital transfers to the private sector. These capital transfers take the form of participation in and support of private-sector investment by the public sector. The recent increase in capital transfers reflects the intention of maintaining a larger role for public policy as a provider of investment incentives for the private sector (Figure 1.10; the spikes during 2010 and 2012 were largely caused by public-sector support for financial institutions). They also receive support through the RRF (Table 1.2).

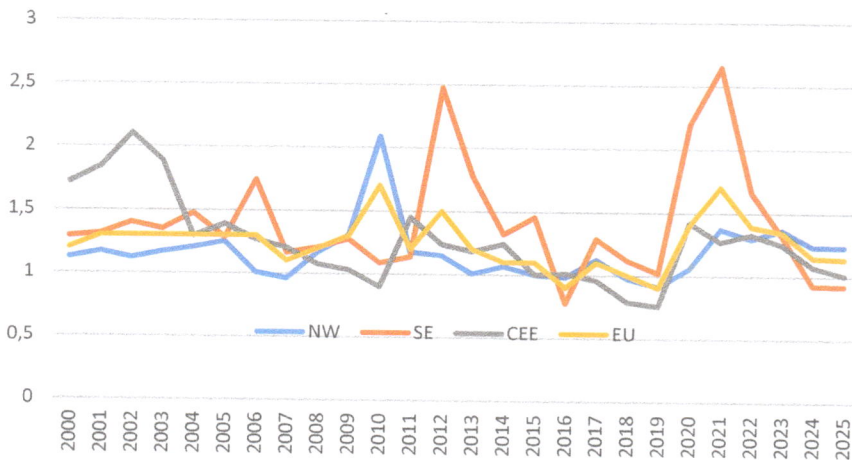

Fig. 1.10 EU capital transfers, % GDP.
Source: AMECO online, EIB calculation based on MS Stability and Convergence plans.

Table 1.2 General Government capital transfers, % GDP

		2021	2022	2023	2024	2025
Germany	Capital Transfers	1.9	1.8	1.8	1.8	1.8
	of which RRF	0.1	0.1	0.1	0.1	0.1
Estonia	Capital Transfers	5.7	7.5	7.6	7.4	6.8
	of which RRF	0.0	0.1	0.4	0.3	0.1
Spain	Capital Transfers	2.1	1.2	0.9	0.6	0.6
	of which RRF	1.0	1.2	0.9	0.1	0.0
Italy	Capital Transfers	3.1	2	1.7	1.1	1.1
	of which RRF	0.1	0.3	0.5	0.1	0
Hungary	Capital Transfers	3.7	2.8	4.1	3.6	3.3
	of which RRF	0.55	0.64	0.8	1.03	0.45
Portugal	Capital Transfers	1.3	1.7	1.2	1.1	1
	of which RRF	0	0.4	0.4	0.4	0.3

Source: AMECO online, MS Stability and Convergence plans

1.5 Security of Energy Supply and the Climate Transition

Security of energy supply is an important issue in designing energy systems and as such it has always been a concern for policymakers and researchers alike (EIB 2007). It covers a wide range of issues, from designing a resilient electricity system to securing reliable import partners. The latter is a particularly difficult aspect for European countries, as most of them rely largely on imported fossil fuels. Furthermore, proximity to Russia, one of the biggest exporters of fossil fuels, has resulted in significant dependencies on Russian fossil fuels across the EU.

The oil crisis in 1973–1974 led to the development of a toolbox for risk management of energy supply security, consisting of mostly market-based tools, used by most Western consuming countries and international oil companies. These tools served the security of energy supply, especially petroleum, well in the period 1980–2000, and relied on relatively abundant oil supplies outside the OPEC. This market structure did not allow the national interests of oil producers to dictate trade on international markets.

With the concentration of oil and gas production in countries in the Middle East, the Caspian Sea region and Russia, where investment in extraction is politically rather than economically motivated, market conditions have changed significantly. The change is reinforced by the rise of high-growth economies like China, India and Brazil, whose demand for energy is increasing seemingly exponentially. Risks for energy supply security in the EU have thus increased.

These changes oblige net importers of fossil fuel to redesign their systems and policies so as to minimise supply disruptions. Frontloading policies and targets aimed at climate change mitigation can become a very important contributor to reducing energy dependence and enhancing energy supply security. The aim of climate-change mitigation policies is to de-carbonise the economy, effectively minimising the use of fossil fuels. As we explain here the EU plan to reduce dependence on Russian energy imports, REPowerEU, effectively frontloads those efforts required in order to achieve a net zero-carbon economy.

1.6 Energy Dependence Indicators

The state of energy import dependence can be mapped with the help of several indicators (EC 2014). While the fossil-fuel import dependence of the EU is well known, there are wide differences between member states (MS). Updating the calculations in EC (2014), Figure 1.11 plots the average 2016–2020 net imports of fossil fuels, as a share of gross inland consumption by fuel, for EU MS. For nineteen MS, net imports of natural gas constitute more than 90% of gas consumption (Figure 1.11a). Thirteen of these import more than 80% of their natural gas from countries outside the European Economic Area (EEA). The number of countries with net import natural gas dependence above 90% has increased, up from seventeen, based on the average values for 2008–2012 (EC 2014).

The high and increasing import dependence on natural gas is even more worrying than that for petroleum and coal due to the structure of the gas market. More than 80% of natural gas imports in the EU are via pipelines, which grants a near monopolistic position for the exporter, at least in the short run. Quickly substituting a substantial portion of pipeline imports with liquefied natural gas (LNG) is virtually impossible due to capacity constraints, long-term contracts of LNG producers and low price elasticity of demand for many high-growth, mostly Asian economies.

a. Natural gas net imports, % of gross inland consumption of natural gas

b. Total petroleum products net imports, % of gross inland consumption of total petroleum products

c. Solid fuels net imports, % of gross inland consumption of solid fuels

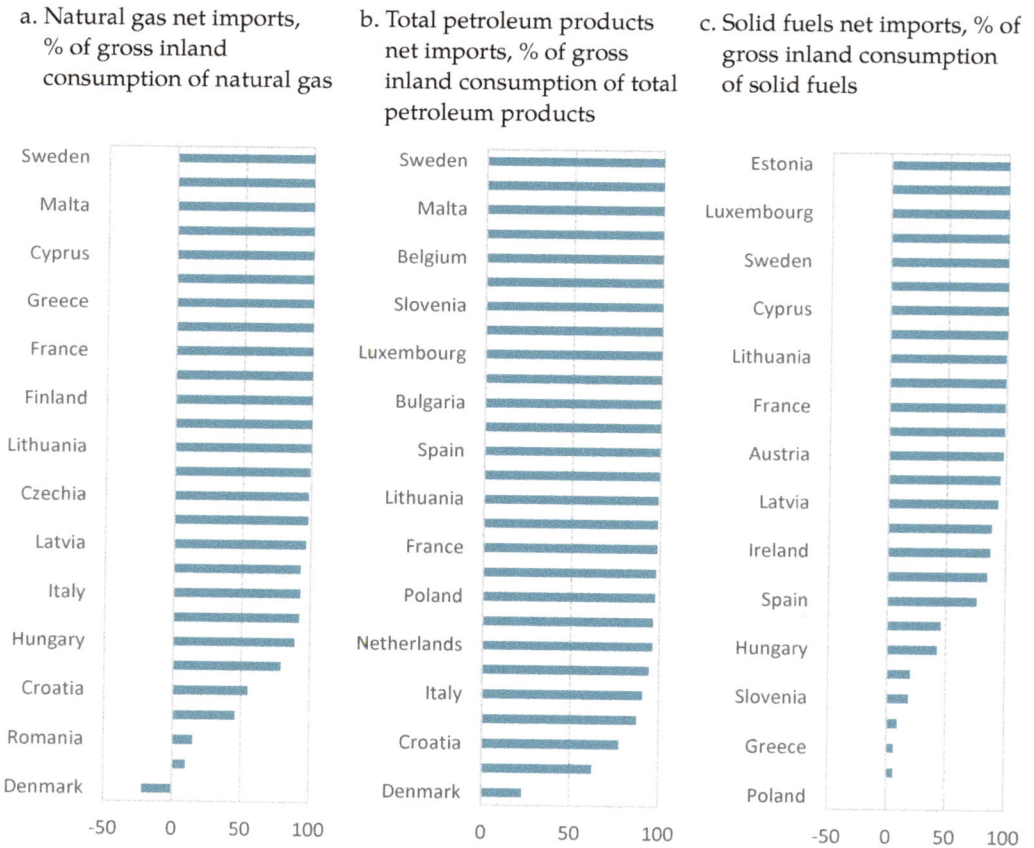

Fig. 1.11 Fossil fuel import dependence in the EU, average 2016–2020.
Source: Eurostat and EIB staff calculations.

Producers of petroleum and solid fuels are more diverse and more geographically dispersed, and these fuels are more easily transported across large distances than gas. These features provide higher flexibility to switch among fuel suppliers. This flexibility notwithstanding, high import dependence and concentration of oil and coal suppliers is a fact for many EU countries. The net import dependence for petroleum products is above 90% in 24 MS. Eight of them import more than 80% of their total petroleum products from countries outside the EEA. The Herfindahl-Hirschman Index (HHI), a measure of market concentration, shows that imports of petroleum products are more diversified than those of gas and solid fuels.[8] Moreover, twelve MS have diversified their sources of oil imports over the past ten years. That said, eight MS have an HHI value above 0.5. Regarding solid fuels, fifteen EU countries depend on imports for more than 90% of their solid fuel consumption and only one of them imports less than 80% from countries outside of the EEA. The HHI values show little diversification in many EU countries—twelve are above 0.5. Furthermore, thirteen countries have increased their HHI over the past ten years.

Fossil-fuel import dependence and the concentration of importers' market shares are more worrying the higher the share of a given fuel in the energy mix of a country. Nearly half of EU MS have very high concentration indices of gas imports (Figure 1.12a), but those with the highest HHI values use less natural gas relative to other fuels. Over the past ten years, many of those countries that are most dependent have worked to diversify the sources of their gas imports. For petroleum products, there is much lower concentration of import sources (Figure 1.12b). Regarding solid fuels, their share of the energy mix has been declining over the few past years and is below 20% for the majority of EU countries.

Imports of solid fossil fuels are also very concentrated among a few importers across EU countries (Figure 1.12c), with twelve countries having an HHI above 0.5. While the use of solid fossil fuels is declining in the EU and is projected to decline even faster in the next decade, there are still countries that use a lot of coal and lignite in their energy mixes. From a pure security of supply perspective, solid fossil fuels are less problematic than coal and gas, as the number of exporting countries is much larger and transportation and storage are fairly easy.

An important tool for smoothing short-term fluctuations in imports is the maintenance of fuel stocks. The importance of this approach grows with the level of a given country's import dependence. Oil storage in the EU is governed by an EU law that mandates the obligation to maintain a minimum reserve of ninety days of average daily net imports of oil and petroleum products, or sixty-one days of daily average consumption, whichever of these two is greater (Council Directive 2009/119/EC). Such storage provides a buffer in the case of short-term supply disruptions (Figure 1.13b). Natural gas storage is much more heterogeneous. Not all countries have the capacity to store natural gas and, for some countries, existing capacity may be low relative to consumption (Figure 1.13a). Even fewer countries have the necessary infrastructure

---

8   Herfindahl-Hirschman index (HHI) of market concentration is calculated by squaring the market share of each exporting country in a country's imports and then summing the resulting numbers. It takes values between 0 and 1. It is difficult to determine a threshold value above which concentration is high. US competition authorities, for instance, consider markets with HHI above 0.25 as highly concentrated.

a. Natural gas

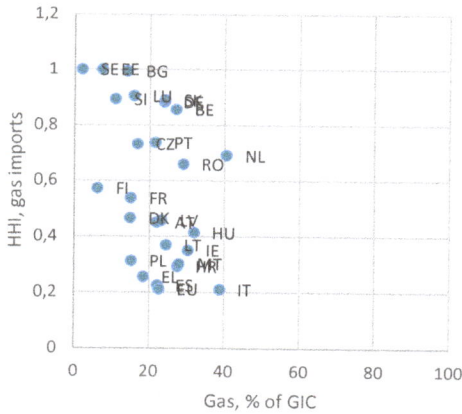

b. Total petroleum products

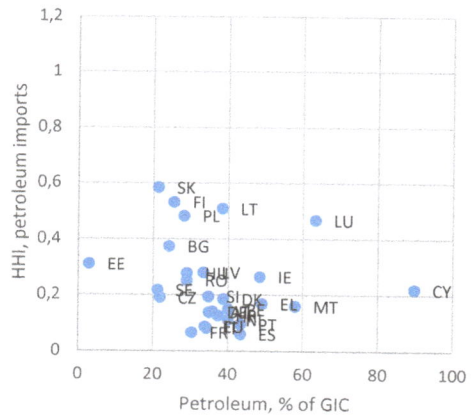

c. Solid fuels

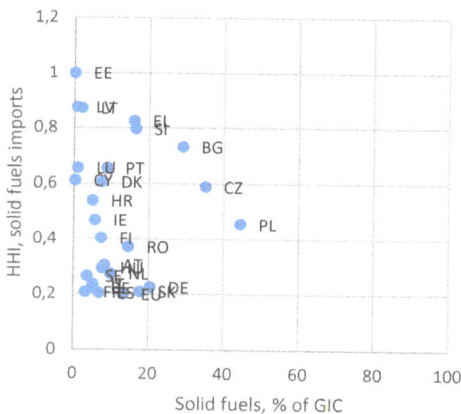

Fig. 1.12 Share of fossil fuels in gross inland consumption (GIC) and concentration index (HHI) for the imports by type of fuel.
Source: Eurostat and EIB staff calculations.

and geographic position to import LNG. This asymmetry in storage capacity and in the capacity to import LNG poses additional challenges to the security of gas supply within the EU, especially in the short term. In the medium term, the security of energy supply in the various EU countries would benefit from better connections between countries, new storage capacity, and clear fuel sharing agreements.

The high import dependence of EU countries makes them more vulnerable to the volatility in energy markets caused by the war in Ukraine. Threats of disruptions and fuel shortages are looming large. An embargo on Russian fossil fuels poses substantial difficulties for many European countries, because Russia is also a large supplier of

a. Natural gas storage and import dependence.

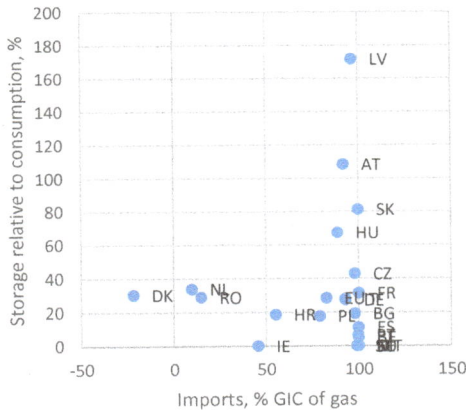

b. Petroleum products emergency stocks and import dependence.

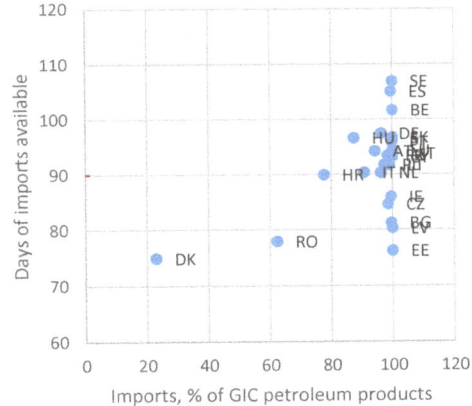

Fig. 1.13 Oil and gas storage in the EU.
Source: Eurostat and EIB staff calculations.

oil and coal for the EU. In 2020, Russian imports to the EU account for about 26% of crude oil imports and 49% of hard coal imports. The EU has already imposed partial bans on coal and oil imports from Russia, which have increased oil and coal prices. These increases have reinforced an upward trend in energy prices that appeared as early as during the second half of 2021. This was due to a confluence of several forces. First, the EU economy rebounded strongly following the easing of restrictions related to COVID-19. In addition, European weather conditions were not very favourable for renewable electricity generation, especially for wind generation. Finally, Russia was reluctant to supply additional quantities of gas on spot markets and deliberately drew down gas stocks from European gas storage facilities owned by Gazprom (IEA, 2021; EC, 2022c). Energy price increases have fuelled inflation around the world, reducing real incomes. The macroeconomic consequences are felt in the EU and elsewhere, as demand weakens and corporations face increasing cost pressures.

High energy prices and potential shortages of natural gas are having signficant negative effects on the European economy by reducing real disposable income, and consequently aggregate demand, and by increasing uncertainty. Weak aggregate demand and uncertainty, in turn, negatively affect investment. As a result, the likelihood of a recession in many EU countries starting in 2022 has increased substantially.

1.7 Improving Security of Energy Supply in the EU: REPowerEU

While diversifying oil and coal imports appears feasible, despite higher prices, diversification of gas imports remains a major challenge. According to Eurostat, in

2020, gas imports from Russia to the EU amounted to around 183 billion cubic metres (bcm), which constituted some 35% of EU total gas imports. Some 169 bcm (92%) came via pipelines and the rest was LNG. The European Commission estimates that it is possible to substitute around two thirds of Russian imports by the end of 2022 and, after implementing the REPowerEU package, to fully substitute Russian gas imports by the end of 2030 (EC, 2022b). With European gas infrastructure oriented towards gas imports via pipelines from Russia and relatively small LNG capacity, it becomes very difficult to diversify gas suppliers. Thus, diversification will ensure the substitution of about a third of Russian gas imports by the end of 2022. The remaining one third should be substituted with improved energy efficiency and reduced demand for energy.

After 2022, the last third of Russian imports could be gradually replaced by a number of different energy sources and savings. About 60 bcm can be replaced by diversification of imports, notably LNG (Figure 1.14). The use of green hydrogen and biogas could replace another 73 bcm. The remaining Russian gas imports could be substituted by stepping up energy efficiency and deployment of renewable energy sources, as well as further electrification of industrial processes.

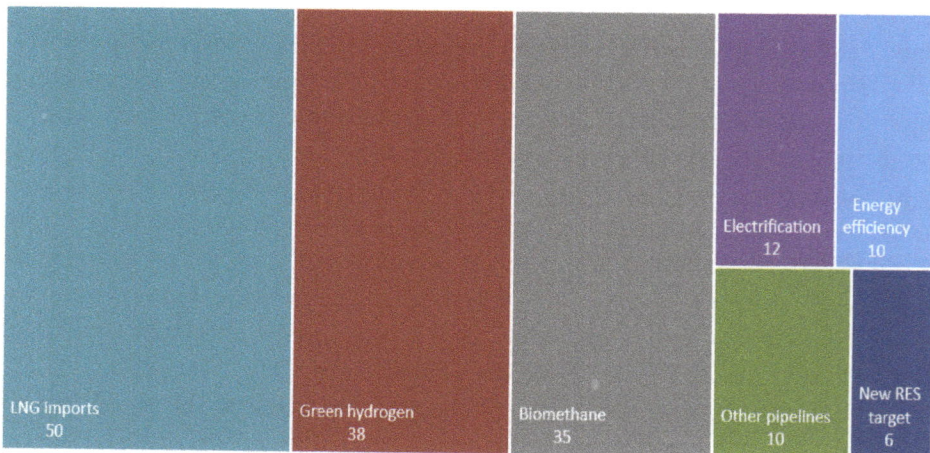

Fig. 1.14 Replacing natural gas imports from Russia by 2030, billion cubic metres.
Source: European Commission. The target for Renewable energy sources (RES) is expected to increase from 40% to 45% by 2030 (new RES target in the figure).

The REPowerEU plan is ambitious and comes on top of the EC Fit for 55 policy package, which aims to reduce greenhouse gas (GHG) emissions in the EU by 55% relative to 1990 by 2030. The measures of REPowerEU can be classified broadly in three main categories: energy savings, diversifications of fossil fuels suppliers and acceleration of the transition to renewable energy sources. Some of these measures involve the implementation of large and complex investment projects. Others are easier to implement. In the short term, by the end of 2022, the focus will be on the latter.

One such measure is the diversification of gas imports away from Russia. This could be achieved mostly through increased LNG imports, as well as pipeline imports from Azerbaijan and Algeria. This diversification also comes with a requirement to fill gas storage capacity to at least 80% by the beginning of the winter 2022–2023. Common purchases of gas via the EU energy platform will help achieve better deals. Energy saving measures, such as nudging citizens and businesses to reduce energy consumption, where possible, are another short-term measure with a potentially significant effect. Ramping up the production of biogas is a further route to achieving this measure.

In the medium to long term, measures will focus on investment in renewable generation capacity and transmission infrastructure, both for electricity and natural gas, with the requirement that gas infrastructure shall be used later for transport of hydrogen and other renewable gases. A concrete step towards the promotion of renewable projects is the proposed increase of the target for renewable electricity generation from 40% to 45% by 2030. Increasing the target for energy efficiency from 9% to 13%, another proposal in REPowerEU, will help to reduce energy demand in the medium term. Measures to decarbonise industry using more hydrogen and biogases are also envisaged.

The European Commission estimates that these measures will cost about €300bn by 2030, of which some €210bn should be spent by 2027. Compared to investment needs for the implementation of the Fit for 55 policy package, this amount is not so large, but it is nevertheless in addition to this ambitious policy initiative. Financing will come from various sources, like additional grants and unused loans from the Recovery and Resilience Facility, from transfers of up to 12.5% from Cohesion Funds and the European Agricultural Fund for Rural Development, and from selling GHG emission permits from the market stability reserve.

There are significant bottlenecks in the implementation of REPowerEU and these are addressed via a number of measures. Planned rapid deployment of solar capacity should be supported by initiatives like the mandatory installation of rooftop photovoltaics for all new commercial and public buildings by 2025 and for new residential buildings from 2029. Furthermore, an initiative to identify and promote "go-to areas" for renewable energy infrastructure, with fast-tracked permitting, short planning times, and without foregoing environmental due diligence, should help speed up the deployment of renewable generation capacity.

The significant scale-up of new renewable generation capacity requires the availability of skilled workers to install and maintain it. Similarly, more skilled workers are needed to install and maintain other technologies available to consumers and industries, like heat pumps or hydrogen installations. The EC plans to address this problem with retraining and reskilling programmes such as Pact for Skills, ERASMUS+ and the Joint Undertaking on Clean Hydrogen.

1.8 Conclusion

The need for investment remains huge: In addition to the resources needed for REPowerEU, the EC assessed that the (existing) investment needs amount to €650 billion per year up to 2030 for the twin transition, of which €520 billion accounts for the green transition alone. This amounts to 20% of EU GFCF in 2021, or 4.5% of GDP in 2021. But the question of whether public investment will increase sufficiently to meet these investment needs has become less certain since the war in Ukraine began. In addition, public investment might focus more on increasing the economy's resilience to shocks. Certain investments in resilience, such as in military resilience, have little or no impact on average growth.

Member states predict that their public investment expenditures will rise over the coming years. The EU will provide substantial support in particular for Eastern and Southern European countries. The challenge is now to effectively deploy those funds. The fact that only 3% of the targets and milestones of the RRF have been met so far, when all investments need to be implemented by the end of 2026, illustrates the difficulties that member states face in implementing the projects. Financial conditions have become constrained, particularly for Southern European countries, and may reduce their ability to fund investment spending domestically.

Since the start of the Ukraine war, investments in energy security have become a new priority. Clearly, REPowerEU is well co-ordinated with policy actions related to the EU 2050 target of a net-zero carbon economy and the intermediate target of a 55% reduction of GHG by 2030. It stresses the role of EU leadership and co-ordination, but also emphasises the important role of national governments. Political economy constraints, however, may undermine the ambitious plan. Until now, the responses of national governments to skyrocketing energy prices, partly caused by the war in Ukraine, have been mixed, and have not always aligned with the green transition, or in some cases have even outright postponed it. The increasing share of coal electricity generation, as a reaction to high natural gas prices is one such development. The implementation of policies, providing general subsidies for fossil fuel consumption in many countries, is another. While these are inefficient because part of the subsidy ends up with the sellers, they are also detrimental to the goal of reducing the use of fossil fuels.[9]

At the macroeconomic level, the focus of public policy needs to remain on stimulating investment in the private sector. This support does not necessarily have to involve subsidies. Turning the proposals of the Fit for 55 policy package into legislation will go a long way in incentivising private investment. An important element of generating investment will be the continued implementation of reforms that lower the barriers for private-sector investment. Some of the necessary policy reforms also feature in member

---

9   Pisani-Ferry and Blanchard (2022) argue that targeted transfers to lower-income citizens are a superior policy option.

states' plans for implementing the Recovery and Resilience Fund. Aside from regulatory reforms, streamlining administrative processes is one pathway that member states have already embarked on in order to accelerate the green and digital transitions.

References

Brasili, A., G. Musto and A. Tueske (forthcoming) "Complementarities between Public and Private Investment in European Regions", presented at the workshop: *Scarring, hysteresis, and investment in Europe* in Bruges Nov. 23–24.

Cerniglia, F., F. Saraceno, and A. Watt (2021) *A European Public Investment Outlook*, Cambridge: Open Book Publishers, https://doi.org/10.11647/obp.0222.

EC. (2014) "Member States' Energy Dependence: An Indicator-Based Assessment", *European Economy Occasional Papers 196*, European Commission: Brussels, https://ec.europa.eu/economy_finance/publications/occasional_paper/2014/pdf/ocp196_en.pdf.

EIB (2007) "An Efficient, Sustainable and Secure Supply of Energy for Europe", *EIB Papers* 12, https://www.eib.org/en/publications/eibpapers-2007-v12-n02.

EIB (2022) "Recovery as a Springboard for Change", *EIB Investment Report 2021/2022*, European Investment Bank: Luxembourg, https://www.eib.org/en/publications/investment-report-2021.

EC (2022a) *Fiscal Policy Guidance for 2023*, European Commission: Brussels, https://ec.europa.eu/info/sites/default/files/economy-finance/com_2022_85_1_en_act_en.pdf.

EC (2022b) *RePower EU Plan*, Communication from the Commission to the European Parliament, the European Council, the Council, the European Economic and Social Committee and the Committee of the Regions, European Commission: Brussels, https://eur-lex.europa.eu/resource.html?uri=cellar:fc930f14-d7ae-11ec-a95f-01aa75ed71a1.0001.02/DOC_1&format=PDF.

EC (2022c) *Quarterly Report on European Gas Markets*, 14 (3). European Commission: Brussels, https://energy.ec.europa.eu/system/files/2022-01/Quarterly%20report%20on%20European%20gas%20markets%20Q3_2021_FINAL.pdf.

EC (2022d) *Digital Economy and Society Index (DESI) 2022: Thematic Chapters*." European Commission: Brussels.

EFB (European Fiscal Board) (2019) *Assessment of EU Fiscal Rules with a Focus on the Six and Two-pack Legislation*. European Commission: Brussels, https://ec.europa.eu/info/sites/default/files/2019-09-10-assessment-of-eu-fiscal-rules_en.pdf.

IEA (2021) *What is behind Soaring Energy Prices and What Happens Next?*, International Energy Agency: Paris, https://www.iea.org/commentaries/what-is-behind-soaring-energy-prices-and-what-happens-next.

Pisani-Ferry, J. (2019) "When Facts Change, Change the Pact", *Project Syndicate*, April 29, https://www.project-syndicate.org/commentary/europe-stability-pact-reform-investment-by-jean-pisani-ferry-2019-04?barrier=accesspaylog.

Pisani-Ferry, J. And O. Blanchard (2022). "Fiscal Support and Monetary Vigilance: Economic Policy Implications of the Russia-Ukraine War for the European Union", *Peterson Institute for International Economics Policy Brief* 22–05, https://www.piie.com/publications/policy-briefs/fiscal-support-and-monetary-vigilance-economic-policy-implications.

2. Public Investment and Low-carbon Transition in France

Not Enough of a Good Thing?

Meriem Hamdi-Cherif, Paul Malliet, Mathieu Plane, Frederic Reynes,
Francesco Saraceno, and Alexandre Tourbah

Introduction

Infrastructure policies are an essential lever in efforts to reduce greenhouse gas emissions and adapt territories to the consequences of global warming. These policies cover many fields that structure our lifestyles, such as mobility, electricity production and transport, telecommunications, and water networks. They significantly influence the patterns of energy production and consumption in the territories, as well as their degree of resilience to natural hazards. Thus, given the need for environmental transition in France, significant investment will have to be made in the coming years to transform, renovate, and maintain infrastructures throughout the country. In view of the amounts involved, these investments imply major socio-economic changes on a national scale, which it seems essential to anticipate in order to inform political decisions regarding infrastructure.

2.1 Public Investment before the Pandemic: On a Downwards Trend since 2010

What is referred to as public capital covers a wide variety of assets, such as land, residential buildings, ports, dams, and roads, but also intellectual property rights. It is necessary to break down the "wealth of the state" into these different components to understand its dynamics, considering that price (most notably land price) and volume effects may play a significant role in explaining the evolution of the different components and of aggregate figures.

 https://doi.org/10.11647/OBP.0328.02

We use public data from the INSEE national accounts; our analysis covers the period 1978–2021 for the decomposition of net wealth and investment. INSEE reports the consolidated level (general government) and its components, distinguishing between the central government, local governments, social security administrations, and other government agencies.

Public investment in France has seen contrasting trends in recent decades. While it was rather dynamic until the late 2000s, at the turn of 2010, the fiscal stance changed, and a substantial part of the fiscal adjustment during the sovereign debt crisis was achieved by reducing capital expenditure. Indeed, the reduction of public investment has contributed to almost a third of fiscal consolidation even though investment only represented 6% of public expenditure. The share of public investment in GDP, which had largely been above 4% since the 1960s, fell below that level in 2011 and, during the period 2015–2018, reached its lowest level since 1952.

In 2021, the consolidated public sector had a positive net wealth despite the negative impact of the COVID-19 crisis (Table 2.1). Total assets held represented 169 % of GDP, of which 102 % was for non-financial assets. Financial liabilities totalled 154% of GDP. The net worth in 2021 was, therefore, 15 % of GDP, around 5,500 euros per capita.

Table 2.1 Decomposition of General Government Net Wealth

	As a % of GDP			In euros per head
	1978	2007	2021	2021
Non-financial assets	60.8	90.4	101.9	37 570
Financial assets	27.6	52.6	67.2	24 780
Financial liabilities	33.7	84.9	154.1	56 820
Net worth	**54.7**	**58.1**	**15.0**	**5 530**

Source of data: INSEE and authors' calculations.

While positive, the consolidated net wealth is close to its lowest level since 1978. Indeed, after reaching a record level in 2007 (58% of GDP), it has lost more than forty points of GDP in the space of fourteen years. The reasons for this sharp drop are to be found on the net financial liabilities (debt) side, which increased substantially while non-financial assets increased slightly (Figure 2.2).

This net worth is unevenly distributed among different levels of government. Indeed, it is very positive for local administrations (70% of GDP in 2021), very negative for the state (-73 % of GDP in 2021), and slightly positive for social security administrations and other government agencies (8% and 10% respectively). Broadly speaking, the central government—which runs recurrent deficits —has accumulated public debt; low-debt local governments hold non-financial assets, be they land, buildings, or civil engineering works. With the economic and financial crisis from 2008 on, the net worth of the central government deteriorated considerably as public deficits and debt

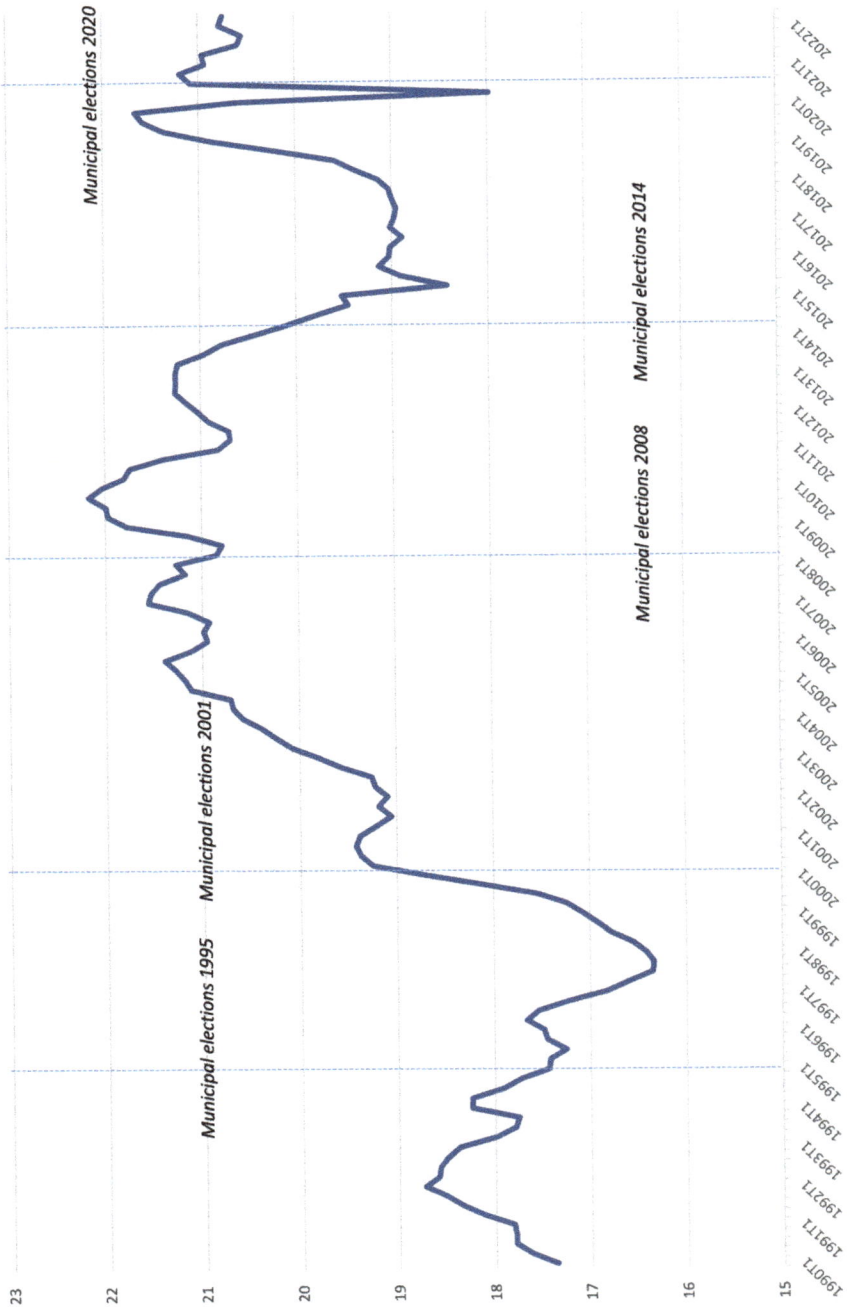

Fig. 2.1 General government investment Constant prices, in billions of euros.
Sources: Insee.

increased. On the other hand, the net worth of local governments remained high and relatively stable over the same period due to a stable value of non-financial assets and their debt.

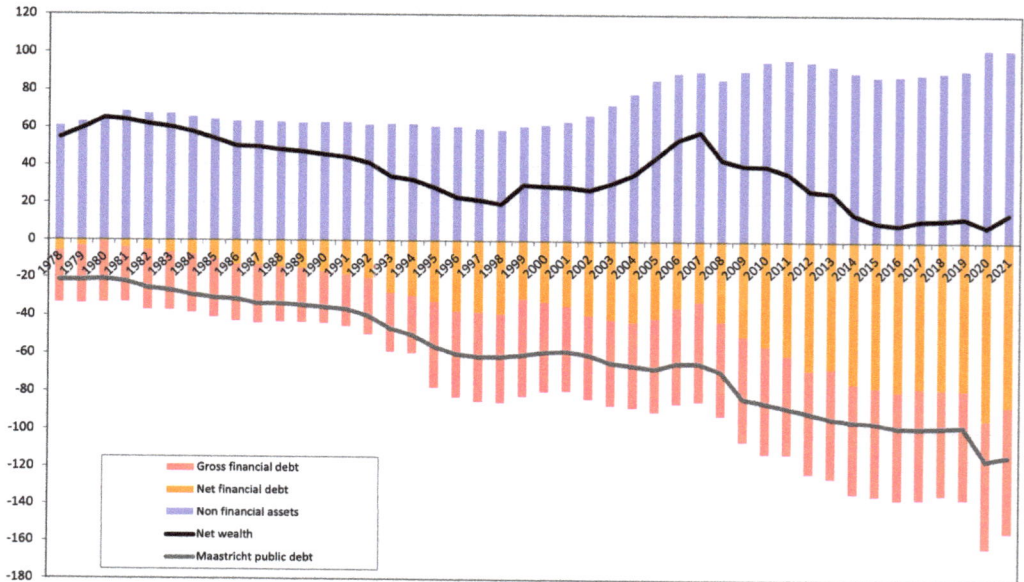

Fig. 2.2 Evolution of General Government Net Wealth as a Percentage of GDP.
Source of data: Insee. Figure created by the authors.

The analysis of gross investment needs to be complemented by the net flow of fixed assets (net investment) to assess the dynamics of the capital stock (abstracting from the effects of revaluation of the existing stock). Thus, if gross investment is greater (lower) than the depreciation of capital (consumption of fixed capital, CFC, in national accounts nomenclature), then net investment increases (decreases), and the stock of capital increases (decreases). Unlike fixed assets, non-produced NFAs (land) and inventories may experience changes in value but are not subject to the consumption of fixed capital. CFC only applies to fixed assets.

Over the period from the late 1970s to the first half of the 1990s, general government net investment was strong, averaging more than 1% of GDP per year (Figure 2.3). It even experienced a strong boom over the period 1987–1992, averaging above 1.4% of GDP per year. From 1993 to 1998, general government net investment declined sharply, reaching 0.5% of GDP in 1998, which amounted to a decrease of 1% of GDP in the space of six years. As in other European countries, this is mostly due to the effort to meet the Maastricht criteria in the run-up to the adoption of the euro: the cyclically adjusted deficit for France decreased from 4.6% of GDP in 1993 to 1.8% in 1998. Past this phase, net investment recovered, then fluctuated between 0.7% and 0.9% of GDP

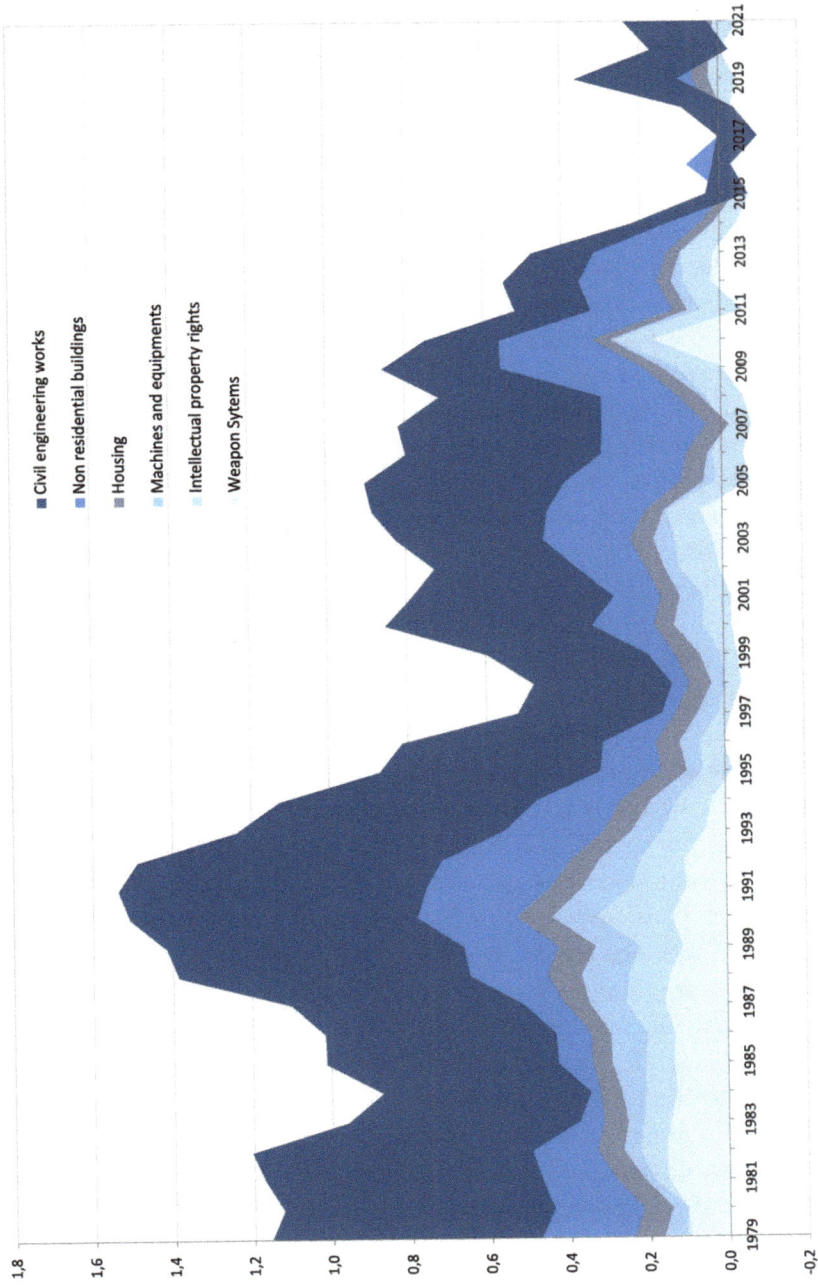

Fig. 2.3 Net General Government Investment by Component as a % of GDP.
Source of data: Insee. Figure created by the authors.

over the 2000–2010 period, without ever returning to the level observed during the 1980s and the first half of the 1990s. But it is mainly since 2011, following the Global Financial Crisis, that net investment has experienced a break. Then, it has been at its lowest level since the late 1970s, when wealth accounts were introduced.

Thus, during the period 2014–2018, France spent about 0.7 percentage points (pp) of GDP (about 17 billion euros per year in constant 2021 euros) less on net investment than it did during the period 2000–2010, and 1.4 pp (approximately 35 billion euros per year in constant 2021 euros) less than during the period 1990–1992.

The picture that emerges from the analysis of stocks and flows is rather consistent and gives two main messages: the first is that public investment and the stock of capital have been largely affected by the macroeconomic cycle. In the two significant phases of fiscal consolidation—the run-up to adopting the euro in the 1990s and the aftermath of the sovereign debt crisis—investment was strongly reduced. Especially in the latter case, net investment turned negative to zero for all levels of government, thus reducing the stock of capital that, before the pandemic, had dropped to an all-time low. The second message that emerges, in particular from the analysis of stocks, is that despite these trends in investment, the capital stock in France is still significant (and larger than in other countries). One might ask then if the effort of consolidation, and the disproportionate burden that it has laid on public investment, at least led to more sustainable public finances.

If we compare the evolution over the last twenty years of non-financial assets' net flows in relation to the primary net financial flow (financial assets—financial liabilities—interest expenses), which we consider here as a proxy of the net worth, two sub-periods clearly emerge. The first, which runs from 1996 to 2008, can be seen as a period in which the additional public net financial debt (excluding interest expense) was more than offset by the net accumulation of non-financial assets, leading to a positive net value in this period, which means that the general government stock of wealth increased in value over this period, even abstracting from price effects. The second period, which runs from 2009 to 2021, displays a new pattern in which the net debt increase is no longer offset by an increase in public non-financial capital, generating a sharp deterioration in government net worth. The economic and financial crisis has led to a sharp increase in public debt. The fiscal consolidation began to be implemented in 2011: while, on the one hand, it has partly reduced new financial commitments, on the other hand, it has been more than offset by a reduction in the net accumulation of non-financial assets. This is yet further proof that the burden of fiscal consolidation was disproportionately laid on the shoulders of public investment. The sharp reduction in net worth, therefore, casts doubt on the effectiveness of fiscal consolidation in strengthening the public finances outlook for France.

2.2 Public Investment during the Pandemic

A recovery in public investment began in the two years before the COVID-19 crisis, with an increase of nearly 14% between the end of 2017 and the end of 2019. This shift was linked to the electoral cycle of municipal elections and the government's desire to preserve investment within the framework of the targeted budget contract with local communities. While a partial reversal in public investment was to be expected after the municipal elections, the drop observed in the first half of 2020 is out of proportion with that observed in previous electoral cycles (Figure 2.1).

Indeed, the COVID-19 crisis and the lockdown led to a drop of 11% in public investment during the first half of 2020 compared to the last half of 2019 (with a fall of 16% during the second quarter of 2020). By comparison, the three strongest half-yearly decreases observed for the previous seventy years were between 5% and 6%. The fall in public investment during the first half of 2020 was, therefore, twice as strong as the most severe reversals since 1950.

However, from the third quarter of 2020, public investment returned close to the pre-COVID-19 level and was, at the end of the year 2020, just 2 % under its level at the end of 2019, despite the second lockdown in November and December 2020. In addition, the government voted in September 2020 on a hundred-billion-euro recovery plan (*Le Plan de Relance*, see Plane and Saraceno 2021), partially financed (40 billion euros) with Next Generation EU funding. The *Plan de Relance* includes a section on public infrastructure, with particular emphasis on the thermal renovation of public buildings, with increased planned investment from the start of the year 2021. Moreover, a new investment plan, "Build the France of 2030", was announced in October 2021. This latter plan is intended to meet the long-term challenges, in particular the ecological transition, through massive investment to help the future technological champions of tomorrow to emerge and to support the transitions of our sectors of excellence: energy, automotive, aeronautics, and even space. Investment is therefore considered by President Macron to be as central to reviving and strengthening the economy, as well as to meeting the major challenges of tomorrow, first and foremost that of ecological transition.

2.2.1 The Paradox of an Investment-less Investment Plan

Beyond the stated ambitions of the government, the macroeconomic analysis is rather disappointing. Indeed, while public investment could be expected to be a driving force behind the catch-up in activity that began in the summer of 2020, the data from national accounts show the opposite. True, public investment was 2% below its pre-crisis level at the end of 2020; but then it contracted throughout 2021 (-3% year-on-year at the end of 2021), reaching 5% less than at the end of 2019 (which represents more than one billion euros less investment per quarter compared to the pre-crisis situation). At the same time, GDP recovered by 4.9% (year-on-year at the end of 2021) and private investment by 4.2%, the latter being well above its pre-crisis level from the second quarter of 2021 (Figure 2.4). While the start of 2022 shows a slight rebound in public investment, it remains 4 % below its pre-crisis level in mid-2022.

This contrasts particularly with the pattern observed during the subprime crisis; at the time, the weak rebound had been driven in part by public investment, with private investment falling sharply during this period of crisis. Indeed, one year after the onset of the economic crisis (during the first quarter of 2008), public investment was at a higher level than its pre-crisis level and, after two years, was 4% above its level at the start of 2008 (before the drop documented above, during the fiscal consolidation period). Conversely, two years after the start of the subprime crisis, private investment was 12% below its pre-crisis level, and GDP was still at -3%.

The contrast between the evolution of investment during the quarters following the start of the COVID-19 crisis and the subprime crisis is striking. If the measures taken by public authorities in support of incomes and of firms' liquidity during the COVID-19 crisis have made it possible to preserve private investment, the evolution of public investment is more surprising; its weak dynamism is surprising given the recovery and investment plans announced.

2.3 Challenges and Perspectives of Low-carbon Investment: The Case of Infrastructures

In the following sections, we analyse the macroeconomic consequences of additional investment in infrastructure necessary to achieve the objectives of the French National Low-Carbon Strategy (SNBC)[1] and the Multi-Year Energy Program.[2] The former is France's roadmap for fighting climate change. It defines a trajectory for reducing greenhouse gas emissions up to 2050 and sets short- and medium-term objectives through carbon budgets. The latter expresses the public authorities' orientations and priorities for action in managing all forms of energy in the country.

We carry out a prospective analysis[3] based on the development of possible scenarios constrained by physical flows and by France's carbon budget as defined in the National Low-Carbon Strategy. We consider two credible yet contrasting scenarios designed to achieve carbon neutrality by 2050 and to ensure compliance with the short and medium-term carbon budgets. The first, the "Pro-Techno" scenario, is based on a world without major changes in current consumption and production patterns, relying mainly on technological developments and the deployment of innovations to

---

1   "La Stratégie Nationale Bas-Carbone (SNBC)", https://www.ecologie.gouv.fr/strategie-nationale-bas-carbone-snbc.

2   "La Programmation Pluriannuelle de l'Energie (PPE)", https://www.ecologie.gouv.fr/programmations-pluriannuelles-lenergie-ppe.

3   This analysis is not intended to predict the future, nor to document a decision in a comprehensive manner. It is intended to shed light on a range of possibilities and to provide input for decisionmakers on the path of transformation.

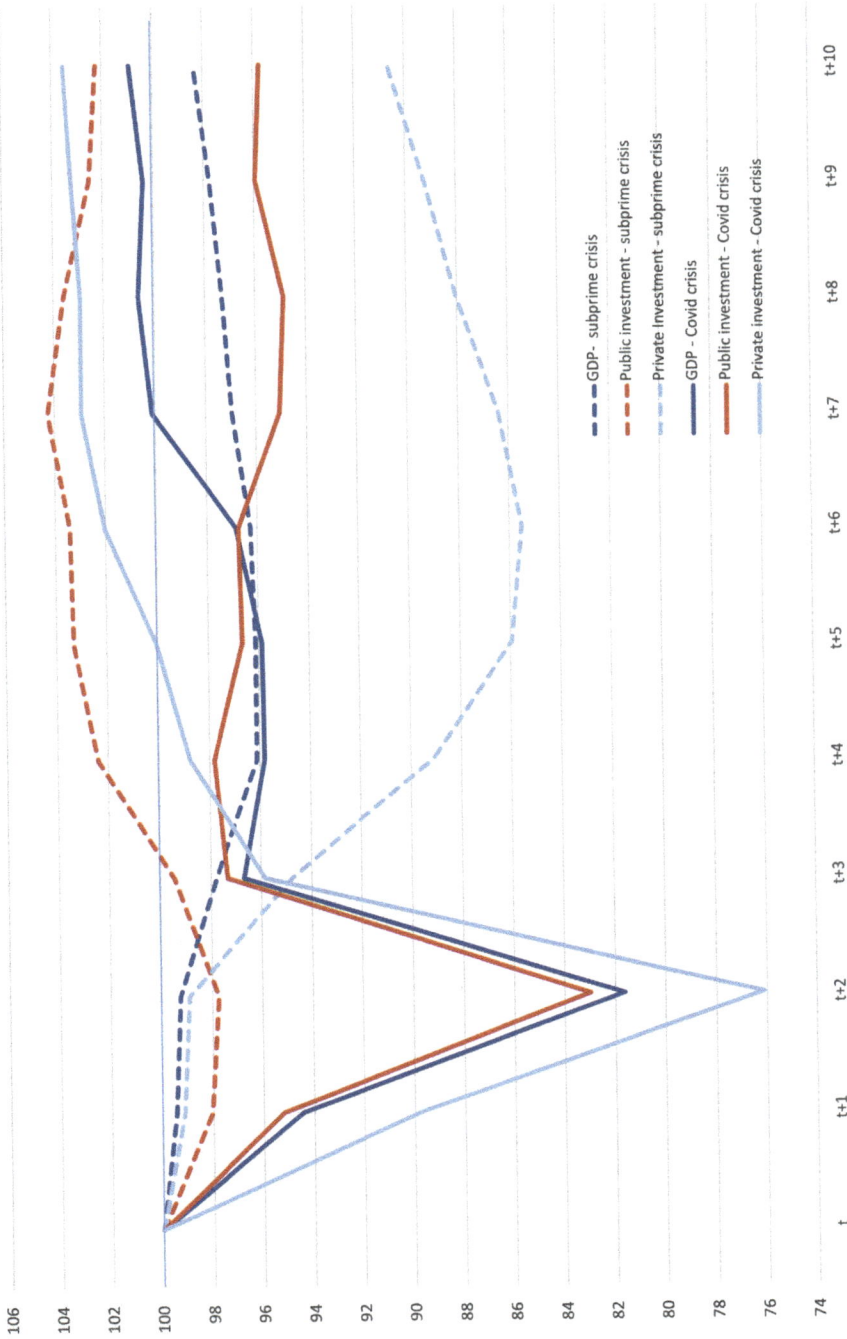

Fig. 2.4 Comparison between trajectories of GDP and investment during the COVID-19 crisis and the subprime crisis.
Sources: Insee, authors' calculations.

achieve climate objectives. The second scenario, the "Sobriety" scenario, is based on a decrease in energy consumption and involves a profound change in lifestyles and consumption patterns, whether in terms of housing, mobility, or industrial production. It involves a limitation or even a significant reduction in the consumption of certain types of goods and services (e.g., individual vehicles, air transport, increased use of digital technologies, etc.).[4] These two scenarios have been designed in the same way as the contrasted energy transition scenarios developed by the French public Agency for the Environment and Energy Management (ADEME 2021) and RTE, the electricity transmission system operator (RTE 2021). The Pro-Techno and the Sobriety scenarios highlight how different factors (technological or social) can concur in different proportions to the objective of carbon neutrality. These stylised scenarios could be hybridised to define a wider range of scenarios, but they nevertheless allow us to analyse the underlying macroeconomic mechanisms triggered by massive investment in low-carbon infrastructure.

This assessment only considers the additional investment compared to a scenario without low-carbon ambitions. Thus, the annual investment amounts reported below, and used as input for a macroeconomic and multi-sectoral model, are investment surpluses compared to those made in the so-called "reference" scenario. This latter scenario provides the trend path of investment in the absence of the implementation of policies compatible with respect to the SNBC objectives. The results of the macroeconomic simulations are therefore also compared to the reference scenario, and all results are given in absolute or relative variations with respect to the reference scenario.

Figure 2.5 shows the additional infrastructure investment amounts for the Pro-Techno and Sobriety scenarios by public works activity for the different components.[5]

Both scenarios imply an increase in investment in public works, including a significant share of site development work (earthworks, demolition, drilling ...). However, some important differences appear:

- The amounts of additional investment in the Pro-Techno scenario are larger than in the Sobriety scenario: over the period 2021–2050, 27 billion euros (1.1 points of GDP) per year in the Pro-Techno scenario versus 14 billion euros (0.6 points of GDP) in the Sobriety scenario.

- The investment trajectory is also different. It increases over time in the Pro-Techno scenario, while it peaks in 2030 before decreasing in the Sobriety scenario. It increases from 23 (respectively 20) to 32 (respectively 9) billion

---

4   For a detailed description of the narratives of these scenarios, see Carbone 4, OFCE, NEO (2021), *The Role of Infrastructure in France's Low-carbon Transition and Adaptation to Climate Change* [*Le rôle des infrastructures dans la transition bas-carbone et l'adaptation au changement climatique de la France*], www.carbone4.com/publication-infrastructures-france.

5   These amounts are based on the calculations of the authors whose methodology and data are detailed in Carbone 4, OFCE, NEO (2021).

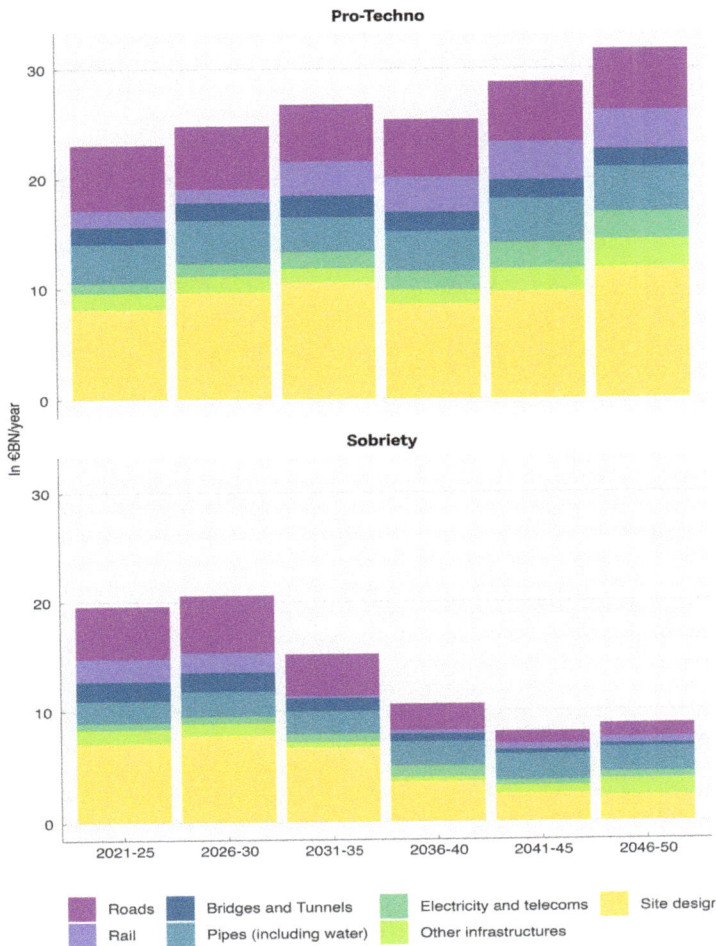

Fig. 2.5. Additional investment by scenario and by sector of activity (average annual amounts for each period).
Source: author's calculation (based on Carbone 4, OFCE, NEO 2021).

euros between 2021 and 2050 in the Pro-Techno (respectively Sobriety) scenario. Thus, the investment trajectories are similar in the two scenarios up to 2030 but diverge significantly over the following decades.

- In the Sobriety scenario, the distribution of total investment among the different segments of public works activity shows significant changes in infrastructure investment choices compared to the Pro-Techno scenario, especially after 2030. In particular, investment decreases sharply in the road and rail sectors due to a lower need for mobility. Similarly, investment in site development decreases significantly after 2030 in the Sobriety scenario, which is explained in particular by a lower need for brownfield recycling and soil de-artificialisation.

2.4 Modelling Framework: The ThreeME Model

In order to quantify the socioeconomic impacts of these two infrastructure investment scenarios, we use ThreeME, a multi-sector macroeconomic model designed to assess the economic impact of energy and environmental policies (Malliet et al. 2020; Landa et al. 2018; Bulavskaya et Reynès 2018). Developed by ADEME (the French Public Agency for the Environment and Energy Management), OFCE (the French Economic Observatory), and NEO (the Netherlands Economic Observatory) in 2008, the ThreeME model has played a leading role in France's inter-administrative and inter-ministerial debates on issues related to the macroeconomic evaluation of energy and climate policies, whether through its mobilisation during the National Debate on Energy Transition (DNTE), the evaluation of energy transition scenarios by ADEME, or the provision of this tool to the Ministry of Ecological Transition.

ThreeME is a country-level,[6] hybrid, dynamic, open-source CGE model. Its sectoral disaggregation allows for analysis of the shifting of activities from one sector to another, particularly in terms of employment, investment, energy consumption, or balance of trade. An important feature of the ThreeME model is that prices are determined in a framework of imperfect competition by profit maximisation so that they do not adjust instantaneously to clear markets (prices and quantities adjust slowly). Furthermore, producers adjust their supply according to demand, and production costs include the costs of intermediate consumption, labor, and capital. These features have the advantage of allowing for situations of market disequilibrium, particularly the presence of involuntary unemployment. Note also that wages are determined by an inverse relationship between the rate of wage growth and the unemployment rate. Wages are also indexed to inflation. This framework is particularly well-suited to policy analysis. In addition to providing information about the long term, it allows for the analysis of transition phases over the short and medium terms, which is especially relevant when assessing the implementation of low-carbon policies.

2.5 Macroeconomic Consequences of Additional Investment in Low-carbon Infrastructure

In both the Pro-techno and Sobriety scenarios, the increase in public investment has both a direct and indirect positive effect on economic activity. It results in increased activity in the public works sectors, with an indirect effect of increased activity in other sectors from which the public works sectors source. This growth in activity, in turn, leads to increased employment, increased household income, and increased consumption.

---

6   For a detailed description of the ThreeME model, see https://www.threeme.org. We use here the French version of the ThreeME model, but other versions of the model have been developed and are used by other regions and countries such as Mexico, Indonesia, the Netherlands, Tunisia, and Occitania.

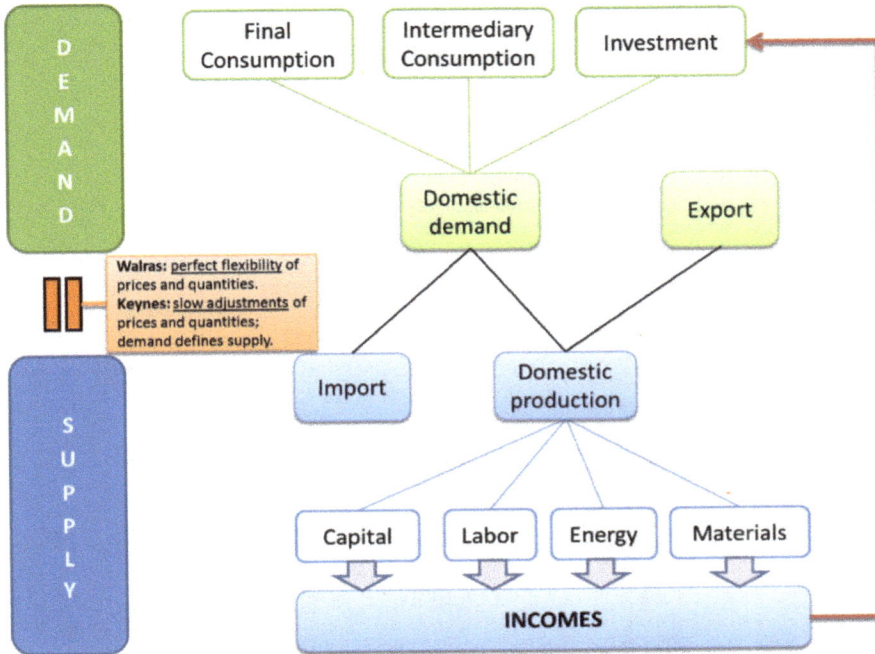

Fig. 2.6. The ThreeME model.
Sources: OFCE, NEO.

This set of impacts is often referred to as the "multiplier effect" because the effect on GDP is greater than the initial investment. However, this increase in activity is offset by a deterioration in the trade balance, which is the result of two effects. The first is a wealth effect: the increase in demand is partly met by the increase in imported products. The second is a substitution effect: the increase in activity generates a rise in inflation and, thus, a deterioration in competitiveness *vis-à-vis* foreign producers, which leads to an additional increase in imports and a decrease in exports.

Considering all of the effects (multiplier and inflationary), the Pro-Techno scenario leads to an increase in GDP of 1.2% on average with respect to the baseline over the period 2021–2030 and of 1% over the period 2030–2050, compared to the reference scenario. In the Sobriety scenario, the increase in GDP is comparable over the period 2021–2030 (1% compared to the baseline scenario) but considerably lower over the period 2030–2050 (0.4%). The effects on GDP follow the trends of the trajectories of the additional investment amounts, with these amounts in the Sobriety scenario being relatively close to those of the Pro-Techno scenario over the first decade and less so over the second period.

In both scenarios, **infrastructure investment significantly increases the number of jobs in the French economy**. Compared to the reference scenario, the Pro-Techno scenario would create 325,000 additional jobs between 2021 and 2025 and 410,000

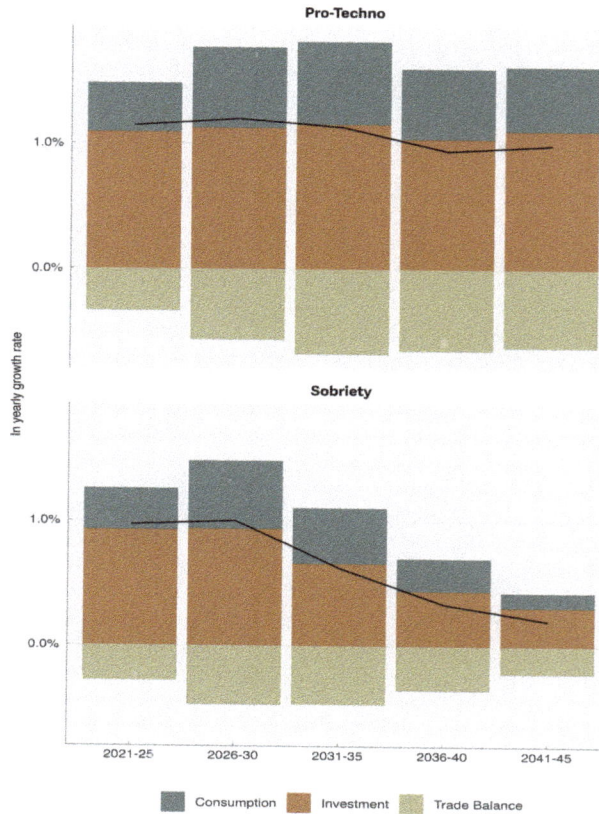

Fig. 2.7 Contribution of consumption, investment, and trade balance to additional GDP in both scenarios (model results).
Sources: ThreeME model simulations results.

between 2026 and 2030. The Sobriety scenario would generate a similar increase in employment over these periods, although slightly less (270,000 additional jobs over the period 2021–2025 and 340,000 over the period 2026–2030). These figures correspond to net job creation (the difference between the number of jobs created and the number of jobs destroyed). This significant result reflects the magnitude of the investment made in the first decade in both scenarios, which generates many new jobs. From 2030 onwards, however, there is a significant divergence in the number of jobs created. In the Pro-Techno scenario, investment amounts remain close to those of the first decade, resulting in a similar increase in employment (of around 300,000 jobs) between 2030 and 2050.

Conversely, the Sobriety scenario is characterised by a marked decrease in investment from 2030 onwards, which leads to a more limited increase in employment in the following two decades compared to the baseline scenario (200,000 additional jobs between 2031 and 2035, and then about 60,000 additional jobs over the period

2036–2050). Overall, therefore, employment follows the initial investment trajectory in public works. The impact is positive in all sectors apart from product manufacturing and agriculture, where the number of jobs falls very slightly in the period 2036–2045.

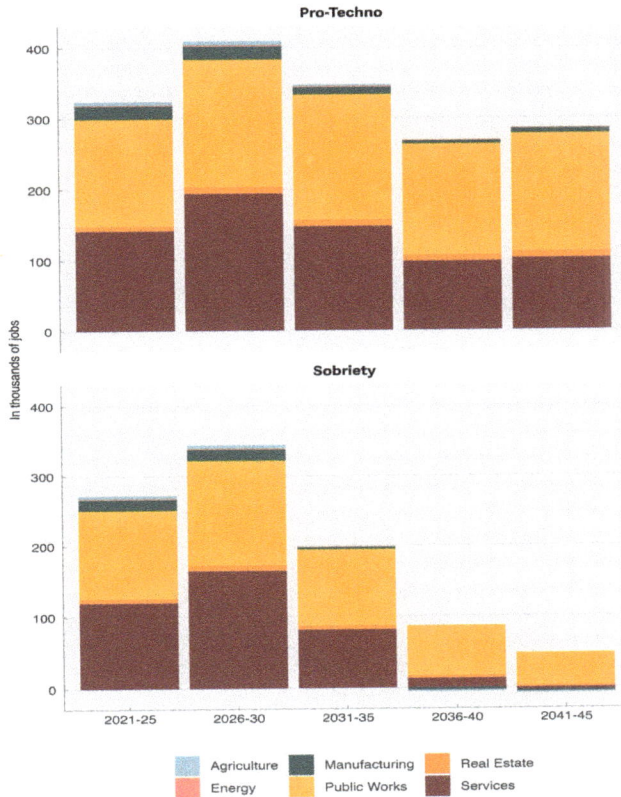

Fig. 2.8 Additional jobs by scenario and sector (model results).
Sources: ThreeME model simulations results.

The estimated economic impacts of the Pro-Techno and Sobriety scenarios are relatively similar, but a divergence appears, especially after 2030. This divergence is the direct result of the higher investment amounts in the Pro-Techno scenario, which generate higher economic activity. However, one should bear in mind that these results do not include all economic effects underlying each scenario. The choice between the Pro-Techno and Sobriety scenarios cannot be made solely based on the difference in direct GDP impact. It is, above all, a societal and, therefore, political choice. Moreover, the choice between these scenarios should be guided by other evaluation criteria, starting with their effects on health and social inequalities.

Moreover, while both scenarios lead to positive economic effects, particularly in terms of employment, they imply major changes in the various sectors of the economy, particularly in the public works sector. This implies that the increase in employment, in either scenario, is conditioned by companies' ability to adapt their offers and supply to the new investment needs.

Finally, it should be noted that the question of financing investment in each scenario is a major one. In particular, it requires a European-level perspective and an in-depth reflection on the possible ways of financing it. The state will have to take its share of the additional effort. However, it will also strongly encourage the other players (such as local authorities and public or private operators) to invest in infrastructure. The development of innovative financing methods could also benefit infrastructure policies. In the field of water management, for example, aid schemes or charges linked to services rendered could be envisaged so that users or local authorities could jointly finance actions to protect aquatic environments or prevent natural hazards: e.g., development of flood expansion zones, alternative drilling to protect an overexploited water table, road maintenance, and support for less polluting agricultural practices.

Conclusion

While public investment slowed down over the last decades, reaching a low point with the COVID-19 crisis in 2019, French public authorities have launched a public investment plan to revive demand and pave the way toward sustainable and long-term-oriented emission reduction targets. In fact, in the context of the Paris Agreement, France has designed the French National Low-Carbon Strategy that provides guidelines for implementing the transition to a low-carbon economy. There are many ways to achieve this transition, and they imply potentially conflicting political and social choices. In particular, significant investment will be necessary in the years to come to transform, renovate and maintain infrastructures, leading to important socio-economic evolutions at the national level. The analysis carried out in this chapter investigates the macroeconomic impact of two contrasting scenarios where additional investments are injected into the economy to develop the necessary infrastructures needed to achieve carbon neutrality by 2050. The Pro-Techno scenario relies on massive technological development and innovations while the Sobriety scenario is based on a change in lifestyles and a reduction in energy consumption. Both scenarios lead to a positive impact on economic activity in the medium term, while being compatible with the long-term objective of a carbon-neutral economy. However, since the Pro-techno scenario assumes a larger public investment in infrastructure beyond 2030 (technological deployment), the positive macroeconomic impact is greater in the long run than in the Sobriety scenario. These two scenarios are extreme and contrasting, they have allowed an analysis of the effects of investment shocks compatible with carbon neutrality at mid-century, and thus inform public decision-making. The actual implementation transition-oriented policies will certainly have to go through a combination and co-existence of innovations of different natures, whether technological or behavioral, and have effects that are somewhere in the middle between the two extreme scenarios.

This will depend, among other things, on the political framework in which things take place. In particular, questions of financing and coordination with other countries and within the EU framework will be essential.

References

Agence de l'Environnement et de Maîtrise de l'Énergie-ADEME (2021) *Prospective Transition(s) 2050 Report*, https://transitions2050.ademe.fr/en.

Bulavskaya, T. and Reynès, F. (2018) "Job Creation and Economic Impact of Renewable Energy in the Netherlands", *Renewable Energy*, 2018–04 (119), 528–38, https://www.sciencedirect.com/science/article/abs/pii/S0960148117309011.

Carbone 4, OFCE, and NEO (2021) *The Role of Infrastructure in France's Low-carbon Transition and Adaptation to Climate Change* [*Le rôle des infrastructures dans la transition bas-carbone et l'adaptation au changement climatique de la France*], www.carbone4.com/publication-infrastructures-france.

Landa, G., Malliet P. Reynès, F. and Saussay, A. (2018) "The State of Applied Environmental Macroeconomics", *Revue de l'OFCE, 2018, Whither the Economy?*, 3(157), 133–49, https://hal-sciencespo.archives-ouvertes.fr/hal-03443474.

Malliet, P, F. Reynès, G. Landa, M. Hamdi-Cherif, and A. Saussay (2020) "Assessing Short-Term and Long-Term Economic and Environmental Effects of the COVID-19 Crisis in France", *Environmental & Resource Economics*, 2020-08-04 76(4), 867–83, https://link.springer.com/article/10.1007/s10640-020-00488-z.

Plane, M. and F. Saraceno, "From Fiscal Consolidation to the Plan de relance: Investment Trends in France", in F. Cerniglia, F. Saraceno, and A. Watts (eds), *The Great Reset: 2021 European Public Investment Outlook*. Cambridge: Open Book Publishers, pp. 33–46, https://doi.org/10.11647/OBP.0280.02.

Réseau de Transport d'Électricité-RTE (2021) *Energy Pathways to 2050: Key Results*, https://assets.rte-france.com/prod/public/2022-01/Energy%20pathways%202050_Key%20results.pdf.

3. Public Investment in Germany

Squaring the Circle

Katja Rietzler and Andrew Watt

3.1 A Decade of Investment

In Germany the huge investment needs for the modernisation and transformation of the economy following decades of under-investment in infrastructure and other public goods have become a prominent topic, as already discussed in previous issues of the European Public Investment Outlook (Dullien et al. 2020; Rietzler and Watt 2021). In its coalition agreement of November 2021, Germany's new government of social democrats, greens and liberals acknowledges Germany's tremendous investment needs and promised "a decade of investment" (SPD et al. 2021). Under the title "Mehr Fortschritt wagen" (Dare to make more progress) the coalition agreement sets out ambitious spending plans that go beyond the modernisation of Germany's infrastructure and speeding up the decarbonisation of the economy. They include among other things a replacement of the Hartz-IV social benefit system, a general transfer to ensure the subsistence level for children ("Kindergrundsicherung"), support for additional housing, and federal support to address the problem of over-indebted municipalities. The latter is particularly noteworthy as in Germany's federal system, it is local authorities that are responsible for more than a third of total public investment and almost 60 % of public construction investment.

At the same time the coalition government is determined to return to the German debt brake—which like the European rules is currently suspended—in 2023 without reforming it and without raising taxes. In both cases the liberal party, FDP, the coalition partner with the least seats in the Bundestag, but whose leader is the new finance minister, has had its way. At first sight it seems nearly impossible to increase spending substantially with no additional public borrowing or tax increases. The coalition government hopes to square the circle by resorting to substantial operations using off-budget funds and reserves. The federal government still has reserves built-up from surpluses before the pandemic ("allgemeine Rücklage") amounting to €48 billion. It has recently taken on new debt, making use of the suspension of the debt brake, and

    https://doi.org/10.11647/OBP.0328.03

transferred €60 billion to the Energy and Climate Fund (EKF), which is to be renamed Climate and Transformation Fund (KTF). In total the EKF/KTF will have reserves of almost €80 billion at the end of 2022 which can be spent in the years from 2023. At the same time more use is to be made of public companies and off-budget entities, such as the state railway company, the federal real estate agency (BImA) and the German development bank KfW. An additional scope of about €6 billion results from postponing the repayment of the federal debt incurred in the pandemic until after 2027. The coalition agreement also foresees that additional fiscal room for manoeuvre will be created by reforming the cyclical adjustment mechanism in the debt brake.

The German debt brake differs in several respects from the European fiscal rules, the two most important being the scope and the deficit concept. Whereas the European Fiscal rules focus on the total government sector as defined in the ESA 2010, the German debt brake includes the core budgets and selected off-budget entities. Unlike the Stability and Growth Pact, the debt brake focuses on net new debt instead of the fiscal balance. As a consequence, operations with reserves and off-budget entities can be used to enable additional borrowing while at the same time complying with the debt brake. The IMK estimates the additional room for manoeuvre created by the agreement between the three parties to be in the low three-digit billions in the legislative term ending in 2025 (Dullien et al. 2022a), if the supply of additional funds to the EKF/KTF under the escape clause of the debt brake is not ruled unconstitutional by the federal constitutional court (Bundesverfassungsgericht) in a lawsuit filed by the conservative CDU/CSU group in the Bundestag. As the additional funding of the EKF/KTF accounts for a substantial share of the additional scope for public investment, a negative court ruling would place the "decade of investment" at risk. The cycle of greater investment, but no additional borrowing or taxes could no longer be squared.

3.2 Some Progress since 2019

"A decade of investment" is exactly what an influential report assessing the requirement for public investment had called for (Bardt et al. 2019) It put the public investment backlog at €457 billion over ten years, or 1.3% of GDP per year, a finding endorsed by trade unions and employers alike and considered plausible by the scientific council of the German Ministry of Economy and Energy (Wissenschaftlicher Beirat beim BMWi 2020). However, the report requires an update, particularly because climate policy has become much more ambitious since 2019. The EU's target for the reduction of greenhouse gas emissions until 2030 has been raised from 40% to 55%. Accordingly, Germany aims to reduce greenhouse gas emissions by 65% before 2030 (instead of 55%). This implies that the transformation of the German economy towards zero or even negative emissions will have to be accelerated tremendously. Investment in the decarbonisation of production, housing and transport will have to be frontloaded, leading to higher spending requirements in the short term.

A recent study by Krebs and Steitz (2021) estimates that €460 billion will have to be spent on public investment in climate protection and related fields alone in the coming ten years. As this more recent study excludes a large part of the public investment requirement, like overcoming the investment backlog at the local level, which is estimated at €159 billion (Raffer and Scheller 2022), the overall requirement is significantly higher. It makes sense to combine the results of the two studies by Bardt et al. and Krebs and Steitz. Allowing for the substantial overlap of more than a third (about 0.5% of GDP) between them, a total requirement emerges of approximately 2.1% of GDP per year. Only part of this spending is direct public investment according to the national accounts' definition; a substantial share consists of support for private investment in the socio-ecological transformation of the economy via investment grants and other instruments. Out of the € 460 billion that Krebs and Steitz (2021) identify as investment spending needs over ten years, €200 billion are support to private investment.

Since the publication of Bardt et al. (2019) German public investment spending has continued to increase not only in absolute terms, but also as share of GDP. The public investment ratio has risen by 0.2 percentage points and investment grants as percentage of GDP have even increased by 0.4 percentage points (Figure 3.1). Part of the increase can be explained by the fall in nominal GDP due to the pandemic, however. If nominal GDP had risen in 2020 and 2021 as in the ten years to 2019—i.e., by 3.6% annually—the ratios would be lower, particularly in the case of direct public investment. Most progress in government investment spending has come via the support for investment in other sectors through investment grants. They include, among others, payments from the federal government to the state railway company and support to non-financial corporations by local governments.

Given the recent higher ratio of investment spending, it can be argued that some 0.4 to 0.6 percentage points of the additional requirement have already been reached; this higher investment ratio would need to be sustained in order to reach a sufficient level of investment. At the same time, the studies mentioned above, both following a bottom-up approach, do not include all public investment needs. The pandemic has shown that the health sector requires massive modernisation investment, which neither study mentions. In addition, climate protection and adaption spending in local communities probably requires substantial spending beyond the amounts gauged in the studies, if climate targets are to be achieved; neither study includes energy efficiency of public buildings at the local level, for instance. The Ministry of Economy and Energy (BMWi 2018) estimates the number of properties owned by local communities at 176,000 and states that the local level consumes two thirds of the public sector's final energy use. In addition, climate adaption requires modernising civil and flooding protection and numerous other climate adaption measures (Rietzler 2022a). Thus, as a very rough estimate it can be concluded that investment requirements (including investment grants to the private sector) still amount to sustained spending of 1.6–2.1% of GDP, or roughly €600–800 billion over ten years.

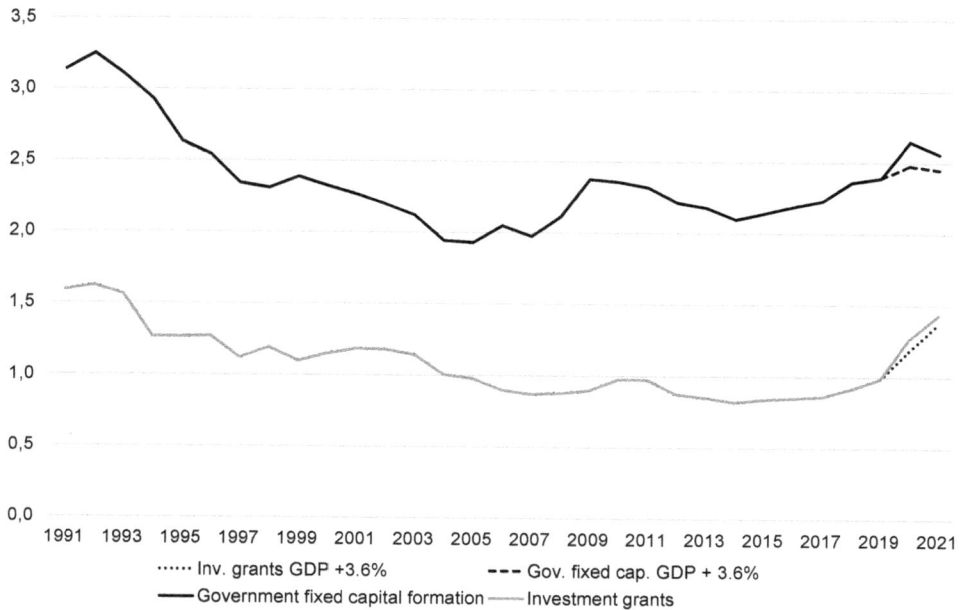

Fig. 3.1 Public Investment and Investment Grants (% of GDP).
Source: Destatis (national accounts), calculations of the IMK.

3.3 War in Ukraine and High Inflation

Just a few months after the government was formed, it faced an unexpected and severe additional challenge in the form of the war in Ukraine and surging energy prices that distract it from its original agenda. From spring 2022 Germany, like other European countries, has experienced monthly inflation rates at a level not seen since the 1950s. Private consumption expenditure was burdened by surging energy prices in the very moment when pandemic-linked restrictions were lifted, which should have supported a recovery of consumer spending. The government saw an urgent need to cushion the effects of high energy prices, particularly for those most affected. Within two months the government launched two "relief packages" amounting to more than €30 billion. Overall, the packages are socially balanced with a substantial share of one-off payments both to recipients of transfers as well as employed persons and households with children (Dullien et al. 2022b). At the same time roughly 10% of the total relief is provided via a temporary reduction of the energy tax on transport fuels, which counteracts the national carbon price introduced in 2021 and largely benefits households with higher incomes and substantial fuel consumption (Rietzler 2022b).

Meanwhile a third relief package has been announced. It consists of more than twenty individual measures including one-off payments to pensioners, income tax reductions as well as an electricity price cap. Although a lot of details remain to be specified, the government puts the overall amount at €65 billion, twice that of the previous two packages. A partial cap on household gas prices is now being specified in detail after group of experts submitted its final report (ExpertInnen-Kommission Gas und Wärme 2022). Depending on its exact parameters, this cap would imply additional fiscal costs of around € 90 billion. Additionally, the major gas importer Uniper was taken into state ownership to prevent its insolvency. Substantial unforeseen public investment is needed, notably to provide, as quickly as possible, a facility to import liquified natural gas and more generally to accelerate the transition away from fossil fuels, specifically those imported from Russia. Beyond the first three relief packages the German government is making an additional € 200 billion available.

As the debt brake is still suspended in 2022, debt finance of the relief measures via an extra-budget is not a problem. However, more than half the measures stretch beyond 2022. At the same time forecasts for economic growth have been substantially revised downwards, putting pressure on government revenues (Dullien et al. 2022c). Under such conditions, unforeseen when the coalition agreement was signed, a further extension of the suspension of the debt brake looks increasingly likely.

The war in Ukraine has also returned military spending to the political agenda. Germany has committed itself to increasing military spending substantially in the coming years so as to meet its NATO commitments. On the one hand military spending in the regular budget is to increase by 7.3% or €3.4 billion according to the budget plan for 2022. In addition, an off-budget fund of €100 billion (Sondervermögen "Bundeswehr") has been created to finance increased military spending in the coming years. As it is to be debt-financed, its implementation required a change of the constitution, which took place with wide parliamentary support. In the short run, this arrangement implies that military spending, of which a large part will be classified as investment in the national accounts, can be increased alongside the investment for other purposes mentioned above and will not crowd out the latter. However, the debt of €100 billion is to be repaid "over a reasonable period" starting in 2031. The repayment will then coincide with the repayment of the federal debt incurred under the pandemic over thirty years beginning in 2028, and this will then inevitably create tensions with other spending priorities in the longer run.

3.4 Stability Programme Suggests that Additional Investment Is Mostly Military

Whereas the coalition agreement contains no quantified fiscal parameters and the government's use of reserves and off-budget funds and entities lacks transparency, the German Stability Programme 2022 submitted under the European Semester provides a complete picture with projections for the whole government sector based on the national accounts. The Stability Programme announces a substantial increase both of direct public investment and investment grants to other sectors from 2022 onwards.

The combined increase in the period from 2021 until 2023 adds up to roughly 0.8 percentage points of GDP (Table 3.1). At first sight this seems impressive as it would be more than one third of the investment spending requirements discussed above within just two years.

Table 3.1 German stability programme (% of GDP)

Year	2019	2020	2021	2022	2023	2024	2025	2026
Government sector gross fixed capital formation	2,4	2,6	2,6	3	3	3	2 ¾	2 ¾
Additional military investment	-	-	-	0,4	0,5	0,5	0,5	0,5
Government sector investment grants	1,0	1,3	1,4	1 ½	1 ¾	1 ¾	1 ¾	1 ½

Source: Federal Ministry of Finance (2022), pp. 54, 57, Additional information provided by the Federal Ministry of Finance, Destatis.

However, closer analysis reveals that the additional investment spending is of the same order of magnitude as planned additional military investment. Furthermore, government gross fixed capital formation is expected to decline again relative to GDP in 2025 and 2026, while the share of military investment is expected to remain unchanged. It must be taken into account that data on annual additional military investment in the German Stability Programme 2022 reflect a "technical assumption". Actual spending may be spread less evenly across the years of the planning period. Most probably, additional military spending will remain significantly below 0,4 % of GDP in 2022 and 2023. According to the draft federal budget, which is currently being discussed in parliament, military spending from the off-budget fund will be €8.5 billion or 0.2% of GDP in 2023.

As discussed in last year's report, the previous German government had announced substantial additional investment as part of its stimulus and future package. Now the coalition government of social democrats, greens and liberals has promised a massive increase of public investment. However, this is not reflected in the government's Stability Programme 2022. The Stability Programme contains no increase of direct public investment beyond additional spending on military procurement. According to the programme, non-military direct public investment will be even lower as a share of GDP in 2025 and 2026 than it was in 2021. This major contradiction is partially explained by the fact that substantial public funds will be made available to support private investment.

3.5 The Critical Issue of Local Government Financing

Assessing public investment in Germany, one has to look beyond federal investment spending. Local communities play a particularly important role. They are responsible for school buildings and local roads, which account for a large share in the public investment backlog. In addition, they also play an important role in local public transport and face additional investment needs for climate protection and adaption. Based on the studies mentioned above, a conservative estimate puts local-authority investment needs at €250–300 billion out of the total of €600–800 billion. To enable local governments to invest enough, long-standing problems of municipal finances have to be solved. One issue is a large burden of liquidity credits piled up primarily in the early 2000s. Some federal states have already implemented their own support programmes for indebted local authorities, but the federal government needs to step up, as a large part of the debt incurred is a consequence of federal legislation transferring more and more responsibilities to the local authorities without providing the necessary funding. At the same time these problems must be prevented from recurring. Additional responsibilities for the municipalities require corresponding funding. Local investment spending differs very widely between regions. Figure 3.2 shows tangible investment of state and local government investment governments in the German states ("Länder") per inhabitant for the year 2021. In Bavaria (BY) the state and local government levels taken together[1] invested €957 per inhabitant, the comparable figure for Saarland (SL) was only €431, less than half. Although there might be differences in the price level and the scope of outsourcing to the private sector, the difference is striking and persistent. During the last ten years Baden-Württemberg, Bavaria, Saxony and in most years Hamburg exhibited public investment above the German average, whereas public investment in North Rhine-Westphalia and Saarland was the lowest among all states excluding the three city states. Besides a weak revenue base, high social spending is a major contributor to low municipal investment (Beznoska and Kauder 2020; Bremer et al. 2021). It has also contributed to the high liquidity credits. Although the federal government has gradually increased its support of local social spending, further improvements are necessary (Rietzler 2022a).

---

[1] For comparability between states it is important to aggregate the state and local levels as the division of responsibilities between state and local levels differs between the German states. (State abbreviations: BW = Baden-Württemberg, BY = Bavaria, BE= Berlin, BB = Brandenburg, HB = Bremen, HE = Hesse, HH = Hamburg, MV = Mecklenburg-Vorpommern, NI = Lower Saxony, NW = North Rhine-Westphalia, RP = Rhineland-Palatinate, SL = Saarland, SN = Saxony, ST = Saxony-Anhalt, SH = Schleswig-Holstein, TH = Thuringia).

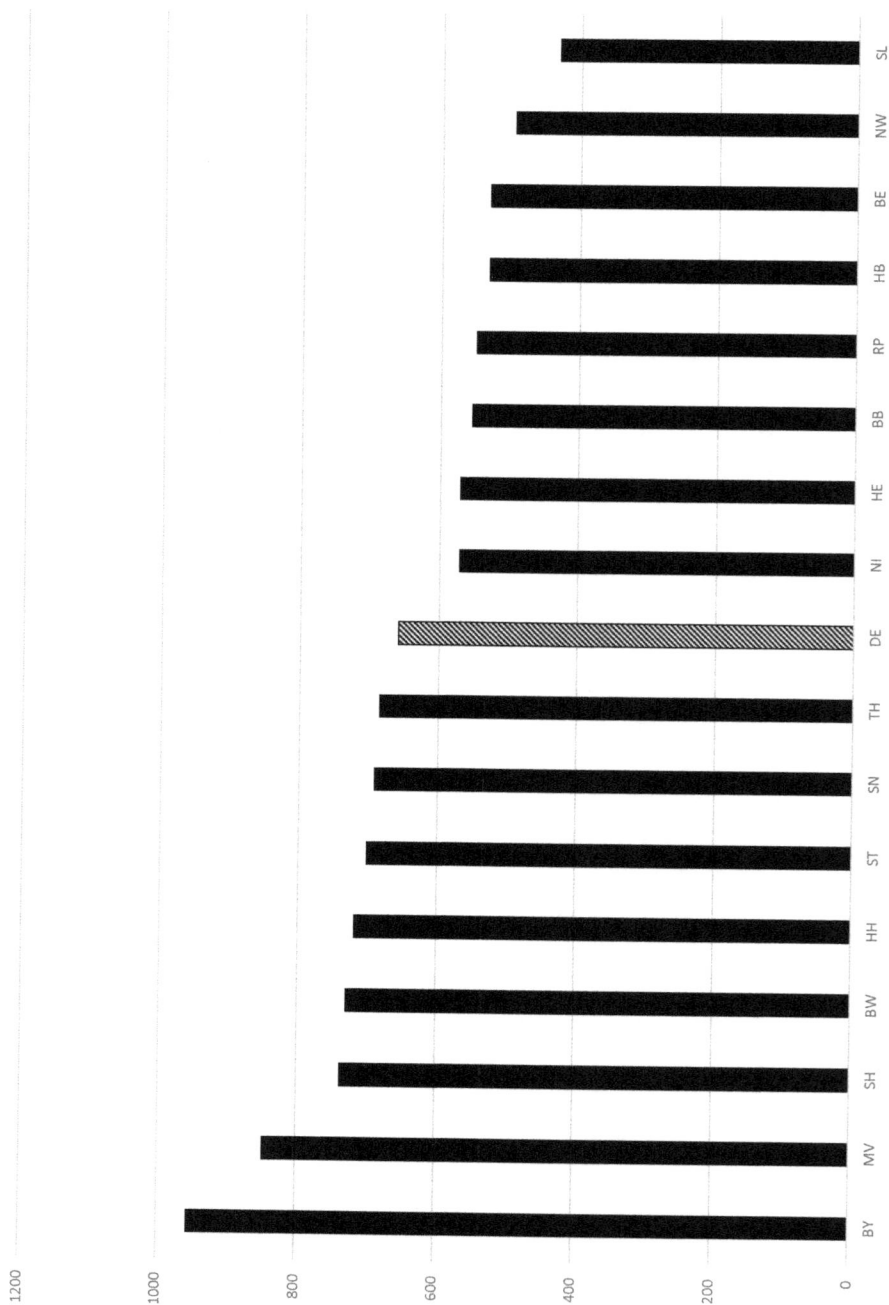

Fig. 3.2 Tangible Investment of Local and State Governments in 2021 (Euro per inhabitant).
Source: Destatis, Fachserie 14 Reihe 2, Statistische Ämter des Bundes und der Länder, calculations of the IMK.

The foreseen return to the debt brake in 2023 will make it more difficult to increase public investment—not so much at the federal level, where the use of loopholes created additional fiscal space, but at the regional and local level. Whereas the federal government is allowed to incur some additional new debt even under the debt brake, the states must stick to a strict zero (structural) debt limit. In addition, the states start paying off the additional debt incurred in the pandemic much earlier than the federal government and some have chosen a short repayment period. This is likely to have repercussions for local finances.

3.6 The German Recovery and Resilience Plan

As discussed in detail in last year's EPIO, Germany submitted its application for RRF funding—the Deutsche Aufbau und Resilienzplan, DARP—on time in 2021. Meeting the requirements in terms of the proportions devoted to decarbonisation and—by a long way—digitalisation, and respecting country-specific recommendations, the plan was swiftly approved by the EU Commission and the Council. Because of the redistributive nature of the RRF, which favours lower-income countries and those more severely affected by the COVID-19-related crisis and the fact that Germany's public debt sets the interest-rate benchmarks in Europe and thus it had no incentive to avail itself of RRF loans, Germany's national RRF Plan is of limited macroeconomic relevance. The overall volume of the DARP is around €25 billion (around 0.7% of annual GDP) to be spread over three years. Germany also faces less stringent constraints from EU fiscal rules than many other countries, such that it is of limited importance compared to the national spending programmes discussed in this chapter. As last year's analysis showed it mainly served to bring forward and expand projects that were due to be implemented under national investment and climate-related initiatives.

One of the consequences of the limited size of the DARP—and thus also public interest in the details—compared to countries such as Italy, which have taken advantage of loans and sought to front-load investment and reform initiatives, is that, at the time of writing, very little information has been made available on the progress of DARP projects. As early as August 2021 pre-financing was disbursed, amounting to 9% of the total (€2.25bn). As, by its nature, pre-financing is not conditional on member states having achieved agreed milestones (and thus requiring reporting on results achieved) this has not generated publicly available data. As of September 2022, the European Commission's RRF Scoreboard does not indicate that any further disbursements have been made nor milestones achieved. While the exigencies of coping with the impact of the Ukraine war offer a plausible explanation for delays, it is noteworthy that, by the summer, Italy, for instance, had already received two payments and submitted a claim for a third, for a total of around €66bn.

The European Commission is conducting a comparative review of progress by the member states in implementing their national plans based on an agreed set of common indicators. Countries were to report by February 2022 and a cross-sectional analysis was to be made available in April. However, difficulties in obtaining fully comparable information from all member states have delayed publication of this information.[2]

In short, an assessment of the national RRF plan's actual—as opposed to potential—contribution to meeting Germany's public investment needs will have to await next year's EPIO.

3.7 The Way to Sufficient Investment Spending

Compared to the additional public investment needs, the amounts that can be expected to be forthcoming will clearly be insufficient, particularly concerning the government sector's own investments. It may be easier in the short run to increase investment grants to the private sector, but direct public investment (excluding military spending) also needs to increase very substantially and in a sustained manner. An increase of the required magnitude requires, of course, not only the provision of financial resources, but also sufficient supply-side capacities, both in the business sector and in public sector planning departments. In recent years Germany has faced significant bottlenecks in the construction sector that slow down public investment projects and cause sharp price increases (Scheller et al. 2021), the price deflator of public construction investment rose by 19.4% between 2017 and 2021, much faster than the GDP deflator (+9.3%). The price hikes in the construction sector were driven by capacity constraints, as capacity has risen only slowly since the construction sector's ten-year crisis after the reunification boom came to an end in 2005. At the same time there is an acute lack of staff in public sector planning departments, particularly at the local level, where insufficient funds had caused more than a decade of net negative local-government investment. Moreover, local authorities with the highest needs have tended to face the tightest fiscal constraints on their investment.

Now, even where sufficient funds are being made available, it remains difficult to increase public investment in the short run, as the existing bottlenecks cannot be removed overnight. Both the construction industry and local authorities need a long-term perspective to invest in additional capacities. Recently, public investment has tended to be procyclical, increasing with rising revenues in good times. A more sensible approach would be to stabilise public investment at a high level, providing reliable and adequate funding over the long term.

In the current fiscal framework such a stable long-term perspective is difficult to implement and becomes particularly challenging when the government rules out both tax increases and additional deficit spending. Then the only remaining option

---

2   Personal communication from EU Commission country desk.

for the federal government is to use whatever room for manoeuvre can be created by making use of loopholes in the debt brake—mostly through off-budget operations or procedural changes such as a reform of the cyclical adjustment method. At least the use of the EKF/KTF and public institutions like the state railway company or BImA has the advantage of favouring investment spending. However, this approach makes public investment much less transparent and results in higher financing costs compared to investment via the core budget. Further, it is currently unknown to what extent fiscal space can be increased and it is vulnerable to legal challenges.

It is time for Germany to implement a more investment-friendly fiscal framework. As public investment increases the public capital stock and facilitates economic growth that future generations can benefit from, there is a strong case for a "golden rule" of investment allowing public investment to be credit-financed. This is all the truer for investment in climate protection and renewable energy, which, in addition to its ecological benefits, is also vital for Germany's future competitiveness. The German government should use the opportunity of the current review of the European fiscal rules to support the introduction of a golden rule, alongside other reforms (Dullien et al. 2020), and adjust the German debt brake accordingly as well as making it more compatible with the European rules.

In the current high-inflation environment additional price pressures should be avoided. Investment affects both the supply and the demand side of the economy. It increases the capital stock and thus strengthens capacity, but in the short run it also increases demand. In theory, a cyclical golden rule that allows higher deficit-financed investment in bad times would be a good idea. However, well-known problems with cyclical adjustment methods may make the practical implementation difficult (Truger 2015). To avoid excessive debt and risks associated with creating excess demand, part of the additional investment spending could be financed by an income tax surcharge or temporary wealth levy. The combination of a golden rule and additional tax revenues would enable a long-term stabilisation of public investment in Germany.

References

Bardt, H., S. Dullien, M. Hüther, and K. Rietzler (2019) *For a sound fiscal policy: Enabling public investment!* IMK Report No. 152e, https://www.imk-boeckler.de/de/faust-detail.htm?sync_id=HBS-007619.

Beznoska, M. and B. Kauder (2020) *Schieflagen der kommunalen Finanzen: Ursachen und Lösungsansätze.* Institut der Deutschen Wirtschaft, IW-Policy Paper 15, https://www.iwkoeln.de/studien/martin-beznoska-bjoern-kauder-schieflagen-der-kommunalen-finanzen.html.

Bremer, B., D. di Carlo, and L. Wansleben (2021) *The Constrained Politics of Local Public Investments under Cooperative Federalism.* Max-Planck-Institut für Gesellschaftsforschung, MPIfG Discussion Paper No. 21/4, https://pure.mpg.de/rest/items/item_3327622_1/component/file_3327623/content.

BMWi (Bundesministerium für Wirtschaft und Energie, Ministry of Economy and Energy) (2018) *Energieeffizienz in Kommunen. Energetisch modernisieren und Kosten sparen: Wir fördern das.* BMWi, Berlin, https://www.foerderdatenbank.de/FDB/Content/DE/Download/Publikation/Energie/energieeffizienz-in-kommunen-broschuere.pdf?__blob=publicationFile&v=2.

Dullien, S., C. Paetz, A. Watt, and S. Watzka (2020) *Proposals for a Reform of the EU's Fiscal Rules and Economic Governance.* IMK Report No. 159e, Düsseldorf, https://www.imk-boeckler.de/de/faust-detail.htm?sync_id=HBS-007716.

Dullien, S., A. Herzog-Stein, K. Rietzler, S. Tober, and A. Watt (2022a) *Transformative Weichenstellungen.* IMK Report No. 173, Düsseldorf, https://www.imk-boeckler.de/de/faust-detail.htm?sync_id=HBS-008218.

Dullien, S., K. Rietzler, and S. Tober (2022b) *Die Entlastungspakete der Bundesregierung. Sozial weitgehend ausgewogen, aber verbesserungsfähig.* IMK Policy Brief No. 120, Düsseldorf, April, https://www.imk-boeckler.de/de/faust-detail.htm?sync_id=HBS-008296.

Dullien, S., A. Herzog-Stein, P. Hohlfeld, K. Rietzler, S. Stephan, S. Tober, T. Theobald, and S. Watzka (2022c) *Energiepreisschocks treiben Deutschland in die Rezession. Prognose der wirtschaftlichen Entwicklung 2022/2023.* IMK Report No. 177, September, https://www.imk-boeckler.de/de/faust-detail.htm?sync_id=HBS-008421.

Dullien, S., E. Jürgens, and S. Watzka (2020) "Public Investment in Germany. The Need for a Big Push", in F. Cerniglia and F. Saraceno (eds), *A European Public Investment Outlook.* Cambridge: Open Book Publishers, pp. 49–62, https://doi.org/10.11647/obp.0222.

ExpertInnen-Kommission Gas und Wärme (2022): Sicher durch den Winter. Abschlussbericht. Berlin 31 October 2022.

Federal Ministry of Defence (2022) *Kabinett einigt sich auf mehr Geld und Sondervermögen für die Bundeswehr,* 16 March 2022, https://www.bmvg.de/de/aktuelles/deutlich-aufgestockt-verteidigungshaushalt-5372564.

Federal Ministry of Finance (2022) *German Stability Programme 2022. 2022 Update (and updated German Draft Budgetary Plan 2022),* Berlin, https://www.bundesregierung.de/breg-de/suche/german-stability-programme-2022-2028432#:~:text=On%2027%20April%20 2022%2C%20the,government%20will%20ensure%20fiscal%20soundness.

Krebs, T. and J. Steitz (2021) „Öffentliche Finanzbedarfe für Klimainvestitionen im Zeitraum 2021–2030", *Forum for a New Economy,* Working Paper No. 03/2021, https://newforum.org/wp-content/uploads/2021/09/FNE-WP03-2021.pdf.

Raffer, C. and H. Scheller (2022) *KfW-Kommunalpanel 2022,* Kreditanstalt für Wiederaufbau, Frankfurt am Main, https://www.kfw.de/PDF/Download-Center/Konzernthemen/Research/PDF-Dokumente-KfW-Kommunalpanel/KfW-Kommunalpanel-2022.pdf.

Rietzler, K. (2022a) "Kommunen zentral für Jahrzehnt der Zukunftsinvestitionen. Beitrag zum Zeitgespräch: Haushaltspolitik der neuen Bundesregierung", *Wirtschaftsdienst,* Jg. 102, H. 1., 27–30, https://www.wirtschaftsdienst.eu/inhalt/jahr/2022/heft/1/beitrag/kommunen-zentral-fuer-jahrzehnt-der-zukunftsinvestitionen.html.

Rietzler, K. (2022b) *Vorübergehende Energiesteuersenkung klima- und verteilungspolitisch fragwürdig. Ausweitung pauschaler Zahlungen oder Gaspreisdeckel sinnvoller. Written statement for the parliamentary hearing on the temporary decrease of the energy tax on May 16, 2022.* IMK Policy Brief No. 122, Düsseldorf, May, https://www.imk-boeckler.de/de/faust-detail.htm?sync_id=HBS-008321.

Rietzler, K. and A. Watt (2021) "Public Investment in Germany: Much More Needs to Be Done", in F. Cerniglia, F. Saraceno, and A. Watt (eds), *The Great Reset: 2021 European Public*

Investment Outlook. Cambridge: Open Book Publishers, pp. 47–62, https://doi.org/10.11647/obp.0222.02.

Scheller, H., K. Rietzler, C. Raffer, and C. Kühl (2021) *Baustelle zukunftsfähige Infrastruktur. Ansätze zum Abbau nichtmonetärer Investitionshemmnisse bei öffentlichen Infrastrukturvorhaben,* WISO-Diskurs No. 12/2021, Bonn/Berlin, https://library.fes.de/pdf-files/wiso/17978.pdf.

SPD, Bündnis90/Die Grünen, FDP (2021) *Mehr Fortschritt wagen. Bündnis für Freiheit, Gerechtigkeit und Nachhaltigkeit, Koalitionsvertrag 2021–2025 zwischen der Sozialdemokratischen Partei Deutschlands (SPD), BÜNDNIS 90 / DIE GRÜNEN und den Freien Demokraten (FDP),* https://www.spd.de/fileadmin/Dokumente/Koalitionsvertrag/Koalitionsvertrag_2021-2025.pdf.

Wissenschaftlicher Beirat beim Bundesministerium für Wirtschaft und Energie (2020) *Öffentliche Infrastruktur in Deutschland: Probleme und Reformbedarf,* Berlin, https://www.bmwk.de/Redaktion/DE/Publikationen/Ministerium/Veroeffentlichung-Wissenschaftlicher-Beirat/gutachten-oeffentliche-infrastruktur-in-deutschland.html.

4. NRRP—Italy's Strategic Reform and Investment Programme

Sustaining an Ecological Transition

Giovanni Barbieri, Floriana Cerniglia, Giuseppe F. Gori,
and Patrizia Lattarulo

Introduction

The intention of this chapter is to provide an overview of the Italian National Recovery and Resilience Plan (NRRP), and more specifically, the investment intended to ensure an ecological transition. Implementing the NRRP is particularly challenging in the Italian context and transcends the short-term goal of a prompt post-pandemic economic recovery. On the one hand, it entails a profound overhaul of the type and aim of sectoral investments with the objective of supporting a radical technological transformation for the country. On the other hand, it forces a change of pace, through reforms, in the modernisation process of its institutions and the operating procedures of the economic system. Relaunching public investment is at the heart of the decade-long scientific and institutional debates associated with attempts—in Italy—at reforming the normative framework within which public and private actors operate. Considerable effort has been made to delineate a system that can both facilitate the immediate implementation of construction plans in order to foster economic growth in the short run, and ensure completion within a reliable timeframe, thus guaranteeing that the infrastructures also support growth in the medium and long run.

In the past, reform initiatives clashed with the limited availability of resources and the complexities of multi-level public policy. The NRRP's funds, and related push for reforms, will enable the country to face, in a coordinated and effective manner, one of the main bottlenecks that have dampened Italy's economic growth for decades. Against this backdrop, the investments planned through the NRRP aim to ensure an ecological transition, which is one of its three main strategic axes along with digitisation/innovation and social inclusion.

    https://doi.org/10.11647/OBP.0328.04

Ecological transition touches upon various normatively sensitive issues, involving a plurality of actors, and represents the most substantial aspect of the NRRP in financial terms. Supporting a green economy is a priority for the European Commission, as can be seen from the approach it has required of national systems to tackle their long-term environmental and economic challenges. In fact, the first years of the von der Leyen Commission have been characterised, COVID-19 aside, by a change in European environmental policy, especially with the European Green Deal and heightened activism on legislation which kicked off a notable series of initiatives all centred around making Europe the first continent to become carbon neutral by 2050.

The European Green Deal is supported by Next Generation EU and obliges member states to earmark at least 37% of resources from their NRRPs for measures that contrast climate change, and in addition, to apply the general principle of Do No Significant Harm (DNSH), which stipulates that the overall measures of the NRRPs—even those that are not specifically connected to ecological transition—do not undermine the EU's environmental goals. The Conte II government began redacting the Italian NRRP in the summer of 2020, it was later finalised by the Draghi government in April 2021, and subsequently approved by Parliament. Note that the investments in the Italian Plan are the largest of all the European countries: €191.5bn plus €30.6bn in direct government funding through its Complimentary Fund.[1]

4.1 Public Investment and the NRRP-Italian Public Works Schedule

Given Italy's protracted recession, public investments have become indispensable for relaunching the economy. The past ten years have been characterised by a deep economic and financial crisis, saddled with public budget constraints aimed at debt consolidation, which resulted in the loss of approximately €200 billion in public investments (Figure 4.1) compared to the trend in the prior decade. In short, the loss is equivalent to about five years' worth of investments, at the 2008–2009 pre-crisis rate.[2]

The European funds for the Italian National Recovery and Resilience Plan earmarked for public investment (approximately equivalent to the amount 'lost' over the previous ten years) represent a unique opportunity that cannot be missed to bridge the infrastructure gap. However, there exist well-known and worrisome shortcomings—like low administrative capacity of the public sector and the extended

---

1   The data in this chapter mostly comes from the government's official website: "Italia Domani, il Piano Nazionale di Ripresa e Resilienza", https://italiadomani.gov.it/en/home.html, which provides a detailed description of the NRRP and the state of implementation through intuitive, constantly updated, fact sheets which monitor the investments made and the reform process. By going to the website, anyone can monitor the information provided on the progress and costs of the various measures and the investments made through the NRRP.

2   A detailed assessment of the fall in public investment in the decade from 2008 to 2018 is available in the previous two editions of this series (2020, 2021) in the relevant chapters on Italy.

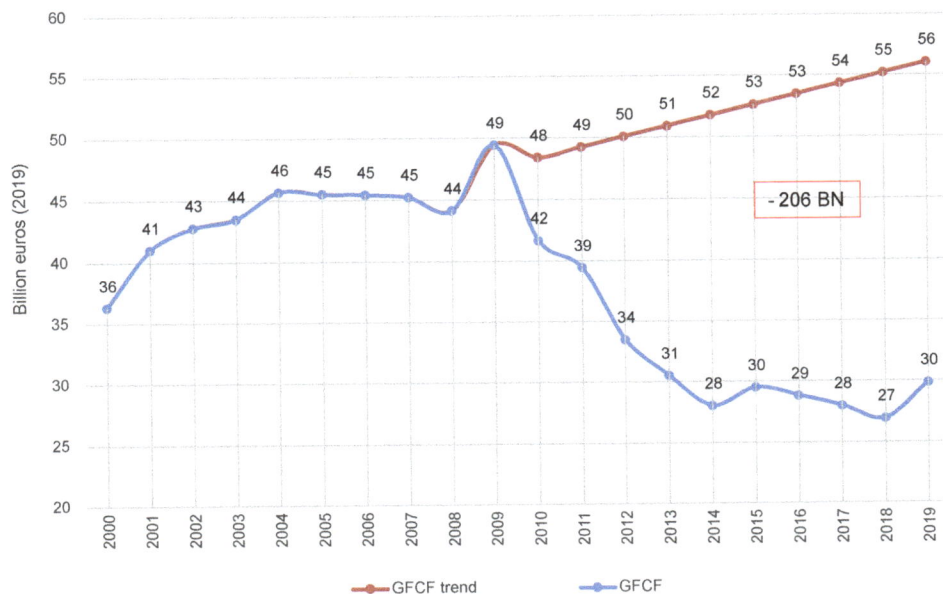

Fig. 4.1 Government gross fixed capital formation (GFCF): real values and trend at constant 2019 prices for Italy.
Source: IRPET calculations based on ISTAT data.

time required to complete public works—that could impede the correct use of funds. The time pressure on projects, from start to completion (end 2026), imposed by the European institutions is due to the realisation that excessively protracted deadlines could not only impact demand in the short-term and countercyclical demand, but if too much time passes, the projects' contributions could wane, or even become irrelevant, if they no longer fulfil the role of dynamic catalysts for the growth and competitiveness of the economic system (Gori and Lattarulo 2022).

It is true that public works in Italy can take a long time from start to finish. Projects greater than €15 million can take up to seven years from the time of award and execution to project completion. The design phase generally takes a large share (from 44% to 56%) of the overall schedule.[3]
The idea of channelling the majority of NRRP resources for investments to "ready-made" or "backburner" projects, for which a large chunk of the planning and design phase has already been done, is aimed at avoiding bottlenecks in the pre-award phase and beating the completion date.

Another important factor to assess the probability of respecting the deadlines established by the NRRP is that the cost of the projects that could start in 2022 represents a significant jump for the public administrations and general contractors

---

3   For an analysis of the determinants of the time scale of public works in Italy, see Gori et al. (2022).

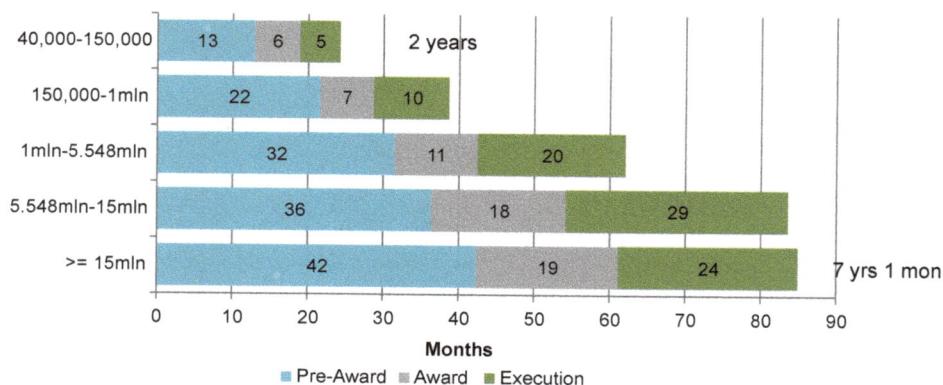

Fig. 4.2. Average time for project phases of public works in Italy (lots) by amounts, 2012–2021 average.
Note: Definitions. Pre-award phase: from the first design phase to the date of publication of the
bid/notice. Award phase: from the date of publication of the bid/notice to the date of publication of
the adjudication report. Execution phase: from the date of publication of the adjudication report to
the date set for project completion. Lot is the part of a public work which is the subject of a tender.
Source: IRPET calculations based on ANAC data.

with respect to previous years. Figure 4.3 compares the average annual cost of projects
undertaken by municipalities and other contracting entities from 2018 to 2020 and the
overall cost of the procedures available through the NRRP in 2022. The funds available
have quadrupled for municipalities and are one and a half times greater for other
contracting entities.

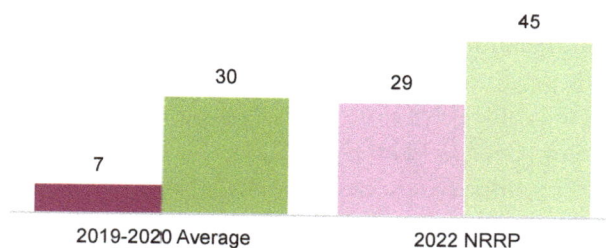

Fig. 4.3. Resources for Construction and Civil Engineering.
Public funding of works undertaken by Italian contractors and funds provided by the NRRP in 2022.
Source: IRPET calculations based on ANAC data.

Dealing with such a large spike in funds and therefore a high project complexity is
challenging for contractors who mainly work with municipalities.[4] The two most
important challenges are connected to the increase in administrative procedures
related to the award phase, and the amount of spending generated by the procedures
and spread over subsequent years. Such a large increase in funds has led to legislative

---

4   On the time for performance of local contractors see Gori et al (2017).

measures being put in place to provide technical, organisational, and accounting support to ensure the effective implementation of investments over the five-year period. These include:

- selection procedures with centralised rankings of senior technical, legal and administrative personnel (approximately 1,000 professionals spread throughout the country);
- simplified budget procedures for municipalities;
- design costs covered by the NRRP;
- other procedural support measures like developing platforms for e-procurement and tenders.

These measures are the result of intense academic and political-institutional debates over the past years. The main reason for the decade-long stagnation of investments by municipalities, besides the limited availability of resources, is the reduced ability to adequately handle an appropriate number of projects, which over time have become increasingly technically complex.

This factor naturally depends on the experience gained over the years and the availability of qualified personnel. However, small and medium municipalities (<= 10,000 residents, which represent 85% of all municipalities) generally award less than three contracts per year with an average cost of less than €300,000, which is hardly enough to guarantee having obtained the needed and necessary specialised technical experience for the size of the current tenders. This matter was already an issue and object of reform before the NRRP.[5]

Starting precisely from these considerations, the NRRP provides a clear framework of reforms and spending strategies. The Italian National Recovery and Resilience Plan is consistent with the EU Commission's indications and provides equal weight to the allocation of resources and to the necessary reforms not only to ensure rapid economic recovery but also to improve the effective management of infrastructure expenditure. In this respect, the NRRP prevalently concentrates on "horizontal" reforms in the public administration and those which "enable" simplification and rationalisation of legislation aimed at managing public contracts for the environment and the accounting of auditing firms.[6] As for public investment, the measures which accompany the expenditure of NRRP resources are especially aimed at ensuring that deadlines are met, hence they focus on two key aspects: strengthening the administrative capacity of contracting authorities and simplifying procedures both upstream at the planning and design stage and downstream at the award stage. A first step was taken with the

---

5 For example the Contract Code (Codice dei Contratti) of 2016 (D.Lgs 50/2016) and other regulatory interventions, which aimed to simplify procedures for public administrations.

6 For a discussion on procurement reforms in Italy see G. Gori, L. Landi, and P. Lattarulo, "Il procurement dei lavori pubblici alla luce delle recenti riforme", Nota di lavoro 2/2020.

extension and consolidation of measures aimed to simplify awarding and authorisation procedures (Simplification bis Decree). However, a more incisive reform is expected with the new Contracts Code which should be approved by 31 March 2023.[7]

4.2 Ecological Transition
and Green Investments in the Italian NRRP

The slump in Italian public investments over the past decade has been associated with an initial significant decrease in its environmental component. In fact, the capital expenditure of public administrations decreased steadily from 2008 to 2014; in 2014 it settled at around 30% less than what was spent in 2000. Today, this gap has not yet been closed. In particular, the decrease in the government's contribution persists; however, it must be noted that the liberalisation/privatisation process has progressively assigned large parts of these investments to state-owned and private enterprises.

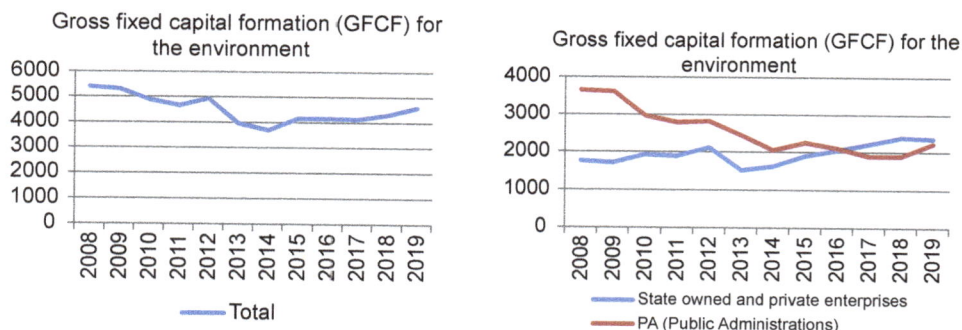

Fig. 4.4 Capital expenditure for environmental services, REAL VALUE.
Source: Calculations based on ISTAT data.

The Italian NRRP has six main missions (Figure 4.5) which follow the six-pillar structure defined by Regulation 2021/241 of the European Parliament and the European Council.[8] The six missions are: 1. Digitisation, innovation, competitiveness, culture and tourism; 2. Green revolution and ecological transition; 3. Infrastructure for sustainable mobility; 4. Education and research; 5. Inclusion and cohesion; 6. Health. The €191.5bn budget is allocated throughout the plan as follows: 21% for Mission 1; 31% for Mission 2; 13.3% for Mission 3; 16.1% for Mission 4; 10,4% for Mission 5 and 8.2% for Mission 6.[9] These missions are in turn further broken down into sixteen components covering a

---

7   The draft law "Government Proxy in Matters of Public Contracts" is in the pipeline, and thanks to the NRRP, it will enable a thorough review of the Call for Tender Code, given the numerous amendments made in the recent years, and ensure Italian legislative compliance with the EU regulatory framework.
8   https://eur-lex.europa.eu/legal-content/EN/TXT/?uri=CELEX%3A32021R0241.
9   For a first sketch of the NRPP see Barbieri and Cerniglia 2021, namely the chapter on Italy in the 2021 volume, pp. 63–78, https://doi.org/10.11647/OBP.0280.

variety of fields and areas of intervention. Its prevalent resource is capital expenditure (62%), followed by incentives for private investments (19%), running expenditure for things like reforms (12%), and the rest for direct transfers and social protection (7%).[10] It is an impressive plan, especially for infrastructure projects (approximately €108bn), which are very important given the significant drop in public investment in previous years.

In this respect, the strong ecological imprint of the NRRP represents an important factor in rebalancing investments in favour of those with significant green content. Mission 2 of the Italian NRRP is dedicated to ecological transition (and green revolution), €59.5bn[11] have been earmarked with the aim to bridge the current gap, €27bn of which will be for existing projects. It has the most funding of all the missions, with no less than 31% of the total NRRP resources (€191.5bn).

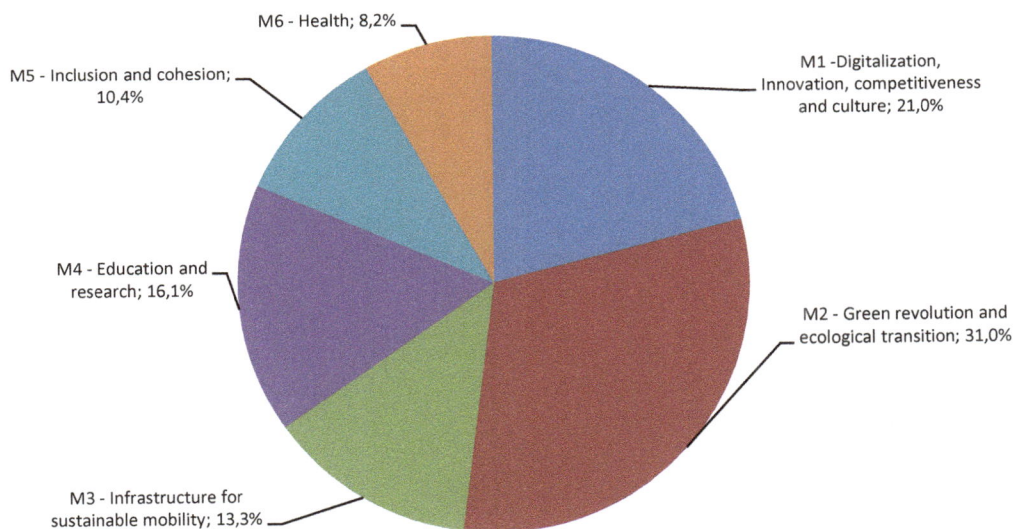

M6 - Health; 8,2%

M5 - Inclusion and cohesion; 10,4%

M1 -Digitalization, Innovation, competitiveness and culture; 21,0%

M4 - Education and research; 16,1%

M2 - Green revolution and ecological transition; 31,0%

M3 - Infrastructure for sustainable mobility; 13,3%

Fig. 4.5 Percentage of NRRP funding by Mission.
Source: Calculations based on Italia Domani data.

However, further funds will also be used through measures more generally directed at climate objectives, which define the broader set of green investments. For each measure, whether or not it falls under Mission 2, the European Commission has associated a climate target coefficient of zero, 40% or 100%. While not all the measures under Mission 2 have a 100% compliance coefficient with the climate objectives, other

---

10 Corte dei conti, Relazione sullo stato di attuazione del Piano Nazionale di ripresa e resilienza, March 2022.

11 The National Complimentary Fund (Fondo Nazionale Complementare) has allocated an additional €9.6bn of its €30.6bn budget to Mission 2, bringing the total budget for Mission 2 to €68.66bn.

missions can have measures with a positive or even 100% compliance coefficient. For example (Figure 4.6, column chart), the "green" quota of the resources used by Mission 3 (Infrastructure for sustainable mobility) is around 82%, which is higher than that of Mission 2 (78%); however, the green resources for Mission 3 (€20.8bn) are only half of those for Mission 2 (€46.2bn). In short, roughly €71.7bn will be dedicated to green investments, 93.4% of the funds will come from Missions 2 and 3 (64.4% and 29%, respectively) and will be divided into 108 actions (Figure 4.6, pie chart).

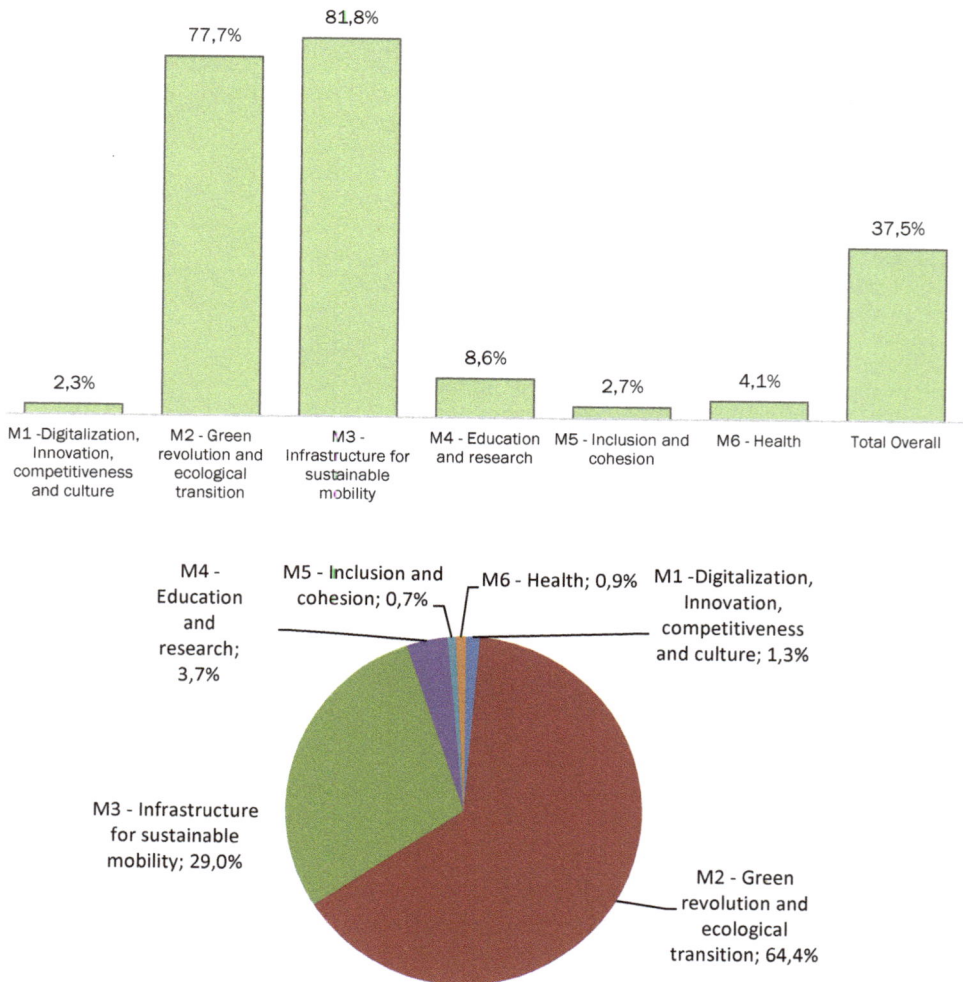

Fig. 4.6 Percentage of green investment by Mission (column chart) and breakdown of green investment by mission (pie chart).
Source: Calculations on Italia Domani data.

Out of the total funding allocated to the Italian NRRP, green investment accounts for 37.5%, which is slightly above the minimum threshold set by the EU. However, in absolute terms, it is by far the most significant investment of all the EU countries.

The overall policy mix for green investment in the NRRP includes proper public investments as well as support for investments by enterprises and private citizens. The breakdown by components (Table 4.1) highlights a major concentration of actions in the fields of renewable energy, hydrogen, networks, sustainable mobility (30.5%) and investments in the national rail network (28.7%).

Table 4.1. NRRP—Green investment by mission and component.

Mission-Component	Description	MM Euro	Share
M2-C1	Sustainable Agriculture and Circular Economy	2.3	3.2%
M2-C2	Renewable energy, hydrogen and sustainable local mobility	21.9	30.5%
M2-C3	Energy efficiency and redevelopment of buildings	12.6	17.6%
M2-C4	Protection and valorisation of land and water resources	9.4	13.1%
M3-C1	High railway speed and road maintenance 4.0	20.6	28.7%
	Other	5.0	6.9%
	Total	71.7	100.0%

Source: Calculations on Italia Domani data.

A more effective classification is proposed by Brugnaro and Orlando (2022), who group investments into four broad categories: transportation and other green infrastructure, efficiency gains, renewable energy, and environmental protection.

The first category (transportation and other green infrastructure) groups the total investments earmarked in Mission 3 for the national rail network (€20.6bn) and in Mission 2 for sustainable mass urban transport and alternative transportation (€9bn).

The second category (energy efficiency) mainly concerns immovable assets and includes measures to reduce energy consumption or substitute existing fossil fuels with green energy. Funding for improving the energy efficiency of public buildings is only a small part (€2.1bn), and the bulk will go to improving the energy efficiency of private buildings (€12.1bn). The latter measure is the most significant green expenditure in the NRRP and consists of renovation incentive mechanisms (110% super-bonus) introduced as early as in the Initial stages of the pandemic. Lastly, another measure that falls into this category is upgrading smart power grids (€3.6bn).

Measures for enhancing green transportation/infrastructure and improving energy efficiency represent 71% of the NRRP's green resources and include individual measures with significant budgets. A partial list of these measures is reported in Table 4.2 with reference to their NRPP mission and component.

The remaining share of resources falls into the categories of renewable energy (approximately 14%) and environmental protection (15%). The primary measures include the construction of solar energy plants (€4.6bn), and measures for developing the bio-methane sector (building new plants and upgrading existing ones), hydrogen (research, production, distribution) wind energy and charging/fuelling

Table 4.2. Main NRRP green measures by budget size.

Measure	Description	BN Euros
M2C2I2.01	Upgrading smart electricity grids	3.6
M2C2I4.02	Development of rapid mass transport (subway, trams, buses)	3.6
M2C2I4.04	Renewal of bus fleets and trains with low environmental impact	3.4
M2C3I2.01	Support for energy efficiency and seismic resistance of private and public buildings	12.1
M2C4I2.02	Interventions for increased resilience, land enhancement and improved energy efficiency of the municipalities	4.2
M3C1I1.01	Construction of new high capacity/high-speed lines along the main routes in the South for passengers and freight	4.6
M3C1I1.02	High capacity/high-speed lines that connect the North to Europe	8.6
M3C1I1.05	Upgrading metropolitan railway junctions and key national rail networks	3.0

infrastructures. A hefty sum (€2.2bn) will also be used for promoting renewables for energy communities and self-consumption. The largest portion of environmental protection—mainly Component 4 of Mission 2—is a mixed bag of measures for adapting to climate change, such as management and prevention of flood risks (approximately €6bn).

Finally, it is worth mentioning the horizontal principle of DSNH (Do No Significant Harm). Respecting this principle as well as exceeding the threshold of 37% of resources allocated to environmental objectives was a precondition for the NRRP's approval. Therefore, the set of measures and reforms in the Italian NRRP was assessed on the basis of six indicators, or environmental objectives: adapting to climate change; sustainable use and protection of water and marine resources; transition to a circular economy; prevention and reduction of air, water, and soil pollution; and protection and recovery of biodiversity and ecosystems. The assessment was conducted with a long-term view, in order to consider all the anticipated effects, both direct and indirect, on the indicators. Based on the analysis, the effects were then placed in four scenarios: (1) the measure has negligible or zero impact on the objective, (2) the measure supports the objective 100%, (3) the measure "substantially" contributes to the environmental objective, (4) the measure requires an overall DNSH assessment.

When evaluations fell into one of the first three scenarios, a simplified DSNH compliance certification procedure was adopted, which required public administrations to draft a brief statement. Evaluations in the fourth scenario—mainly investments and reforms in sectors such as energy, transport, or waste management—required a more in-depth analysis.

Note that most major measures shown in Table 4.2 are associated with a 100% contribution coefficient to climate objectives, which require the simplified DSNH compliance certification procedure.

4.3 Related Reforms

The NRRP's ambitious reform agenda includes three types of reforms: "horizontal reforms" (which concern the public administration (PA) and legal system), "enabling reforms" aimed at ensuring the implementation of the NRRP (including the reform of public procurement contracts), and 'sectoral reforms' specific to each of the six missions.

When considering sectoral reforms, the NRRP does not restrict the use of natural resources, it addresses the challenge of environmental sustainability by introducing measures to provide incentives for disseminating innovative technologies (e.g. hydrogen), prioritising the optimisation of resource management (water and waste), and simplifying procedures, as a strategy to facilitate the widespread and speedy dissemination of energy efficient plants and green technologies. Obtaining authorisations is an important cause of delays in public works and it is also a factor that generates great uncertainty for the overall timetable, which is a problem that has been repeatedly referred to by contractors (Gori and Lattarulo 2021).

The NRRP is committed to boosting interventions through a simplification process aimed at easing the authorisation burden of PAs as well as that of households and businesses. Measures have been provided to support procuring entities and the PA responsible for environmental authorisations. Furthermore, specific actions are foreseen to create synergy between public and private resources. Thus, the main sectoral reforms for a green transition, as identified in the Italia Domani (NRRP) documents, focus on a national strategy for a circular economy and waste management, a legal framework for more efficient water resource management, and the simplification of regulatory procedures for renewable energy, renovations, and local public services. In other words, it addresses the important themes of regulating public services and a myriad of measures aimed at simplifying procedures in many areas (from the promotion and diffusion of hydrogen to speeding up procedures for producing energy from renewable energy sources and for—public and private—energy efficient plants, and measures to contrast hydrogeological risks). The complete list of reforms is in Table 4.3 below.

More specifically, concerning the main fields of action, the "National Waste Management Programme" is aimed at promoting the mechanisation of urban selective waste collection and the proliferation of modern disposal/recycling plants. The plan is expected to be adopted by the end of June 2022, and act as a preliminary step to plant modernisation investments. Technical support will be provided to those local authorities who have difficulty with programming and implementation.

Table 4.3 List of reforms under Mission 2 Green Revolution and Ecological Transition.

Measure	Description
M2C1	Sustainable agriculture and circular economy
M2C1 1.1	National strategy for circular economy
M2C1 1.2	National waste management programme
M2C1 1.3	Technical support to local authorities
M2C2	Renewable energy, hydrogen, infrastructure and sustainable mobility
M2C2 1.1	Simplification of authorisation procedures for onshore and offshore renewable plants; new legal framework to support production from renewable sources and extension of the time frame and eligibility of current support regimes
M2C2 1.2	New legislation for promoting renewable gas production and consumption
M2C2 3	Administratively simplifying and reducing regulatory barriers to hydrogen deployment
M2C3	Energy efficiency and safety of buildings
M2C3 1.1	Simplifying and speeding up procedures for adopting energy efficiency measures
M2C4	Protection of the territory and water resources
M2C4 2.1	Simplifying and speeding up procedures for undertaking initiatives against hydrogeological instability
M2C4 3.1	Adoption of national air pollution control programmes
M2C4 4.2	Measures to ensure full management capacity of integrated water services

Source: Italia Domani Ministry for Ecological Transition (Ministero della Transizione Ecologica) Implementation of NRRP Measures, December 2021.

Facilitating and in general simplifying authorisation procedures is essential. In the energy sector it is important to encourage the use of renewables and the construction of power plants on a regional/national scale—with a focus on promoting hydrogen as the main source of clean energy, and energy efficiency by optimising electricity stocking systems. It is also necessary in the building sector to facilitate renovation authorisations for residential buildings.

"Measures to ensure full management capacity of integrated water services" include strengthening the industrial development of the sector, especially in the lagging South, whose inability to resolve its shortcomings alone has been acknowledged. Regarding hydrogeological risks, the focus is mainly on the simplification of procedures and the provision of support to operators.

4.4 Multilevel Governance and the Role of Local Governments

The NRRP's governance (defined in DL 77/21[12]) is very hierarchical; it focuses on national implementation and the Council Presidency. It is a complex structure nested in a system of oversight and coordination by the Italian Presidency of the Council of

---

12   https://temi.camera.it/leg18/temi/d-l-77-2021-governance-del-pnrr-e-semplificazioni.html.

Ministers, the Ministry of Economy and Finance (MEF), and interactions at various administrative levels for the implementation of measures.

The first level is the European level, which coordinates and monitors measures through relevant technical and political interactions, including the various institutions and social partners. As for the second (national) level, the Ministry for Ecological Transition is "the point Ministry" for all of the measures in the NRRP, while the other ministries are responsible for the various related components. It is in charge of coordinating the work of the other implementing parties and interfacing with the European Commission (EC). The regions, along with the pertinent territorial authorities and other public and private bodies, are the "implementors" of the "assigned projects". The Ministry has a "mission structure" equivalent to that at the national level, which is capable of coordination, oversight, and reporting. It is responsible for stipulating agreements with the implementors. Overall, the governance of the NRRP is highly centralised at the national, executive level, and more specifically in the office of the Prime Minister. Various ministries however have the authority to make important investment and implementation decisions. This also means that the specific identification and location of the projects rests with the ministries through normative provisions.

An important investment role is given to local governments, especially municipalities, in the NRRP. However, these entities have witnessed the significant depletion of their resources and competencies due to a decade of fiscal restrictions, especially the 2008 financial crisis. Consequently, the risks linked to their implementation capability are significant.

The resources assigned to local governments, specifically in Mission 2, are quite considerable (approximately €20bn for regions, municipalities and other governing bodies, see Figure 4.7 and Table 4.4); which means that, as a consequence, so is the increase in responsibility for project implementation. More specifically, €6bn have been earmarked for "Actions aimed at increasing resilience, enhancing land and improving energy efficiency" (M2C3. 2.2); €3bn for "Rapid mass transport development" (M2C2.4.2); and €2.4bn for "Renovation of bus fleets and green trains" (M2C2. 4.4.1).

The main strategy aimed at easing the work of public administrations, especially in the South—the major recipients of the funding—is based on strengthening administrative capacity. More specifically, it concerns those actions that have to do with improving human capital skills and supporting small and remote municipalities with their planning. Thus, the NRRP provides for temporary employment contracts of technical personnel that cover the period of the investment. In order to overcome the lack of resources or planning capacity of small and remote municipalities, resources have been specifically earmarked for recruiting technical personnel. In order to speed up the recruitment procedures, a centralised selection process for specialised personnel has been established. Public authorities who need other types of support can refer to Consip, Invitalia, CdP, Anac, or Sogei for help using resources from MEF. In short, a mix of measures and resources has been established with the intent of bridging the

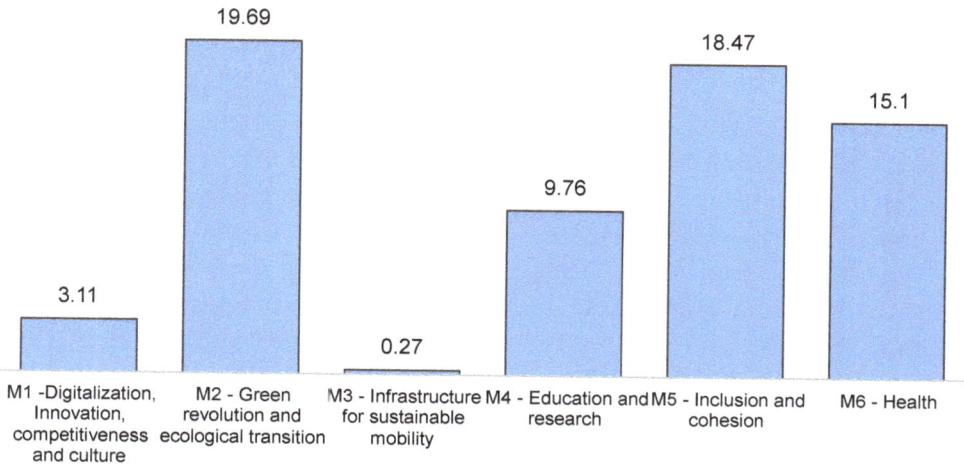

Fig. 4.7 Estimate of resources for territorial authorities by NRRP Mission.
Source: Italia Domani 2021.

various shortcomings of these local administrations. Only municipalities that are regional capitals or joint municipalities can award contracts, while all municipalities can introduce measures that simplify administrative procedures.

However, many limitations to these measures are already beginning to emerge; for example, technical personnel are being recruited at a slow pace due to a lack of adequate administrative skills, public administrations are suspicious of a possible imbalance in resources (investments vs current expenditure), and there is concern that the schedules set by the NRRP may not be respected, leading to refusals of personal responsibility by public administrators. Last but not least, there are price-side tensions caused by a weakened production system and an impoverished public sector following years of economic crises and further worsened by exceptional economic circumstances.

4.5 Conclusions

Linked to the success of Italia Domani, Italy's NRRP, is a huge gamble for the future of the country, and for the general consolidation of European integration, which must increasingly focus on investments to finance European public goods. The gamble for Italy is quite significant due to the resources involved, the structural lags that must be overcome, and the major political consensus required on the overall objectives and/or missions that the NRRP has placed on the political agenda.

Causes for concern include the deadlines set by the European Commission, the insufficient planning and execution capacity of public administrations faced with such huge investment resources, and the laborious cooperation required by the social partners and political parties for the reform process.

Swift implementation of the measures is essential for a rapid economic recovery in the short term and the launch of a solid recovery in the medium to long run, which must contend with major changes in technological innovation, ecological transition and social cohesion. The resources earmarked for ecological transition are a bit (if not much) over the 37% mark imposed by the EU and amount to investments of €72bn in energy efficiency, sustainable mobility, renewable energy, circular economy (which is almost equivalent to Italy's capital expenditure of the previous fifteen years on environmental protection and water and waste management). It should also be noted that the Ministry for Economic Development in its National Integrated Energy and Climate Plan (2019) estimated an overall need for investments for the 2017–2020 period of approximately €1.194bn, €800bn of which are for the transport sector.[13]

The government has thus intervened with multiple instruments to support public administrations, with a preference for supporting human capital and simplifying administrative procedures. On the former point, it has intervened by offering greater recruitment possibilities, the availability of resources, and the pre-selection of qualified personnel. On the latter point, both the enabling reforms and the sectoral reforms related to Mission 2 place significant attention on simplifying administrative and authorisation procedures for measures linked to the environment.

Some of the limits of the measures aimed at supporting public administrations are now emerging, as are the numerous contradictions in the overall process. One is the limited effectiveness of the measures with respect to the huge investments available, especially in the Southern regions, which is even more grave if one considers that rebalancing the territorial divide is one of the NRRP's priorities as well as an urgent national requirement. There is also a need for additional current expenditure to sustain investments made by the public administrations in those cases where the savings obtained are not sufficient to cover future expenditures.

However, the most worrisome prospect for the disbursement of investments is the recent inflationary trend, especially in the energy and construction goods markets. Prices were already increasing before the Ukraine crisis; in fact, the Italian government had responded by creating a price adjustment fund for contractors. Nonetheless, the resources that have been made available through the fund and other government interventions might not be sufficient to cover the local administrations' needs, especially those of municipalities. If costs cannot be covered, procurement authorities will not be in a position to launch tendering procedures, making the risk of a substantial gridlock in the tendering process quite real. In conclusion, this inflationary effect could become embedded in the Italian system, which currently already suffers from significant lags in the entire procurement process.

---

13   https://www.mise.gov.it/images/stories/documenti/PNIEC_finale_17012020.pdf. This plan is in the process of being updated by the Ministry, and more recent data on investment needs will soon be available.

References

Brugnara, L., and C. Orlando (2022) 108 misure Verdi, cosa fa il PNRR per la transizione ecologica, Osservatorio Conti Pubblici Italiani (OCPI), 12 May, https://osservatoriocpi. unicatt.it/ocpi-pubblicazioni-108-misure-verdi-cosa-fa-il-pnrr-per-la-transizione-ecologica.

Cerniglia, F. and G. Barbieri, (2021) "Relaunching Public Investments in Italy", in F. Cerniglia, F. Saraceno, and A. Watts (eds), The Great Reset: 2021 European Public Investment Outlook. Cambridge: Open Book Publishers, pp. 63–78, https://www.openbookpublishers. com/10.11647/OBP.0280.

Cerniglia, F. and F. Rossi (2020) "Public Investment Trends across Levels of Government in Italy", in F. Cerniglia and F. Saraceno (eds), A European Public Investment Outlook. Cambridge: Open Book Publishers, pp. 63–81, https://www.openbookpublishers.com/10.11647/ obp.0222.

Corte dei conti (2022) Relazione sullo stato di attuazione del Piano Nazionale di ripresa e resilienza, March, https://www.corteconti.it/Download?id=ece03c3a-0a39-449a-8d19-3105b75ded32.

Ferretti, C., G. Gori, and P. Lattarulo, (2020) "Tutela dei bisogni e investimenti, il ruolo dei comuni di fronte all'emergenza covid-19", in Ires, Irpet, Srm, Polis, Ires, Liguria ricerche, Aur, (eds) La finanza territoriale, Rapporto 2020, Catanzaro Rubbettino, pp. 23–41.

Gori, G. F., P. Lattarulo, and N. C. Salerno (2022) "L'efficienza temporale nella realizzazione delle opere pubbliche in Italia", Nota di lavoro UPB 2/2022, https://www.upbilancio.it/ nota-di-lavoro-2-2022/.

Gori, G. and P. Lattarulo, (2022) "Decentramento e investimenti pubblici locali negli scenari del PNRR", in N. Antonetti, and A. Pajno (eds), Stato e sistema delle autonomie dopo la pandemia. Bologna: Il Mulino, 203–16.

Gori, G., L. Landi, and P. Lattarulo, (2020) "Il procurement dei lavori pubblici alla luce delle recenti riforme", Nota di lavoro 2/2020, https://www.upbilancio.it/nota-di-lavoro-22020/; http://www.irpet.it/archives/55544.

Gori, G., P. Lattarulo, and M. Mariani (2017) "Understanding the Procurement Performances of Local Government: A Duration Analysis of Public Works", Environment and Planning C: Politics and Space 35(5), https://doi.org/10.1177/0263774X16680109.

Gori, G., L. Landi and P. Lattarulo (2020) "Il procurement dei lavori pubblici alla luce delle recenti riforme, UPB" Note di lavoro 2/2020, https://www.upbilancio.it/wp-content/ uploads/2020/05/Nota-appalti-2_2020.pdf.

Presidency of the Council of Ministers (2021) "Italia Domani. Piano Nazionale di Ripresa e Resilienza". Italian Government, https://italiadomani.gov.it/en/home.html.

Senato e Camera dei Deputati (2022) "Monitoraggio del l'attuazione del Piano Nazionale di Ripresa e Resilienza", Dossier, 30 June, https://documenti.camera.it/leg18/dossier/pdf/ DFP28d.pdf?_1665063471640.

Viesti, G. (2021) "Il PNRR e il Mezzogiorno : 80 miliardi, un totale in cerca di addendi", *Quaderno di Rassegna Sindacale*, 2/2021, https://www.futura-editrice.it/prodotto/qrs-n-2-2021/.

Viesti, G. (2022) "The Territorial Dimension of the Italian NRRP", in A. Caloffi, M. De Castris, and G. Perucca, *The Regional Challenges in the Post-Covid Era*, AISRE, Milan: Franco Angeli, pp. 201–18, https://series.francoangeli.it/index.php/oa/catalog/book/858.

Viesti, G. (2022) "Un piano per rilanciare l'Italia ?", in *L'Italia nella bufera*, Il Mulino 2/2022, 28–38.

5. Current Challenges in the Spanish Energy Market

José Villaverde, Lucía Ibáñez Luzon, Daniel Balsalobre-Lorente, and Adolfo Maza

Introduction

Today, the study of the energy market, and the ongoing challenges, is one of the main topics of discussion in any context, academic or otherwise. And the role played by public initiatives in this framework is beyond doubt. In this chapter, we intend to make a modest contribution to this debate, albeit concerning the particular situation in Spain.

After reviewing the historical evolution of the energy mix in Spain, we pay special attention to the effect that the different energy packages approved by the EC and their implementations (the regulatory changes they entailed) have had on Spain. In the second section, we focus on public policies and specific support plans for a green transition over the period 2020–2030. Subsequently, in the third section, the current scenario after the COVID-19 pandemic and the Russian invasion of Ukraine is scrutinised, focusing on the Spanish government's response to the guidelines set by the EC. To be precise, both the Next Generation EU and the REPowerEU plans are examined. Finally, some conclusions and policy suggestions are made.

5.1 Evolution of the Spanish Energy Sector: A Retrospective Review

During the first decades of the twentieth century (1900–1940), electricity production in Spain was based on imported fossil fuels, especially coal. Great Britain was the world's top coal-producing country (Seo 2008) and the biggest importer of Spain. Then in the years of the Francoist regime (1939–1975), the military regime spread a rhetoric of autarky and self-sufficiency, which they mobilised to build their systems of domestic infrastructures and international connections (Campubrí 2019). Due to the weight given to hydropower, the energy sector in Spain differed from other developed

https://doi.org/10.11647/OBP.0328.05

countries, with greater dependence on imports of fossil fuels and greater susceptibility to drought periods (BP Statistical Review 2020).

Between 1965 and 1975, the generation structure changed substantially: hydroelectric sources' weight decreased from 17% in 1965 to only 9% in 1975. Jointly with coal plants, fuel plants' weight also increased (doubling in ten years) in a low oil price context.

At a global level, two oil crises impacted profoundly global economies, the oil crisis of 1973/1974 and the second major oil crisis of 1979/1980 (Baumenster and Kilian 2016). These crises had an enormous negative impact on the economy and fostered the rise of nuclear energy, whose production increased sixfold between 1970 and 1980. The Spanish Parliament approved the first National Energy Plan in 1975 to deal with Spanish dependence on oil (which accounted for 68% of primary energy consumption in 1974).

The energy policy direction was similar to those in other developed countries. At the end of 1986, coal represented 55% of the energy mix and nuclear energy 11%, while in 1973, they only represented 17% and 3%, respectively (BP Statistical Review 2021).[1]

In the 1990s, the European Union launched a common EU reform promoting a common European energy market. The first liberalisation directives (First Energy Package) were adopted in 1996 (electricity) and 1998 (gas), to be transposed into member states' legal systems by 1998 (electricity) and 2000 (gas). The main objectives of this reform were to gain increased competition and maintain a good quality of service while protecting the environment and fostering renewable energies as part of the plan. A wave of deregulation started with the objective of increasing competition since, in most countries, the public sector controlled the whole supply chain.

The deregulation process was complex, and entry barriers to the energy market were substantial. In some cases, there was a coexistence of horizontally and vertically integrated structures, market distortions, inelastic demand and supply, and high external dependence, among other factors. When the average external sourcing dependence in the EU was 65%, external sourcing dependence reached 80% in Spain.

During the first decade of the twenty-first century, it was clear that it was still necessary to address more market integration and deregulation reforms. European legislation pointed to the development of liquid and efficient internal markets as the solution to achieving a solid and reliable European energy market.

The Second Energy Package promoted by the European Commission was adopted in 2003. Its directives were to be transposed into national law by the member states by 2004, and some provisions entered into force only in 2007. In Spain, some regulatory changes were implemented, and in January 2003, consumers were entitled

---

1   At that point, the level of inflation was high, so the government decided to regulate energy prices. The government intervened in the sector in different ways; one was the transmission of high-voltage lines or the creation of the 1985 *Red Eléctrica de España* (REE) to deal with the electricity system operation. That same year, Spain joined the European Union.

to choose their supplier for the first time. Thus, the level of market concentration in Spain has steadily improved since then due to regulatory and institutional efforts to lower market barriers and improve efficiency in the process. In April 2009, the Third Energy Package drafted by the European Commission sought to further liberalise the internal electricity and gas markets, amending the Second Package and providing the cornerstone for the implementation of the internal energy market. The EC's rationale for increasing competition within internal markets was to transfer the boundaries of increasing efficiency to the consumers through prices.

In June 2019, the European Commission introduced the Fourth Energy Package, composed of the Electricity Directive 2019/944/EU and three regulations. This new regulatory package aimed to bring in new market rules to increase the penetration of renewable energies while attracting investment. It delivers incentives, such as new limits for PPs eligible for subsidies, or other incentives aimed at consumers. It promotes the role of the Agency for the Cooperation of Energy Regulators (ACER) in dealing with cross-border regulatory issues. As well as this, it introduces an obligation for member states to prepare contingency plans for a potential energy crisis related to the Security of Supply. Also, the fourth package recognises the importance of renewable sources and promotes their penetration.

As a summary of all the above, Figures 5.1 and 5.2 present the evolution of the energy mix in Spain in absolute and relative terms. As can be seen, after the transposition of the directives mentioned above into national legislation in Spain, the energy mix has changed significantly. In any case, oil has always been the primary energy source in Spain. Coal played an important role in the second half of the twentieth century, but its weight has been decreasing over the years, like hydropower. The penetration of renewables, especially wind and solar, is remarkable and has been increasing over the last twenty years, mainly due to the role played by subsidies and incentives, which have been determinant factors in the diffusion of renewable energy sources.

Spain is one of the countries in the EU with the most hours of sunshine: on average around 2,500 hours per year and radiation of 1650 kWh/m2. For that reason, electricity generation through solar panels has great potential. As for wind energy, Spain is the fifth country globally in terms of installed wind power after China, the US, Germany and India.

Figure 5.3 focuses on the year 2020. It illustrates the technologies that represented a more significant share of electricity generation in 2020, such as nuclear (23%), wind (22%) and combined cycle (16%), followed by hydro (13%) and cogeneration (11%). Compared to the previous year (although this is not shown owing to space restrictions), the reduction in the shares of generation from natural gas combined cycle (16% in 2020, compared to 21% in 2019) and from coal (2% in 2020, compared to 4% in 2019) stood out due to a lower registered demand due to the health crisis and the greater participation of generation via renewable technologies. The share for generation via renewable technologies stood at 46% in 2020 (39% in 2019).

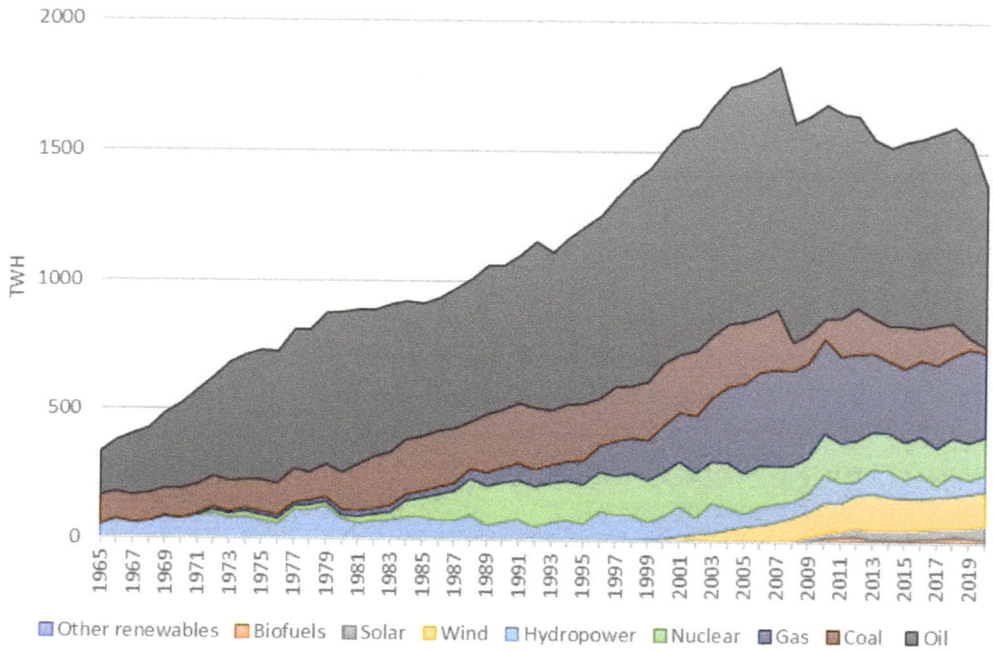

Fig. 5.1 Evolution of the energy mix in Spain in absolute terms (1965–2020, TWh).
Source of data: Own production, BP Statistical Review (2021).

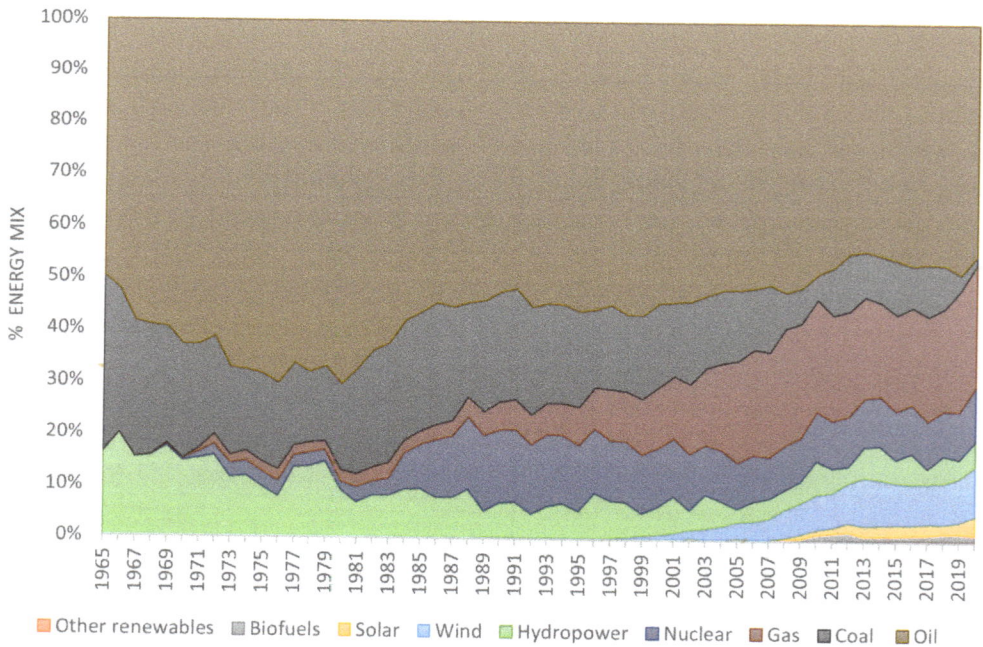

Fig. 5.2 Evolution of the energy mix in Spain in relative terms (1965–2020, %).
Source of data: Own production, BP Statistical Review (2022).

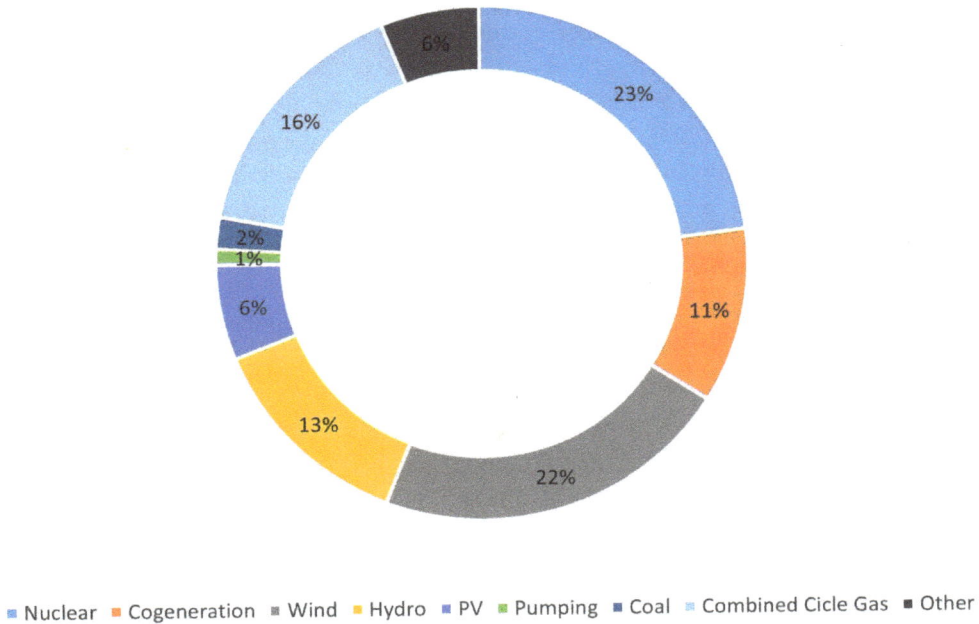

Fig. 5.3 Energy mix in Spain (2020).
Source of data: Own elaboration, CNMC (2022).

Consequently, the peninsular generating park reached 105,683 MW in 2020 due to an increase of 1GW related to the installation of an improved renewable generation capacity (4,735 MW) and the closure of coal-fired power plants (3,723 MW) (CNMC 2022).

5.2 Public Policies for a Green Transition (2020–2030)

Taking action to prevent environmental degradation is a core principle of the Treaty of the European Union and a priority objective for the 'EU's internal and external policies. The Treaty of the European Union sets out its vision for sustainable development based on balanced economic growth combined with a high level of protection and improvement of the quality of the environment. In the fight against environmental degradation, the EC works on different but complementary key points, such as urban environment, sustainable consumption and industrial sustainability.

As part of the EU, Spain follows the same energy policy framework. In line with EU objectives, the aims of the Spanish government are: (1) to reduce dependency and ensure the security of supply, (2) to reduce greenhouse emissions and (3) to reduce energy intensity. It could be said that Spain has been one of the leading EU countries in terms of enactment of the energy transition in recent years. One of the factors for this success has been the significant penetration of renewable energy sources.

The 20–20–20 Strategy provided a set of laws defined by the European Commission to cut greenhouse emissions, increase 'the share of renewables, and improve energy efficiency by 2020. These objectives were settled in 2009 through EU legislation. Spain achieved the last two of these goals, but did not accomplish the goal regarding greenhouse emissions (20% cut in greenhouse gas emissions from 1990 levels). This objective is deferred for 2030, meaning Spain's economy would have to produce no more than around 230 million tons of CO_2 equivalent in nine years.

Consequently, in 2020 the Spanish government presented an ambitious plan to cut the country's net carbon emissions to zero by 2050. The goal to decarbonise the Spanish economy and achieve carbon neutrality by 2050 will be achieved, on the one hand, by reducing emissions and, on the other, by offsetting the emissions that continue to be produced with mitigation actions. The so-called Long-Term Decarbonisation Strategy will allow a 90% reduction in greenhouse gas emissions in 2050 compared to those emitted in 1990. The remaining 10% will be absorbed by carbon sinks (about 37 $MtCO_2$eq by 1950), as the government details.

As for the second goal (more specifically, that 20% of the EU's energy comes from renewable energies), Spain has fulfilled its role. At the end of 2020, 21.2% of the final energy demand in Spain was covered with renewables, a percentage slightly below the EU average (22.1%), but above the 2020 objective.

The government's main approach to pushing for renewable energy sources was the introduction of a feed-in tariff (FIT) scheme that was suspended in 2013 in response to the economic crisis. After the suspension of the FIT scheme, the sector initially collapsed. In 2015, however, the renewable energy market pumped once again.

Finally, Spain reached the third objective (20% improvement in energy efficiency). It was significantly exceeded in Spain, achieving 35.4% by 2020. Regarding the energy intensity target previously mentioned (reach 20%), endorsed with the adoption of the Energy Efficiency Directive 2012/27/EU in 2012, between 2017 and 2019, the total energy consumption in Spain was reduced by 14.2%, making Spain the third best country in the EU.

To reach third place, Spanish authorities launched several subsidy schemes to push for energy efficiency measures that would achieve such an improvement. One example was the so-called PAREER-CRECE programme (*Programa de Ayudas para la Rehabilitación Energética de Edificios existentes*), a support scheme for increasing the energy efficiency of existing buildings, launched in May 2015 with a total budget of €200M.

In the same vein, more recently, in December 2020, the European Commission proposed new goals for the following decade as part of the European Green Deal, known as the 2030 climate and energy framework. Its objectives are: (1) to reduce greenhouse emissions to at least 40% compared to 1990, (2) at least a 32.5% improvement in energy efficiency and (3) a minimum 32% share of renewable energy sources in the generation mix. The emissions trading system goes some way towards the 40% reduction of greenhouse emissions.

Following this path, Spain was authorised the *Estrategia Nacional de Energía 2020*, focusing on various measures like improvements in the energy management of public and private lighting, fostering RES in generation (mainly solar, but also wind), innovative projects related to smart grids, local energy communities and electric vehicles and fiscal incentives.

1. **Reduction of emissions:** The measures contemplated in the *Plan Nacional Integrado de Energía y Clima* (PNIEC) seek a reduction from 340.2 million tons of CO_2 equivalent ($MtCO_2$-eq) emitted in 2017 to 226 $MtCO_2$-eq in 2030. The decrease in GHG emissions will be accompanied by a reduction in primary pollutants affecting air quality.

2. **Promotion of renewable energies:** The promotion of renewable energies in the next decade is one of the main vectors for achieving the objectives of the PNIEC. Renewable energies are expected to amount to 42% of the country's total energy use in 2030. In the case of electricity generation, the percentage of renewables is set to reach 74%. Concerning storage, the increase in pumping and battery technologies stands out, with an additional capacity of 6 GW providing greater generation management capacity. Spain is looking at a future of increased electrification of end-use sectors and sector coupling as analysed by the IEA.

3. **Sustainable mobility:** The mobility and transport sector will reduce emissions by 28 $MtCO_2$-eq between 2021 and 2030. The penetration of renewables in the mobility sector will reach 22% in 2030 through the incorporation of around five million electric vehicles and advanced biofuels. Based on this commitment, a Comprehensive Support Plan for the Automotive Sector 2019–2020 has already been established, and allocated €562 million.

4. **Energy efficiency:** As a result of applying the measures defined in the PNIEC, energy efficiency is expected to achieve a 39.5% share by 2030, which equates to an improvement in primary energy intensity of 3.5% per year until 2030. Among the measures proposed in this regard, priority is given to energy rehabilitation of existing buildings, in line with the objectives of the Spanish Urban Agenda, which also includes the fight against energy poverty and improving universal accessibility, especially for vulnerable consumers. The PNIEC forecasts an average annual rate of energy rehabilitation of 120,000 houses in the next decade. Public investment is articulated, among other mechanisms, through the State Housing Plan.

The 2020 and 2030 objectives have been and will be accomplished through public policies and specific support plans. Apart from the specific funding plans mentioned in the previous paragraphs, RD&D programmes have been an essential pillar of the energy transition and are important for securing competitiveness in the provision of clean energy in Spain. Two examples are the Strategic Energy Technology Plans (SET-Plans) that endorse collaborative RD&D engagement, and the National Energy and Climate Plans (NECPs) that shape the EU's energy sector governance and ensure it meets its climate and energy targets. NECPs also address the need to align state research and development activities, particularly those that target renewable energy technologies (EU 2019; IEA 2020).

In December 2015, the European Union and twenty-four governments signed the Mission Innovation (MI) initiative in conjunction with the Paris Agreement. They committed to double public R&D support for clean energy technologies up to 2020 (Cunliff 2019). Additionally, the European Green Deal (EU 2019) and the European Commission's research and innovation programme 'Horizon Europe' (2021–2027), have configured a powerful organ with a total budget of €95.5 billion. This policy instrument is the largest ever transnational research and innovation programme, 35% of whose funding will be allocated to correcting climate change.

The advances in the Spanish energy sector have been supported by the relevance of public research and development funding for renewable energy technologies, increasing public RD&D investment. Figure 5.4 presents the evolution of RD&D investments in the energy sector in Spain between 1974 and 2019.

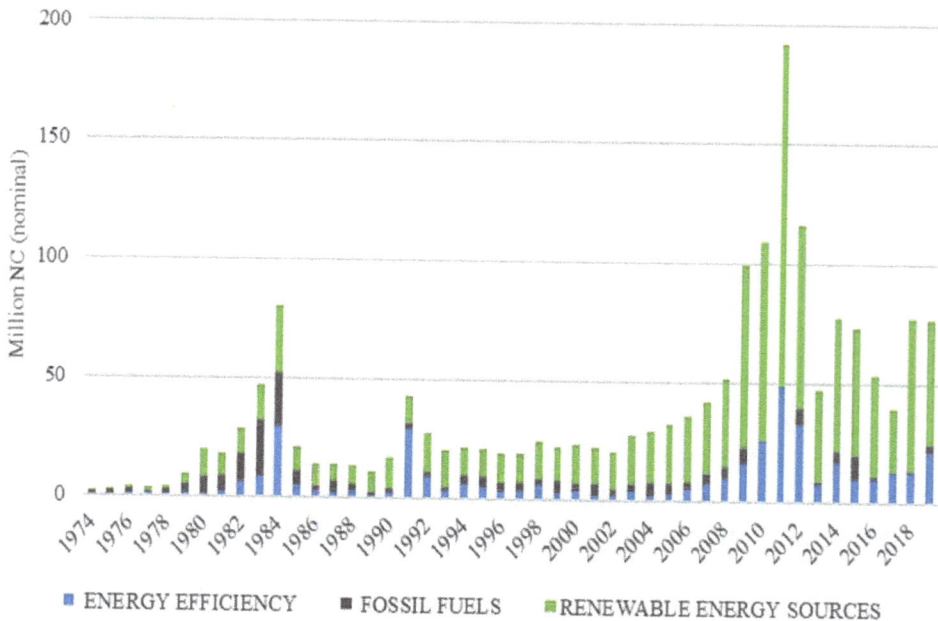

Fig. 5.4 RD&D investments in the energy sector in Spain.
Source of data: Own production, OECD (2022).

As shown in Figure 5.4, since the beginning of the twenty-first century, RD&D investments in energy in Spain have gradually increased, reaching their highest values between 2009 and 2012. RD&D dedicated to developments in the fossil fuel sector was significant, especially during the 1980s, but is nowadays marginal. In the last decades, most of the RD&D invested in energy has been in renewable energies development (around 70% in 2019) and energy efficiency (around 28% in 2019). The increase in RD&D between 2000 and 2019 has multiplied by 4.3 in the case of energy efficiency and by 2.3 in the case of RES, taking into account European Guidelines.

Recent R&D funding that targeted RE technologies and was issued through the Horizon 2020 (2014–2020) funding programme did not vary strongly across most NUTS 2 regions. However, economically strong regions profited significantly more than others. Spain received 46% of its total public RD&D support from the EC for renewable energy technologies from the European Commission.

5.3 Current Scenario after the COVID-19 Pandemic and the Russian Invasion of Ukraine

Energy markets worldwide have been subjected to the greatest supply and price tensions in recent decades. This situation is explained as the result of a cumulative set of circumstances, beginning in 2019 with the health crisis caused by COVID-19, which brought an evident slowdown in investment in all economic sectors, followed by the energy crisis caused by Russia's invasion of Ukraine. The EC designed the Next Generation EU Plan and the REPowerEU Plan to deal with both crises, in order to achieve major independence from external producers while increasing the efforts towards the green transition. Here, as is pertinent, we will pay specific attention to the Spanish case.

5.3.1. Next Generation EU

The Recovery and Resilience Facility (RRF) is the central pillar of the European recovery plan called Next Generation EU, designed to provide financial aid to EU member states in order to combat the economic and social effects of the COVID-19 pandemic and to make the European economy more resistant to future shocks. The RRF has a financial provision of €672.5 billion. The RRF is translated into separate national Recovery and Resilience Plans (RRPs), which must be aligned with the strategic priorities of the EU and should also support the green and digital transitions, allocating 37% and 20%, respectively, of their total value to these areas.

In Spain, there was an overall reduction in electricity and natural gas demand during 2020 due to the COVID-19 pandemic. Electricity demand in Spain in 2020 was 223 TWh, which meant a decrease of 6% compared to 2019, while natural gas demand was 358 TWh, 10% lower than it had been in 2019. This reduction had a greater impact on the SMEs, and industrial segments, which saw 12% and 9% drops, respectively (CNMC 2020). On the contrary, the demand for electricity in the domestic sector increased by 6%, due to confinement and of the need for teleworking.

To fight the economic slowdown, Spain will receive a total of €69.5 billion to handle its RRP. The plan supports the green transition through investments of over €7.8 billion in the energy efficiency of public and private buildings, including new social housing. Furthermore, €13.2 billion will be invested in sustainable mobility in urban and long-distance transport, notably by improving railway infrastructure, creating low-emission zones in urban areas, financing green public buses, deploying electric charging stations and developing urban public transport more generally. The plan supports the decarbonisation of the energy sector by investing €6.1 billion in clean technologies and infrastructure (including storage and electricity grids) and accelerating the development and use of renewables, including renewable hydrogen. Finally, the plan also includes measures to help mitigate the adverse effects of climate change by preserving coastal spaces, ecosystems and biodiversity. It promotes the circular economy by improving water and waste management in the country. The plan comprises a law on climate change and energy transition, enshrining in law the renewable targets for 2030 and the objective of climate neutrality by 2050, including a 100% renewable electricity system. It also includes a Renewable Hydrogen Roadmap, new strategies for building rehabilitation, decarbonisation and energy storage, and new procurement auctions for renewable electricity.

5.4 REPowerEU

The occupation of Ukraine by Russia, which started in February 2022, has had a tremendous impact on energy markets, pushing the resilience capacity of European countries to the limit, mainly due to the high dependence of Central European countries on Russian gas. Looking at the numbers, the EU imports 90% of its gas consumption, with Russia providing around 45% of those imports at varying levels across member states. Furthermore, Russia also accounts for around 25% of oil imports and 45% of coal imports (Eurostat 2022).

As presented in Chapter 1 of this book, in response to the Russian invasion, the European Union imposed strong economic sanctions on Russia, a move to which Russia responded with energy supply cuts to central European countries. Consequently, Europe is contending with fossil fuel prices that have never been seen before in the leading national and international trading hubs. The rise to hitherto unknown levels in the price of gas throughout Europe has dragged down the electricity market price. In the case of natural gas in the Iberian Peninsula, the average price of the D+1 product at the virtual balance point—PVB—in the first four months of 2022 stood at €95.98/MWh, a value nine times higher than the average price of the same product during 2020, and two times higher than the price during 2021. On March 8 2022, the D+1 product stood at €241.36 /MWh, a historical record that is reflected in the other counterpart European trading parks (CNMC 2022). According to the CNMC, electricity prices increased over 200% compared to the previous year, due to the multiplication of natural gas versus electricity prices, owing to the weight of natural gas combined cycles within the energy mix.

This geopolitical reality made it necessary to draft a new EU-level energy policy strategy. The European Commission created the REPowerEU Plan, intended to make Europe unreliant on Russian oil, gas and coal by 2030, while contributing to the clean energy transition.

Delivering REPowerEU objectives requires an additional investment of €210 billion between now and 2027. In the words of the EC, this is a down payment on our independence and security. Cutting Russian fossil fuel imports can save us almost €100 billion per year. These investments must be met by the private and public sectors and at the national, cross-border and EU levels.

To support REPowerEU, €225 billion is already available in loans under the RRF. The Commission adopted legislation and guidance for member states on modifying and complementing their RRPs in the context of REPowerEU. The plan highlights the importance of replenishing gas stocks before next winter and proposes several measures to respond to increasing energy prices. Among the emergency measures to mitigate high prices are financial support for companies and individuals, a plan to keep underground gas storage replenished by 90% before 1 October each year, investigation options to optimise the electricity market design taking into account ACER's recommendations, diversifying natural gas sources via higher LNG imports and biomethane or hydrogen production, boosting energy efficiency, fostering electrification and promoting a higher penetration of renewable energies (45% by 2030). By taking these steps, the European Commission expects EU demand for Russian gas to be reduced by two thirds by the end of 2022.

All of these objectives are of great importance to Spanish authorities. The security of supply is a real threat since Spain is still heavily dependent on external producers to meet its demand.[2] Natural gas sources are diversified in Spain, as presented in Figure 5.5 (NG comes from sixteen countries, via pipelines or in the shape of LNG). However, the country is highly dependent on Algerian gas.

The leading natural gas supplier for Spain is Algeria (which provides 43% of Spain's total demand). After Algeria, the most prominent suppliers are the USA (14.2%), Nigeria (11.5%), Russia (8.9%) and Qatar (6.3%). Internal production is small (1.418 GWh) and equates to 0.34% of total demand.

In comparison with 2020, the price of natural gas imports increased by 337% in 2021, according to CNMC (2021), changing from 13€/MWh in December 2020 to 58€/

---

2   Security of supply was threatened on 1 November 2021, when there was a supply cut due to the lack of any agreement between Algeria and Morocco to renew the gas transit contract related to the Medgaz pipeline.

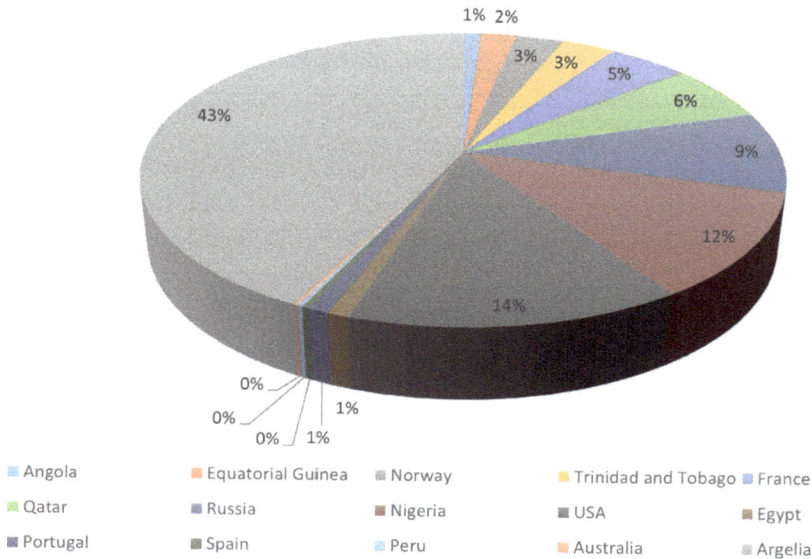

Fig. 5.5 Spain. Natural gas sourcing by origin in 2021.
Source of data: Own production, CNMC (2021).

MWh in December 2021. 45.5% of total imports arrived by pipeline; 81.66% of them came from Algeria and 18.34% from the European internal market. The remaining 54.5% of the gas supply arrived in the form of LNG.

Prompted by Algeria and the current situation caused by the Russian occupation of Ukraine, the Spanish government settled on new measures to ensure greater security of supply in the country. Spanish objectives are aligned with EC goals; achieving greater sourcing diversity and independence through higher electricity production from renewable energy sources, greater diversification of natural gas sources and reduced energy demand through energy efficiency measures.

Nonetheless, interconnectivity with other neighbouring countries within the EU will be crucial. At the moment, there are only two low-capacity pipelines connecting Spain to France, and thus to the rest of the EU, but the current situation has revived the debate of building a third natural gas interconnector between Spain and France, called STEP (previously called MidCat), whose purpose would be to bring gas from Algeria to the rest of Europe in order to end the energy isolation of the Iberian Peninsula. Besides its interconnection with Algeria, Spain has six terminals for regasifying liquefied natural gas (more than any other European country). These facts, together with a gas port in Portugal, could make the peninsula a prime gateway for gas into the EU in efforts to reduce EU dependence on Russian fossil fuels.

5.5 Final Conclusions and Policy Recommendations

Energy policies designed at the European level and transposed by EU governments have meant significant advances in market competitiveness, development and openness. However, not all the work is yet done, as demonstrated by the demand crisis caused by the COVID-19 pandemic and the energy crisis caused by the Russian occupation of Ukraine.

The main objective of the European Commission is to achieve an independent, sustainable and resilient internal energy market. These objectives were made explicit in the signing of the European Union Treaty, and later, in the 2020 and 2030 strategies, they were converted into solid figures.

As shown in the previous sections of this chapter, Spain has managed to achieve several of the objectives proposed by the 2020 strategy, but not all of them, since it is now focused on achieving the newly devised 2030 strategic objectives. All efforts to achieve these objectives are essential for the green transition and in order to reduce dependence on external fossil fuel producers and ensure good levels of security of supply.

From our perspective it is significant to note, as is always important from a political point of view, that citizens agree with using public funds to achieve these objectives. According to data from the *Barómetro del Real Instituto Elcano* (Real Instituto Elcano 2020), Spanish citizens consider the fight against climate change to be a priority in terms of foreign policy, as they feel that we are facing a climate emergency (61%) or a serious situation in relation to climate change (31%). We have, therefore, a clear blueprint for a joint strategy between politicians, on the one hand, and business, trade unions and citizens' organisations, on the other. We need a system that is capable of combining these different actors' interests while facing up to the fear of change and the uncertainties that exist in the current energy context.

Hence, energy policies in Spain will need to continue to increase internal production via renewable energies, fostering energy efficiency to reduce the country's internal energy needs and promoting different measures to reduce atmospheric pollution levels, such as fostering electric mobility. More extensive efforts will need to be made to accelerate these processes given the current situation, and the EU will be a great contributor of public funding. However, it is essential to note that the previous increase in EC contributions has compensated for decreasing national budgets. There is a need to stabilise total public RD&D support for renewable energy technologies and energy efficiency practices in the forthcoming years; otherwise, significant progress will be difficult to achieve.

Apart from those technologies currently available, policymakers need to promote technological development and complementary actions between public RD&D and private sector or international funding schemes and enhanced country-level accessibility and categorisation.

References

Baumeister, C. and L. Kilian (2016) "Forty Years of Oil Price Fluctuations: Why the Price of Oil May Still Surprise ", *Journal of Economic Perspectives* 30(1): 139–60.

BP (2020) *BP Statistical Review of World Energy 2019*. UK: BP, https://www.bp.com/content/dam/bp/business-sites/en/global/corporate/pdfs/energy-economics/statistical-review/bp-stats-review-2019-full-report.pdf.

BP (2021) *BP Statistical Review of World Energy 2020*. UK: BP, https://www.bp.com/content/dam/bp/business-sites/en/global/corporate/pdfs/energy-economics/statistical-review/bp-stats-review-2020-full-report.pdf.

BP (2022) *BP Statistical Review of World Energy 2021*. UK: BP, https://www.bp.com/content/dam/bp/business-sites/en/global/corporate/pdfs/energy-economics/statistical-review/bp-stats-review-2021-full-report.pdf.

Camprubí, L. (2019) "Whose Self-sufficiency? Energy Dependency in Spain from 1939", *Energy Policy* 125: 227–34, https://doi.org/10.1016/j.enpol.2018.10.058.

CNMC (2018) *Spanish Energy Regulator's National Report to the European Commission*. Spain: CNMC, https://www.cnmc.es/sites/default/files/2168599_3.pdf.

CNMC (2021) *Informe de supervisión de los mercados minoristas de gas y electricidad*. Spain: CNMC, https://www.cnmc.es/sites/default/files/3981989.pdf.

CNMC (2021) *IS/DE/013/21: Informe de supervisión mercado peninsular mayorista al contado de electricidad año 2020*. Spain: CNMC, https://www.cnmc.es/sites/default/files/3722490_0.pdf.

CNMC (2022) *Boletín informativo del mercado mayorista de gas y aprovisionamiento*. Spain: CNMC, https://www.cnmc.es/sites/default/files/4351303.pdf.

CNMC (2022) *Boletín informativo del mercado minorista de gas, Primer trimestre de 2022*. Spain: CNMC, https://www.cnmc.es/sites/default/files/4304039.pdf.

Cunliff, C. (2019) *Omission Innovation 2.0: Diagnosing the Global Clean Energy Innovation System*. Information Technology and Innovation Foundation. Research Gate, https://doi.org/10.13140/RG.2.2.21713.15204.

EU European Commission (2019) *Communication from the Commission to the European Parliament, the European Council, the Council, the European Economic and Social Committee and the Committee of the Regions: The European Green Deal. Communication no. COM/2019/640*. Brussels: European Commission, htt ps://eur-lex.europa.eu/legal-content/EN/TXT/?uri=COM%3A2019%3A640%3AFIN.

Eurostat (2022) https://ec.europa.eu/eurostat/web/environment/waste/database.

International Energy Agency (2020) *Spain 2021. Energy Policy Review*. France: International Energy Agency, https://iea.blob.core.windows.net/assets/2f405ae0-4617-4e16-884c-7956d1945f64/Spain2021.pdf.

OECD (2022) https://www.oecd-ilibrary.org/energy/data/iea-energy-technology-r-d-statistics/rd-d-budget_data-00488-en.

Seo, B.S. (2008) "The Political Importance of Coal as portrayed in Punch (1898–1900)", *Korean Minjok Leadership Academy International Program*, https://www.zum.de/whkmla/sp/0910/sbs/sbs2.html.

PART II
CHALLENGES

6. How Big Are Green Spending Multipliers?[1]

Nicoletta Batini, Mario Di Serio, Matteo Fragetta, Giovanni Melina, and Anthony Waldron

Introduction

Fixing the twin climate and biodiversity crises is still possible, but it requires stewarding the global economy within limits set by nature (Rockström et al. 2017; Attenborough 2020; Georgieva 2020; Stiglitz 2020; Carney 2021). Although some have argued that cutting emissions and protecting wildlife clashes with job creation and growth (see, for example, Walley and Whitehead 1994; NERA 2017; and Christian 2021), analysis based on a global survey of experts found that green projects are widely perceived as capable of creating more jobs and delivering higher short-term returns per dollar spent by comparison with traditional fiscal stimuli (Hepburn et al. 2020).

In a recent paper (Batini et al. 2022), we contribute to this debate. To our knowledge, it is the first study directly estimating the effect on GDP of money spent to foster the transition to a zero-carbon, nature-friendly world for a variety of green expenditure typologies. Although 'green' expenditure has historically tended to be defined as spending that helps reduce greenhouse gas emissions, we expand the definition to include examples of nature-based negative emissions technologies ("nature-based solutions" or NBSs) in the form of expenditure on biodiversity conservation and rewilding. These are increasingly regarded by science as solutions that support the Earth's natural capabilities to sequester carbon and mitigate climate change. Moreover, these measures have been shown to be a vital complement of planetary climate and global temperature stabilisation strategies (IPCC 2019; IPBES 2019; Foley et al. 2020; Dasgupta et al. 2021).

Employing a new international dataset, part of which was especially put together for the analysis, Batini et al. (2022) find that every dollar (private and public) spent

---

1   This chapter is based on the findings of Batini et al. (2022). The views expressed in this paper are those of the authors and do not necessarily represent those of the IMF, its Executive Board, the Independent Evaluation Office, IMF management, or the UK's FCDO.

https://doi.org/10.11647/OBP.0328.06

on green activities—from zero-emission power plants to the protection of wildlife and ecosystems—can generate more than a dollar's worth of economic activity: the total increase in GDP is greater than the original increase in green spending. These economic effects appear significantly larger and more long-lasting than 'non-green' spending in alternative energy technologies or land/sea uses, a result connected to the fact that green spending tends to be both more labour intensive and richer in domestic content than non-green spending, as we discuss later. Although green and non-ecofriendly expenditures are not always strictly comparable due to data limitations, the estimated multipliers associated with green spending are found to be generally bigger than those associated with non-green expenditure. In the case of renewable versus fossil fuel energy investments, where country and time samples are homogeneous and allow for a formal statistical comparison, green spending multipliers are about twice as large as their non-green counterparts. The point estimates of the multipliers are 1.1–1.7 for renewable energy investment and 0.4–0.7 for fossil fuel energy investment, depending on horizon and specification.

These findings suggest that, in crafting a post-COVID-19 recovery, investments in energy and land/sea use transitions may be economically superior to those offered by supporting economic activities involving unsustainable ways to produce energy and food.

The remainder of this chapter is organised as follows. Section 2 summarises the empirical results by Batini et al. (2022). Section 3 draws policy implications and concludes.

6.1 Results

While for the details on the construction of the dataset and on the empirical methodology, we refer to Batini et al. (2022), here we summarise the main results. We discuss results by sector, starting with energy then moving to land use, and comparing output effects of green and non-green spending. We use *cumulated spending multipliers*, defined as the cumulative change in GDP divided by the cumulative change in spending on energy or land use, at various time horizons, following the approach proposed by Gordon and Krenn (2010) and Ramey and Zubairy (2018).

Multiplier values should be interpreted in the standard way. For example, a value of the cumulated spending multiplier equal to, say, 1.5 in the third year would indicate that, after three years from the occurrence of the spending shock, the cumulative increase in output, in dollar terms, is one and a half times the size of the cumulative increase in green (or non-green) expenditure. In this case, then, a change of, for example, US$100 in public or private investment in clean energy infrastructure or power generation will have an effect of more than US$100 (and precisely US$150) on the level of real GDP.

6.2 Green Energy versus Non-Green Energy Spending Multipliers

In this subsection we report cumulated multipliers of spending on clean energy (renewable and non-renewable) versus spending on non-green energy (fossil fuel energy generation). It is worth noting upfront that multipliers related to fossil fuel and renewable energy generation are fully comparable because their underlying data cover the same country and time sample. The data on nuclear energy spending cover a smaller set of countries and a larger number of years, therefore they are not strictly comparable.

For both short and longer horizons the green renewable energy spending multiplier is systematically higher than the non-green energy multiplier (Table 6.1). Specifically, the impact multiplier for green renewable energy is 1.19. For non-green energy, the impact multiplier is 0.65, suggesting that these kinds of expenditures tend to crowd out private investment or consumer spending that would have otherwise taken place to a larger extent.

Focusing on the impact multiplier, however, may be misleading because investments in energy can only be implemented over time and the economy may only respond gradually. The cumulative multiplier for green renewable energy spending falls only marginally over the years and plateaus to a five-year value of 1.11, very close to the first-year effect. This may reflect the fact that renewables are built sequentially and the persistence of the multiplier as well as the fact that the composition of their investment vector typically includes different types of activities (construction itself, networks for transmission and distribution, smart meters, etc.). For non-green energy spending, however, the multiplier becomes even smaller at year five (0.52). In other words, when an additional dollar of public or private money is spent to build more fossil fuel energy infrastructure and power generation plants, this expenditure crowds out some other component(s) of GDP (investment, consumption, and/or net exports) by 48 cents in the medium run. When the same dollar is spent on solar, wind or geothermal, 11 cents are instead crowded in. In addition, while the green multiplier is statistically significant up until four years after the shock occurrence, the non-green multiplier loses its significance after three years.[2]

These results are intuitive on two grounds. First, clean energy is more labour intensive than carbon-based fuels spending. In relation to spending within fossil fuel industries, spending on clean energy—including the direct spending on specific projects plus the indirect spending of purchasing supplies—uses far more of its overall investment budget on hiring people, and relatively less on acquiring land (either on- or offshore), machines, and supplies and energy itself (Wiser et al. 2017; IRENA 2016; Garrett-Peltier 2017). In addition to the jobs directly created in the renewable energy

---

2   For the sake of simplicity, we prefer to use the terminology of statistical significance, in analogy to the frequentist approach to inference. However, the Bayesian approach used in the analysis formally leads to credible intervals around the estimates. We consider "significant" those multipliers with credible intervals, delimited by the 16th and the 84th percentiles, that exclude zero.

Table 6.1 Cumulated Multipliers associated to Green (Renewable) and Non-Green (Non-Renewable) Energy Investment Spending

Horizon	Green (Renewable) Energy Investments Multiplier	Non-Green Energy Investments Multiplier
Impact	1.19*	0.65*
1 Year	1.20*	0.64*
2 Years	1.19*	0.62*
3 Years	1.17*	0.59*
4 Years	1.14*	0.55
5 Years	1.11	0.52

Source: Batini et al. (2022).
Note: * denotes multipliers with credible intervals, delimited by the 16th and the 84th percentiles, that exclude zero.

industry, growth in clean energy can create positive economic "ripple" effects. For example, both industries in the renewable energy supply chain and unrelated local businesses benefit from increased household and business incomes (EPA 2020; IEA 2020). Moreover, clean-energy investments produce far more jobs at all pay levels—higher as well as lower-paying jobs—than the fossil fuel industry (E2-ACORE-CELI 2020). For the United States, Muro et al. (2019) find that workers in clean energy earn mean hourly wages that are between 10% and 20% above the national average; and their wages are more equitable, with workers at lower ends of the income spectrum earning up to US$10 more per hour than other jobs. At the same time, clean-energy investments also produce more jobs for a given dollar of expenditure due to the larger number of entry-level jobs relative to the fossil fuel industry. Second, clean energy implies a higher domestic content than fossil fuel energy, which explains the crowding out of demand from spending on the latter, as money spent on fossil fuel plants or generation tends to "leak" abroad.[3] Considering direct plus indirect spending, clean energy spending relies much more on economic activities taking place within the domestic economy—such as retrofitting homes or upgrading the electrical grid system locally—than spending within conventional fossil fuel sectors (IRENA 2016; EPA 2020). These considerations help rationalise the much stronger multiplier effect of clean spending than that of non-green spending on the larger economy.

Table 6.2 reports cumulated spending multipliers of non-renewable clean energy (nuclear energy), indicating that spending on nuclear energy has a large output effect, about six times larger than the output effect associated with spending on fossil fuel energy. However, nuclear spending multipliers lose statistical significance after two years from the occurrence of the shocks.

---

3   In addition, network effects may be important: oil fields and gas wells tend to be economic and geographic enclaves which may lead to smaller multipliers.

Table 6.2 Cumulated Multipliers associated with Nuclear Energy Investment Spending

Horizon	Nuclear Energy Investments Multiplier
Impact	4.11*
1 Year	3.97*
2 Years	3.88
3 Years	3.83
4 Years	3.80
5 Years	3.78

Source: Batini et al. (2022).

Note: * denotes multipliers with credible intervals, delimited by the 16th and the 84th percentiles, that exclude zero.

Although nuclear spending multipliers are not strictly comparable to the other two sets of multipliers, its initially larger values may be linked to their nature. Relative to other forms of clean energy (e.g., solar and wind) investments in nuclear energy may lead to larger employment of both high- and lower-skilled resources for the construction of nuclear reactors relative to lighter energy-producing infrastructure. In addition, while building and operating nuclear reactors tends to take time (5.1 years on average for large reactors of recent construction) spending is not sequential like in the case of renewables and tends to be more frontloaded, which could explain the stronger near-term impact and subsequent loss of statistical significance. Findings in studies comparing a steady-state employment estimate for the generation of electricity using nuclear versus wind power indicate that investment in nuclear power produces about 25% more employment per unit of electricity than wind power (WNA 2020). Moreover, research comparing pay across nuclear, wind and solar direct workforces in the United States in 2017 indicates that pay of nuclear workers is one-third higher than that in the wind and solar sectors, and that they were paid more than twice the mean for power sector workers (Oxford Economics 2019). In the medium term, the point estimate of the nuclear energy spending multiplier is still larger than the renewable energy counterpart, but not being statistically significant, does not allow us to draw definite conclusions.

6.3 Green Land Use versus Non-Green Land Use Multipliers

Lastly, we consider spending on ecosystem conservation (green land use spending) versus a shock of the same size to spending on subsidies to conventional agriculture (non-green land use spending).

Interpreting differences in multipliers from spending in these two land use categories requires caution for two reasons. First the multipliers have been estimated over different country and time samples, and in two separate econometric specifications, because of data coverage and availability constraints explained in Batini et al. (2022). This is also the reason why a statistical test on their difference cannot be constructed. In addition, spending in conservation reflects a mix of public spending in wages, education, training and recreational programming (which are thus part of public consumption) and some public investment,[4] whereas spending on conventional agriculture here reflects primarily public transfers and subsidies to crop and animal producers in industrial farm systems. However, even coarse comparisons of average output effects of spending on sustainable versus unsustainable land uses can be informative, as a consensus is emerging that subsidies to unsustainable land use and conventional agriculture should be quickly redirected toward sustainable uses (see for example UNEP-UNDP-FAO 2021). Getting a sense of the potential economic gains (or losses) of redressing land use subsidies to sustainable and land regenerative goals is key for policymaking and budgetary decisions.

Table 6.3 reporting cumulated spending multipliers on green versus non-green land use shows that, while green land use spending multipliers are not significantly different from zero on impact and over the first year's horizon, cumulated multipliers at horizons greater than one year are large and grow over time. This suggests that spending to sustain natural ecosystems exerts powerful positive ripple effects on the economies that practice it: for every dollar spent in conservation, almost seven more are generated in the larger economy in the medium term, a result in line with findings in bottom-up analyses of local and regional impacts (see Batini et al. 2022).

Table 6.3 Cumulated Multipliers associated to Green and
Non-Green Spending for Land Use

Horizon	Green Land Use Multiplier	Non-Green Land Use Multiplier
Impact	-5.36	0.55*
1 Year	-1.60	0.85*
2 Years	1.45*	0.95*
3 Years	3.75*	0.96*
4 Years	5.45*	0.95
5 Years	6.67*	0.94

Source: Batini et al. (2022).
Note: * denotes multipliers with credible intervals, delimited by the 16th and the 84th percentiles, that exclude zero.

---

4   For example this includes the construction and the maintenance of infrastructure such as fences, boardwalks, observation platforms, and other durable machinery such as communication equipment and optical devices for distant viewing, vehicles or satellite monitoring and GPS tracking devices necessary to perform conservation services.

By contrast, the multipliers of spending to support industrial agricultural production are below one at every horizon. This reflects the high mechanisation of industrial agriculture, the typically low value added associated with high costs of machinery, fossil fuel energy, and imported chemical inputs and foreign-patented GMO seeds, all of which tend to have low domestic content, given the high global market concentration of suppliers of all these inputs (FOLU 2019; UNEP 2020; UNEP-UNDP-FAO 2021).

The high multipliers associated with green land use are expected and can be ascribed to two main determinants. First, as documented by Waldron et al. (2020) the conservation activity has a strong labour intensity. Much of the economic impact of conservation is in driving a visitor economy, with associated creation of opportunity and income in sectors such as hospitality and tourism in rural and coastal communities which, in developing countries, tend to have below average income, a higher marginal utility of income, and thus are more likely to have higher propensities to spend. Second, by limiting land available for agricultural expansion, conservation spending lifts the prices paid to rural producers (Waldron et al. 2020). More generally, protecting biodiversity helps underpin the ecosystem services upon which economic activity and lives depend, such as food production, fresh water, natural resources and the protection from extreme weather events. These activities all create jobs and inspire innovation through biomimicry (Kennedy and Marting 2016; OECD 2020). While keeping in mind the caution on comparability made above, this finding is a potential indication that repurposing spending from unsustainable land uses toward more labour intensive and high-domestic-content sustainable land uses may promise important economic gains and may hold the keys to a successful green recovery.

6.4 Conclusions

Drawing on the work of Batini et al. (2022), in this chapter we discussed empirical evidence about output multipliers of spending in green and non-green energy and land use. Spending on the green economy is both efficient—returning more than the initial investment in all cases—and superior to spending on non-green activities. In the case of renewable versus fossil fuel energy investments, where country and time samples are homogeneous and allow for a formal statistical comparison, multipliers on green spending, at 1.1–1.7, are about twice as large as their non-green counterparts, at 0.4–0.7, depending on the estimation horizon and specification used.[5]

These findings can be rationalised by noting that, compared with fossil fuel technologies, which are typically mechanised and capital intensive, the renewable energy industry is more labour intensive, and investments have a higher domestic content. This feature is highlighted in sector studies, showing that, on average, more jobs are created for each unit of electricity generated from renewable sources than from

---

5   Please see the detailed results and the robustness analysis in Batini et al. (2022).

fossil fuels. Similar results emerge for spending on nuclear energy, for which there is an even greater multiplier than renewable energy—albeit obtained on a different dataset and thus not formally comparable.

Likewise, findings on ecosystem conservation spending show that it is associated with large economic gains. In contrast, spending to support unsustainable land uses—highly mechanised and imported-input-dependent industrial crop and animal agriculture—returns less than the initial expenditure. While these estimates originate in different datasets and preclude a formal discussion on their statistical difference, they are indicative of a potential economic advantage of a sustainable use of land relative to the widespread conventional farming practices.

All in all, these findings lend support to those post-COVID-19 stimulus programmes that prioritise green investments. For instance, the European Union's Next Generation EU plan, approved to help member states repair the economic damages caused by the COVID-19 pandemic, features the green transition as one of its core elements.

References

Attenborough, D. (2020) *A Life on Our Planet: My Witness Statement and a Vision for the Future*, New York: Grand Central Publishing.

Batini, N., M. Di Serio, M. Fragetta, G. Melina and A. Waldron (2022) "Building back Better: How Big are Green Spending Multipliers?", *Ecological Economics* 193: 107305, https://doi.org/10.1016/j.ecolecon.2021.107305.

Carney, Mark (2021) *Value(s): Building a Better World for All*, New York: PublicAffairs Books.

Christian, W. (2021) "Opinion: An Assault from All Fronts on Energy Independence", Speech posted on 5 Jan 2021, *Texas Railroad Commission*, https://www.worldoil.com/news/2021/1/5/opinion-an-assault-from-all-fronts-on-energy-independence.

Dasgupta, P. et al. (2021) *Report of the Independent Review on the Economics of Biodiversity led by Professor Sir Partha Dasgupta*. London: HM Treasury, https://www.gov.uk/government/publications/final-report-the-economics-of-biodiversity-the-dasgupta-review.

Environment Protection Agency (EPA) (2020) *Quantifying the Multiple Benefits of Energy Efficiency and Renewable Energy: A Guide for State and Local Governments*. Washington D.C.: U.S. Environment Protection Agency, https://www.epa.gov/statelocalenergy/quantifying-multiple-benefits-energy-efficiency-and-renewable-energy-guide-state.

Foley, J., K. Wilkinson, C. Frischmann, R. Allard, J. Gouveia, K. Bayuk, M. Mehra, E. Toensmeier, C. Forest, T. Daya, et al. (2020) *The Drawdown Review (2020)—Climate Solutions for a New Decade*. Project Drawdown, https://drawdown.org/sites/default/files/pdfs/TheDrawdownReview%E2%80%932020%E2%80%93Download.pdf.

FOLU (2019) *Growing Better: Ten Critical Transitions to Transform Food and Land Use*, https://www.foodandlandusecoalition.org/wp-content/uploads/2019/09/FOLU-GrowingBetter-GlobalReport.pdf.

Garrett-Peltier, H. (2017) "Green versus Brown: Comparing the Employment Impacts of Energy Efficiency, Renewable Energy, and Fossil Fuels Using an Input-output Model", *Economic Modelling* 61: 439–47.

Georgieva, K. (2020) "The Long Ascent: Overcoming the Crisis and Building a More Resilient Economy." Speech delivered for the 125th Anniversary of the London School of Economics on 6 October 2020. Washington D.C.: International Monetary Fund.

Gordon, R.J. and R. Krenn (2010) "The End of the Great Depression 1939–41: Policy Contributions and Fiscal Multipliers", *NBER Working Paper*, National Bureau of Economic Research.

Hepburn, C., B. O'Callaghan, N. Stern, J. Stiglitz, and D. Zenghelis (2020) "Will COVID-19 Fiscal Recovery Packages Accelerate or Retard Progress on Climate Change?", *Smith School Working Paper* 20–02.

Intergovernmental Panel on Climate Change (2019) *Climate Change and Land: An IPCC Special Report on Climate Change, Desertification, Land Degradation, Sustainable Land Management, Food Security, and Greenhouse Gas Fluxes in Terrestrial Ecosystems.* Geneva: IPCC.

Intergovernmental Science-Policy Platform on Biodiversity and Ecosystem Services (IPBES) (2019) *Global Assessment Report on Biodiversity and Ecosystem Services.* Bonn: IPBES.

International Energy Agency (IEA) (2020) *Renewable Energy Market Update: Outlook for 2020 and 2021.* Paris: International Energy Agency, https://www.iea.org/reports/renewable-energy-market-update.

International Renewable Energy Agency (IRENA) (2016) *Renewable Energy: Measuring the Economics,* https://www.irena.org/-/media/Files/IRENA/Agency/Publication/2016/IRENA_Measuring-the-Economics_2016.pdf.

Kennedy, E. and T. Marting (2016) "Biomimicry: Streamlining the Front End of Innovation for Environmentally Sustainable Products", *Research-Technology Management*, 59(4): 40–48, https://doi.org/10.1080/08956308.2016.1185342.

Muro, M., A. Tomer, R. Shivaram, and J. Kane (2019) *Advancing Inclusion Through Clean Energy Jobs*, Metropolitan Policy Program at Brookings. Washington DC: The Brookings Institution, https://www.brookings.edu/research/advancing-inclusion-through-clean-energy-jobs/.

NERA (2017) *Impacts of Greenhouse Gas Regulations on the Industrial Sector*, Report prepared for the American Council for Capital Formation Center for Policy Research, https://www.globalenergyinstitute.org/sites/default/files/NERA%20Final%20Report%202.pdf.

OECD (2020) *Biodiversity and the Economic Response to COVID-19: Ensuring a Green and Resilient Recovery,* https://www.oecd.org/coronavirus/policy-responses/biodiversity-and-the-economic-response-to-covid-19-ensuring-a-green-and-resilient-recovery-d98b5a09/.

Oxford Economics (2019) "Nuclear Power Pays—Assessing the Trends in Electric Power Generation Employment and Wages", *Oxford Economics*, https://www.oxfordeconomics.com/resource/nuclear-power-pays-assessing-the-trends-in-electric-power-generation-employment-and-wages/.

Ramey, V.A. and S. Zubairy (2018) "Government Spending Multipliers in Good Times and in Bad: Evidence from U.S. Historical Data", *Journal of Political Economy* 126 (2): 850–901, https://doi.org/10.1086/696277.

Rockström, R. J., O. Gaffeny et al. (2017) "A Roadmap for Rapid Decarbonization", *Science* 355(6331): 1269–71, https://doi.org/10.1126/science.aah3443.

Stiglitz, J. (2020) *Green Dealing—The Green Recovery Event*, Project Syndicate, 15 October 2020, https://www.project-syndicate.org/videos/green-dealing-the-green-recovery-event?referral=d582d5.

United Nations Environment Programme (UNEP) (2020) *10 Things You Should Know About Industrial Farming.* Nairobi: UNEP, https://www.unep.org/news-and-stories/story/10-things-you-should-know-about-industrial-farming.

United Nations Environment Programme-United Nations Development Programme-Food and Agriculture Organization (UNEP-UNDP-FAO) (2021) *A Multi-Billion-Dollar Opportunity: Repurposing agricultural support to transform food systems.* Nairobi: UNEP, https://www.unep.org/resources/repurposing-agricultural-support-transform-food-systems.

Waldron, A., V. Adams, J. Allan, A. Arnell, G. Asner, S. Atkinson, A. Baccini, J. E. M. Baillie, A. Balmford, and J. Austin Beau (2020) *Protecting 30% of the Planet for Nature: Costs, Benefits and Economic Implications.* Cambridge: Cambridge University, https://www.conservation.cam.ac.uk/files/waldron_report_30_by_30_publish.pdf.

Walley, N. and B. Whitehead (1994) "It's Not Easy Being Green", *Harvard Business Review*, May-June 1994, https://hbr.org/1994/05/its-not-easy-being-green.

Wiser, R. and M. Bolinger (2017). *2016 Wind Technologies Market Report.* Washington D.C.: U.S. Department of Energy, https://www.energy.gov/eere/wind/downloads/2016-wind-technologies-market-report.

World Nuclear Association (WNA) (2020) *Employment in the Nuclear and Wind Electricity Generating Sectors.* WNA Report No. 2020/006. London: World Nuclear Association, https://www.world-nuclear.org/getmedia/690859bf-ebe6-43a2-bedd-57ddf47ee3ac/Employment-in-Nuclear-Report-Final.pdf.aspx.

7. Europe's Green Investment Requirements and the Role of Next Generation EU

Klaas Lenaerts, Simone Tagliapietra, and Guntram B. Wolff

Introduction

Policymakers have made a clear commitment to use the European Union's post-pandemic recovery plan, Next Generation EU, to accelerate the bloc's green transition. The underlying idea is simple: seize a moment of unprecedented economic and social disruption to reinforce the reorientation of Europe's economic model towards sustainability, and in particular to accelerate the implementation of the European Green Deal.

This idea also reflects a hope that green investments will have high fiscal multiplier effects and that they can achieve in one swoop a so-called 'triple dividend' promoting economic growth, fostering job creation and reducing greenhouse gas emissions (Hepburn et al. 2020). While this might be overly optimistic, it has shaped policymakers' preference and means that significant parts of the EU's recovery fund will be spent on green investments.

In practice, this has meant setting a 37% minimum target for spending on climate objectives under the Recovery and Resilience Facility (RRF), the largest component of Next Generation EU.

For this it is, of course, necessary to define 'green', 'climate' and 'environmental' spending. The regulation establishing the RRF (Art. 18) includes three different requirements that must be met by EU countries' recovery and resilience plans, which are the framework for RRF spending:

1. All proposed measures must respect the 'do no significant harm' principle in relation to environmental objectives, and adherence to this must be demonstrated;

https://doi.org/10.11647/OBP.0328.07

2. Countries must explain how their plans contribute to 'the green transition'. This term refers to both environmental and climate-change objectives and is not subject to a target;

3. At least 37% of a plan's spending must go to measures which are specifically meant to support climate-change objectives, a narrower aim than the 'green transition'. The regulation provides coefficients to be used for the calculation of each measure's contribution to the target. Note that there are also coefficients for 'environmental objectives', but no minimum share of spending was established for these.

Bruegel's dataset of EU countries' recovery and resilience plans, and the European Commission's assessments (2021), show that all countries have met this 37% minimum requirement. However, in some cases the Commission's assessment of the plans reported a different 'climate share' than originally stated by the member states concerned (e.g. higher for Austria while lower for France and Italy). The Commission judged that all plans respected the 'do no significant harm' principle to a great extent.

In this chapter, we look at both the climate and environmental components of the national plans in the RRF framework to understand countries' spending priorities in these fields. Including both of these areas in our analysis is important, as doing so better reflects the encompassing nature of the European Green Deal.

7.1 Overall Priorities

We first looked at each country's green spending, as categorised under the European Commission's green 'flagship areas': *Power up*, *Renovate* and *Recharge and Refuel* (referring, broadly, to cleantech, building energy efficiency and sustainable transport). This provides an understanding of overall spending priorities. Note that the numbers we present here are different from the allocations to climate-change objectives, as reported in the national plans and Commission assessments, since we count the full allocations of measures included in the relevant categories (though some of their components might not contribute to climate objectives) and exclude some measures that contribute to the 37% target but have a non-green primary focus.

When classified this way, national allocations differ significantly (Figure 7.1). For the EU as a whole, *Recharge and Refuel* is the main green spending priority, accounting for more than a third, or €86 billion. For countries including Estonia, Germany, Hungary, Latvia, Luxembourg and Romania, this area even accounts for 50% or more of all green spending. Italy and Spain also have notably high sustainable transport allocations.

The *Power up* priority has been allocated around a quarter of green spending at the EU level, or €55 billion. Shares are, however, much larger in countries including Cyprus, Czechia and Poland, which allocate close to two thirds or more to this area. Though not visible in Figure 7.1, Sweden also spends money on this, but the amount could not be singled out based on the information in the plan, and therefore falls within the 'other green' category. Some spending on renewable energy is included under *Renovate* for Luxembourg.

The smallest green flagship in spending terms is *Renovate* (energy efficiency of buildings), which receives €48 billion in the EU. France, Greece, Latvia, Slovakia and Belgium go against the trend by devoting considerably higher shares to improving their building stocks.

Finally, 'other green' in Figure 7.1 captures spending that either could not be put into one single category, or which is primarily devoted to other items in support of the green transition. This amounts to €34 billion of spending on measures including reforestation and biodiversity protection. For Sweden it includes broad 'climate investments' with many different elements. Luxembourg directs half of its green spending to environmental protection and biodiversity, and Croatia plans relatively high spending on waste and water management and tourism. Finally, a significant share of Slovenia's 'other green' goes to water management and flood prevention.

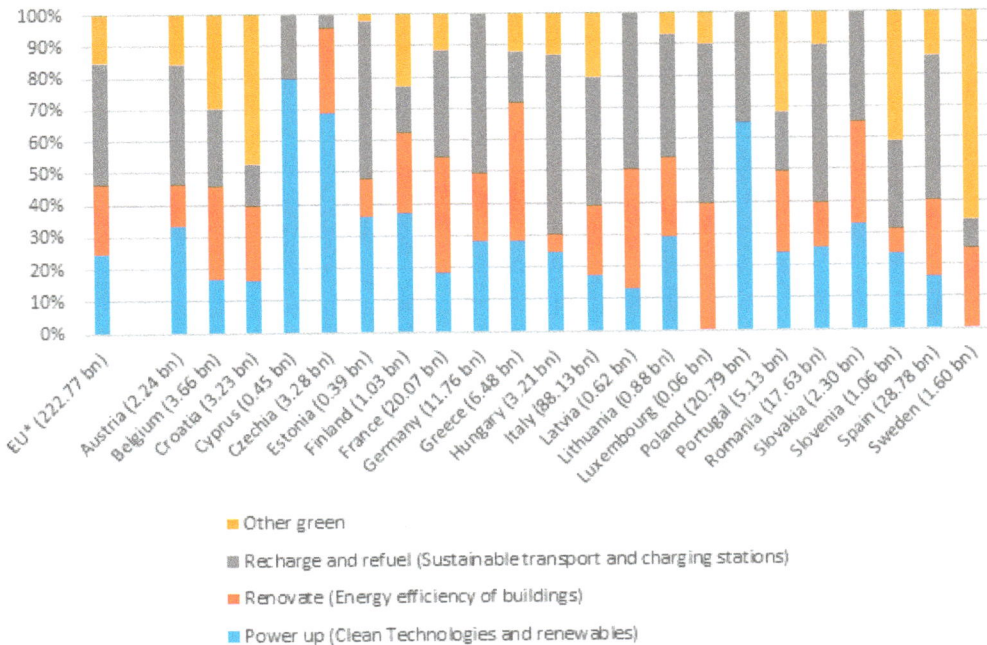

Fig. 7.1 Green spending in the national Recovery and Resilience Plans, counted using the European Commission's flagship classification (% of total green spending).

Source: Bruegel based on submitted national recovery plans. Note: country names are followed by total green spending in € in brackets. These amounts are the sums of spending (grants and loans) categorised under the flagships *Power up, Renovate, Recharge and Refuel*, and a residual category, 'other green'. Some measures that also contribute to the green transition but are aimed primarily at other fields are not included. Total green spending can therefore differ from the total amounts of spending related to climate change objectives as reported by the plans, which are calculated with weights assigned to individual spending items by member states and which should be at least 37% of total RRF spending within a country.* Includes twenty-two countries currently in the dataset.

7.2 A More Detailed Examination

While the Commission's flagship-based classification is useful for getting an overall idea of green spending priorities, a more granular breakdown is required to understand thoroughly the measures countries intend to put in place (Figure 7.2). Bruegel introduced its own classification to allow for this sort of deeper analysis.

Unsurprisingly, this more detailed classification also reveals significantly varying national spending priorities. In EU aggregate terms, spending to increase the energy efficiency of buildings takes the largest share, with €45 billion, almost a fifth of total green spending. This usually concerns both public and private buildings, sometimes explicitly targeting social housing as part of a 'just transition' narrative. Belgium and France have made renovations the largest component of their green spending, devoting around 28% to it. Czechia, Greece, Latvia and Slovakia spend even larger shares on this, reflecting what is shown in Figure 7.1.

The second biggest category at the EU level is public transport, with €34 billion, or 15%. This is a particularly large part of planned green spending in Romania (47%) and also in Austria, Hungary, Latvia and Lithuania, where it accounts for more than a third of green spending.

We created a separate category for high-speed trains, which ranks third in size with €26 billion, or 12%. Almost all the planned investments are in Italy (€24 billion), where it is one of the largest spending categories. The rest of the spending on high-speed trains is planned most notably in Czechia and Germany. Taken together, spending on 'regular' public transport and on high-speed trains surpasses spending on renovations in the EU as the biggest green subcomponent.

The fourth biggest category in the EU is renewable energy sources, which receives €23 billion, or around 10% of green spending. Most of this spending will be concentrated in three countries: it is the biggest green component for Poland with 37% (€9 billion); Spain and Italy will also be big spenders in absolute terms, with €5 billion and €6 billion respectively. Remarkably, renewables don't really feature in the French and German plans, which allocate substantial amounts to hydrogen development instead.

Finally, measures specifically targeting hydrogen come in seventh place at the EU level, behind electric mobility (mostly championed by Germany and Spain) and climate adaptation. Countries will spend in total €11 billion (5% of green spending) on this alternative fuel, with €3 billion of spending planned in Germany, €3 billion in Italy, €2 billion in France, and around €1 billion each in Poland and Romania.

Depending on which classification system is used, at the EU level some €225 billion of the RRF funds is set to be spent on green elements. This is certainly a welcome and necessary effort, but it pales in comparison to the annual investment needed by 2030 to realise the aspirations of the European Green Deal, as illustrated hereafter.

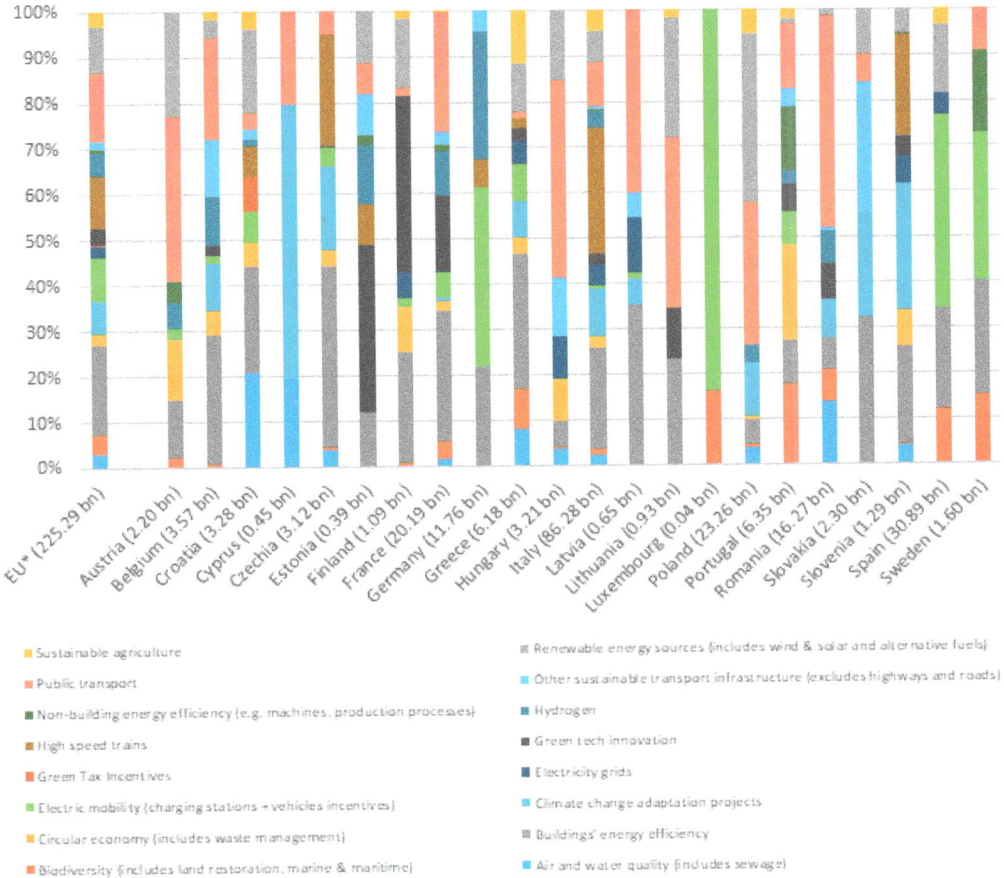

Fig. 7.2: Green spending by Bruegel's own Level 2 classification (% of total green spending). *Source*: Bruegel based on submitted national recovery plans. Note: the classification used is 'Bruegel Level 2, 1st' from the Bruegel dataset. Country names are followed by total green spending (as defined by Bruegel's Level 1 classification) in € in brackets. Some measures that also contribute to the green transition but are primarily aimed at other fields are not included. Total green spending can therefore differ from the total amounts of spending related to climate change objectives as reported by the plans, which are calculated with weights assigned to individual spending items by member states and which should be at least 37% of total RRF spending within a country.* Includes twenty-two countries.

Investment Requirements to Deliver the European Green Deal and Global Net-zero Pledges

To become climate neutral by mid-century, the European Union and other major economies must substantially reduce their greenhouse gas emissions during this decade. The EU aims to reduce its emissions by 55% by 2030 compared to 1990 levels with a wide range of policies proposed in the European Commission's 'Fit for 55' package. Meanwhile, the United States aims to reduce its emissions by 50–52% by 2030 compared to 2005 levels,[1] and China wants its CO_2 emissions to peak before 2030. To achieve this, major investment will be needed.

To understand the investment required to deliver on these pledges it is useful to review the multiple estimates in the field. Global energy investment currently stands at around $2 trillion per year or 2.5% of global GDP, according to the International Energy Agency (IEA). In an illustrative pathway (IEA 2021), this will have to rise to $5 trillion or 4.5% of GDP by 2030 and stay there until at least 2050 to reach net zero CO_2 emissions by 2050 (Figure 7.3). Much of this will be spent on electricity generation and infrastructure to electrify new economic sectors and to make the electricity system more suitable for much higher volumes and variability of renewable energy.

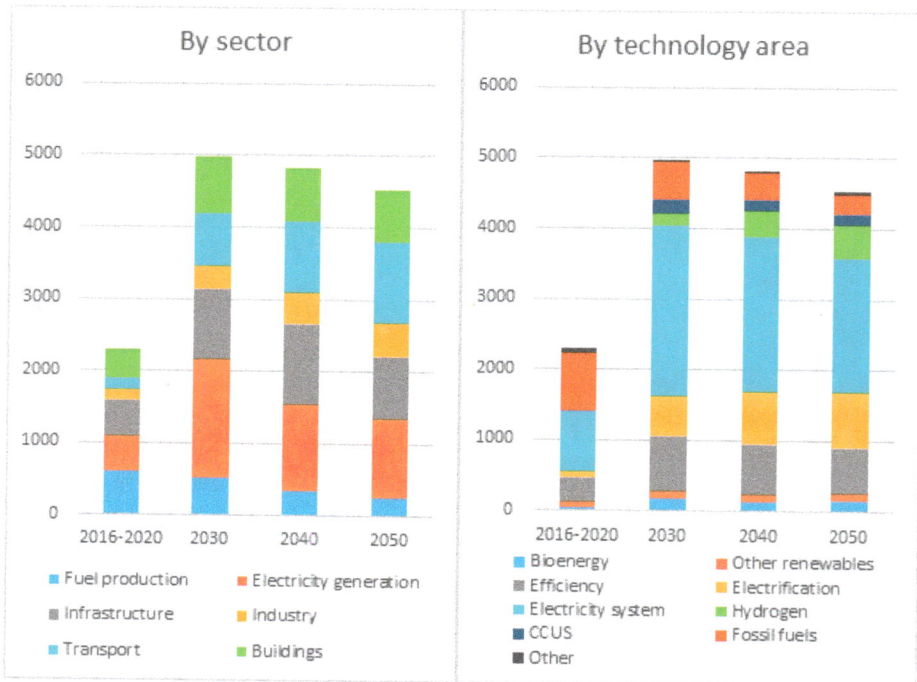

Fig. 7.3 Annual average capital investments worldwide to reach net-zero CO_2 emissions by 2050 ($ billions, 2019 prices).
Source: International Energy Agency (2021).

Other net-zero pathways point to similar orders of magnitude (Figure 7.4). The International Renewable Energy Agency (IRENA 2021) frontloaded the necessary investments into the 2020s, resulting in global investments of $5.7 trillion per year until

---

1   See White House factsheet, 22 April 2021, https://www.whitehouse.gov/briefing-room/statements-releases/2021/04/22/fact-sheet-president-biden-sets-2030-greenhouse-gas-pollution-reduction-target-aimed-at-creating-good-paying-union-jobs-and-securing-u-s-leadership-on-clean-energy-technologies/.

2030, though these decrease to less thereafter. Bloomberg New Energy Finance (BNEF 2021) estimated the average investment requirements to be between $3.1 trillion and $5.8 trillion per year up to 2050.

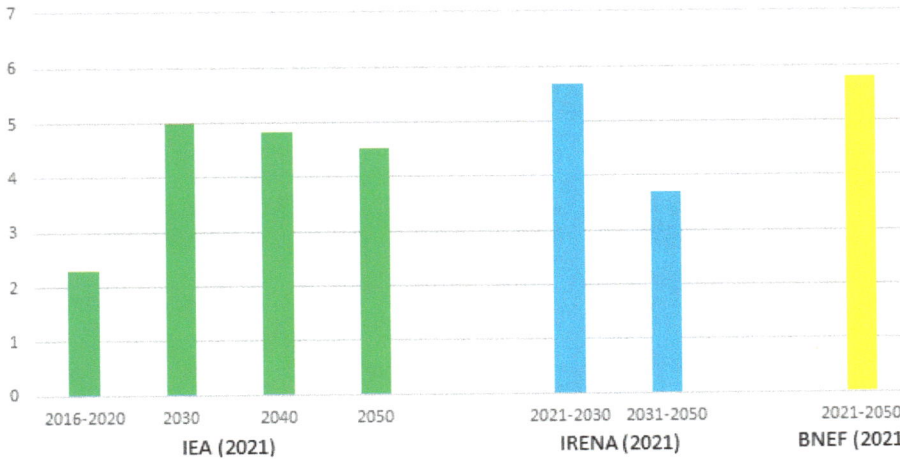

Fig. 7.4 Average yearly global investment needs in order to reach net-zero CO_2 emissions from energy by 2050, different estimates ($ trillions).
Source: Bruegel.

For the EU, the European Commission (2020) estimated that reaching the 2030 climate target will require additional annual investments of €360 billion on average, starting now. This will raise relevant investments from an average of €683 billion per year in the last decade to around €1,040 billion per year. Roughly a third of the additional investment is in transport, by far the largest component because of substantial vehicle replacement needs. Apart from transport, the emphasis seems to lie more on doubling investment in residential heating, but smaller components, such as power grids and plants, still have to increase by a factor of two (Figure 7.5).

According to all of these estimates, reaching climate neutrality by 2050 will thus require investments in energy and transport systems roughly 2 percentage points of GDP higher than current levels. No government can finance this with public money alone, so enabling and incentivising policies such as carbon taxes and green financial regulation will be necessary to mobilise private investments. Governments could also try to focus their spending on areas and initiatives from which viable companies can arise, as part of a green industrial policy (Tagliapietra and Veugelers 2020). The extent to which governments can rely on private funding for these additional investments will vary widely between countries (see, for example, EIB 2021 for EU countries), but given the large overall expansion, global public energy investments may need to double in absolute terms even with significant private participation (IRENA 2021).

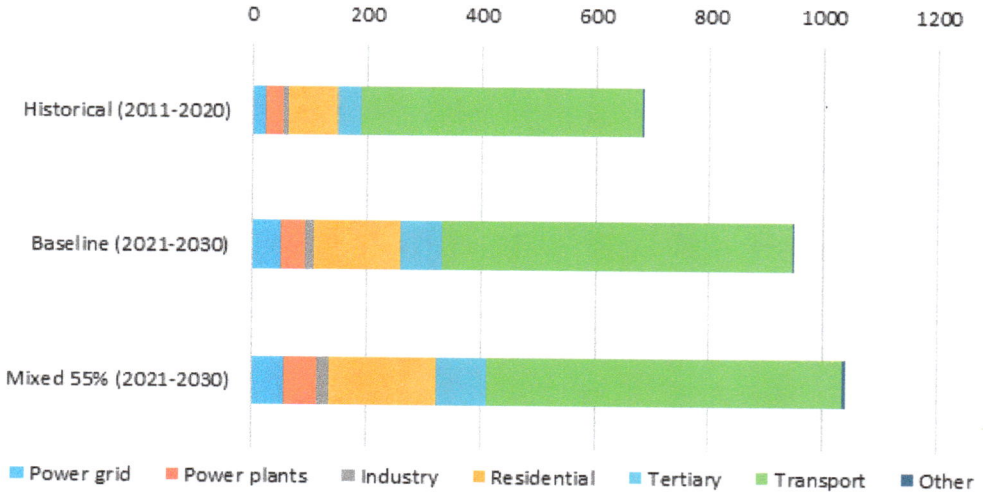

Fig. 7.5 Average annual investment needs to reduce EU emissions by 55% by 2030, compared to baseline trend and historical data (€ billions, 2015 prices).
Source: European Commission (2020). Note: 'Mixed 55%' is a scenario (MIX) that features a combination of expanded carbon pricing and moderately increased ambitions in energy regulations. The baseline is a scenario in which current policies and targets for 2030 continue to apply (-40% emissions).

In the EU, a rough estimate suggests additional public investments of €100 billion per year are required (Darvas and Wolff 2021).

7.3 Conclusion

The green spending financed by the Recovery and Resilience Facility may serve primarily as a short- to medium-term stimulus policy. In reality it will have to be the start of a bigger and sustained investment push to make the European economy climate-neutral and able to prosper in a post-fossil fuel world. The national recovery plans suggest that member states have different needs and approaches, and make choices between, for example, renewables versus nuclear energy or electric cars versus public transport and high-speed trains. All countries have in common however that massive mobilisation of private funding will be necessary, given the limited fiscal space of most governments. Spending choices need to create opportunities for private initiatives to take off, and suitable policies and regulation must incentivise and facilitate.

References

BloombergNEF (2021) *New Energy Outlook 2021*, BloombergNEF, https://about.bnef.com/new-energy-outlook/.

Darvas, Z. and G. Wolff (2021) "A Green Fiscal Pact: Climate Investment in Times of Budget Consolidation", *Policy Contribution* 18/2021, Bruegel.

European Commission (2020) "Impact Assessment Accompanying the Document 'Stepping up Europe's 2030 Climate Ambition. Investing in a Climate-neutral Future for the Benefit of Our People'", SWD/2020/176 final, https://eur-lex.europa.eu/legal-content/EN/TXT/?uri=CELEX%3A52020SC0176.

European Commission (2021) "Recovery and Resilience Facility", https://ec.europa.eu/info/business-economy-euro/recovery-coronavirus/recovery-and-resilience-facility_en#national-recovery-and-resilience-plans.

European Investment Bank (2021) *EIB Investment Report 2020/2021: Building a Smart and Green Europe in the COVID-19 Era*, https://www.eib.org/en/publications/investment-report-2020.

Hepburn, C., B. O'Callaghan, N. Stern, J. Stiglitz and D. Zenghelis (2020) "Will COVID-19 Fiscal Recovery Packages Accelerate or Retard Progress on Climate Change?", *Oxford Review of Economic Policy* 36 (1), 2020: S359–S381, https://academic.oup.com/oxrep/article/36/Supplement_1/S359/5832003.

IEA (2021) *Net Zero by 2050 A Roadmap for the Global Energy Sector*. Paris: International Energy Agency, https://www.iea.org/reports/net-zero-by-2050.

IRENA (2021) *World Energy Transitions Outlook: 1.5°C Pathway*. International Renewable Energy Agency, https://www.irena.org/publications/2021/Jun/World-Energy-TransitionsOutlook.

Tagliapietra, S. and R. Veugelers (2020) *A Green Industrial Policy for Europe*, Blueprint 31, Bruegel, https://www.bruegel.org/2020/12/a-green-industrial-policy-for-europe/.

8. The Public Spending Needs of Reaching the EU's Climate Targets

Claudio Baccianti

Introduction

The European Green Deal has set the clear goal of reaching net-zero greenhouse gas emissions by 2050, bringing climate action centre stage. The revised intermediate 2030 target of reducing greenhouse gas emissions by at least 55% compared to 1990 levels has triggered a comprehensive revision of relevant EU and national legislations and funding schemes. Since then, it has become even more evident that the green transition will have important economic and fiscal effects across the EU even before 2030. While the investment needs of EU climate policy are often discussed, understanding of the fiscal implications is still limited. This article offers an estimate of the climate public spending needs in the EU, based on a review of the evidence and literature for each sector. In the current decade, public expenditures on green investment should increase by 1.8% of GDP in a scenario with a balanced policy mix. Most of the spending will go to the buildings and transport sectors (Fig. 8.1).

The fiscal costs of the green transition can be minimised by making extensive use of carbon pricing, regulation (emission standards), soft loans and de-risking instruments. The regulator can trigger emission abatement by making low-carbon technologies cheaper (e.g. tax incentives) or traditional fossil-based and inefficient alternatives more expensive (carbon pricing), or a mixture of both. Because of political economy considerations, politicians prefer to offer generous financial support to green investment, shifting the burden to public finances.

Even if governments will successfully crowd in as much private capital as possible, the public share of the aggregate investment costs should still be close to 50%. Public budgets are one of the main sources of funding for key infrastructures in the power and transport sectors. Moreover, a large stock of buildings to be renovated is publicly owned, and low-income households will need substantial public support to renovate their homes. During this decade there is also the need to deploy technologies like

https://doi.org/10.11647/OBP.0328.08

green hydrogen and low-carbon industrial solutions that are still expensive and will rely on public funding for a while.

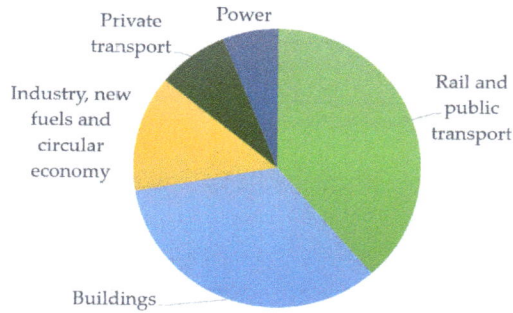

Fig. 8.1 Composition of public spending to support green investment in 2021–2030 in the EU. *Source*: author's calculation.

8.1 A Sectoral View of the Public Spending Needs in the EU

8.1.1 Power Sector

8.1.1.1 Power Generation

The rapid deployment of renewable power generation is essential to displace fossil-based power plants and to feed the growing electricity demand from green hydrogen production and the diffusion of heat pumps and electric vehicles. According to the European Commission, the total renewable energy generation capacity in the EU should reach 1236 GW by 2030, of which 510 GW of wind and 592 GW of solar PV, under the RePowerEU plan. The rate of deployment must increase very quickly (Fig. 8.2 Solar and wind power—Annual change in installed capacity in the EU.). Only 20 GW per year of solar and wind power capacity were added in 2016–2020,[1] and around 40 GW will be installed in 2022, according to the IEA (2022). To reach the 2030 RePowerEU targets, annual capacity additions for renewable power will have to stay close to 85 GW through this decade.

However, tripling or quadrupling the annual renewable capacity additions may still lead to investment flows no higher than what Europe experienced in the 2010–2011 boom. In those years, the EU annual investment in renewable power generation reached 80 billion euros, and then rapidly dropped and hovered around 30 billion in 2013–2019.[2] In the meantime, the investment costs per GW installed for solar and wind power have declined sharply between 2010 and 2020, i.e. 81% for solar PV and 31% for wind globally (IRENA 2021). To reach the 2030 EU climate targets, available studies estimating the power generation investment needed in 2021–2030 put annual capital

---

1   Based on Eurostat data.
2   Baccianti and Odendahl (2022). Values in 2020 prices.

expenditures between 45 and 80 billion euros per year (Baccianti and Odendahl 2022). However, these figures do not account for the revised ambitions of the RePowerEU plan and the current reversal of the long-term renewable investment cost decline, which followed the COVID-19 crisis. As prices of key commodities such as steel, copper and aluminium skyrocketed, the costs of solar PV modules and wind turbines also increased and are expected to remain higher than the pre-pandemic levels until 2023, while remaining competitive with fossil fuels (IEA 2022).

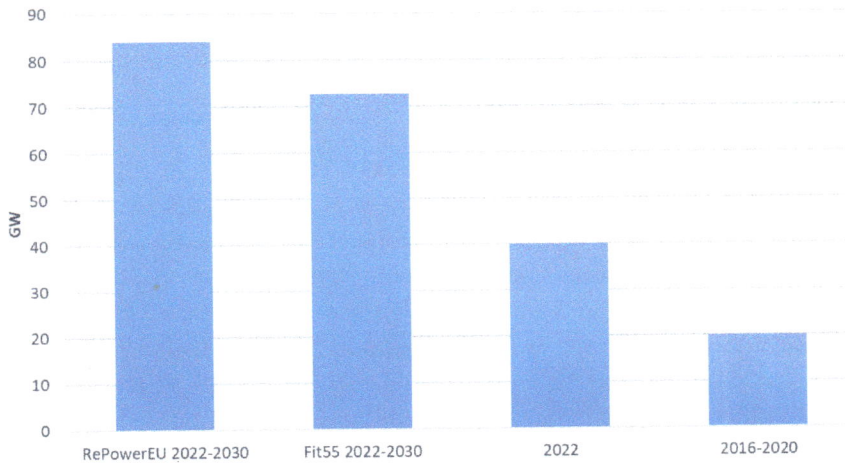

Fig. 8.2 Solar and wind power—Annual change in installed capacity in the EU.
Sources: Author's calculations on European Commission (2022b), IEA (2022), Eurostat data.

New solar and wind power generation projects are much less dependent on public support than in the past, and the private sector is expected to provide a high share of the financing needs. The OBR (2021) and IEA (2021) expect the direct contribution of public funding to renewable power investment to be below 20% in net-zero by 2050 scenarios. Globally, in 2013–2018 the public sector share of total investment financing was 14% on average (around 30% for off-grid renewables). Grants and subsidised loans made only 4% of capital expenditures, with shares up to 10% in Europe (IRENA and CPI 2020). However, IRENA and CPI (2018) point out that, while the share of capex support in Western Europe was 20% in 2015, the public sector contribution to investment costs reached 55% when revenue support (e.g. feed-in tariffs, etc.) is included. Since then, support schemes have been reformed across Europe, shifting to a larger reliance on market-based revenues. Thanks to fast-declining production costs for renewable power, reforms reduced the subsidy rate for new installations. The average subsidy to supported plants dropped from 110.22 €/MWh in 2015 to 97.95 €/MWh in 2019, with solar PV plants still receiving more than 200 €/MWh on average in several countries in 2019 (CEER 2021).[3]

---

3   Values are capacity-weighted averages from CEER (2021). These figures only cover the pool of supported plants and they do not reflect the fact that more and more RES projects do not receive any direct financial support.

Going forward, so much new solar and wind power capacity is needed that part of the new plants will have to be located in less productive locations. Small scale rooftop solar PV, agri-voltaics and off-shore wind power will play an important role to reduce land consumption and their potential is high. Rooftop solar PV in the EU could produce 680 TWh of solar electricity annually, which is equal to around one quarter of the current EU power demand (Bodis et al. 2019). Using just 4% of the arable land in Germany for agrivoltaics—that is the dual use of agricultural land to produce farming products and solar power—could satisfy the entire German power consumption (Trommsdorff et al. 2020). However, these solutions have a higher levelised cost of electricity generation and will demand more direct subsidies than utility-scale solar or onshore wind. Generating electricity on arable farming land and rooftops can be on average twice as expensive over a twenty-year period as using ground-mounted solar PV plants, while the cost disadvantage is less pronounced for agrivoltaics on permanent crops and grassland (Trommsdorff et al. 2020). Agrivoltaics is a new and relatively niche market at the moment, with strong potential for cost-cutting innovation.

The impact that the support of new renewable power generation will have on public finances will depend on the policy design and on market conditions. In twenty-one out of twenty-eight member states, renewable support schemes have been financed via special levies and not general taxation over the last few years (CEER 2021). Charging a levy on the final electricity price relieves the government budget from the cost of supporting renewables, while allowing the possibility to intervene and temporarily ease the burden on consumers. In 2022, Germany joined the group of countries financing the renewables support scheme via the state budget. Furthermore, the policy cost will depend on the dynamics of wholesale power prices and capture, carbon and gas prices, as well as the level of demand over the next two to three decades (Agora Energiewende 2022)

8.1.1.2 Power Grids

Investment in power grids is necessary to enable the electrification of energy demand and the penetration of intermittent renewable power generation. Transmission lines will have to be strengthened to allow renewable power generated in high-performing areas to reach other regions, and to accommodate for higher electricity consumption. The digitalisation and upgrade of distribution networks and adoption of storage technologies will balance the market in the presence of a high share of renewables in power generation.

The investment gap estimates significantly vary across studies, especially regarding the additional needs before 2030 (Fig. 8.3 Cumulative investment in power grids in 2022–2030 and historical.), while all much higher than historical levels. These differences can be explained by disparate views on the rate of electrification. From these and other studies we learn that investment flows into distribution networks will be larger than those into transmission lines (IEA 2021; Goldman Sachs 2022), and that investment should scale up after 2030, as power demand and the share of renewable generation are substantially higher.

The ownership of transmission and distribution system operators varies across EU countries. Power infrastructure companies are all or mostly publicly owned in France, Sweden, the Netherlands and Latvia, while in Spain, Portugal and Italy the ownership is mainly private. Other countries have mixed models (CEER 2022). Governments can in part contribute through grants and direct investment, as for instance with 8.5 billion euros of dedicated investments in different national recovery and resilience plans (European Commission 2022a). But in general, power grid investment is financed through corporate debt and consumer levies, i.e. network charges, and not general taxation. However, as electricity tariffs are regulated, grid operators may experience budget deficits that eventually require governments to step in. In the past, this kind of contingent liability posed a limited risk to public finances even in the most exposed countries (Linden et al. 2014), but the situation should be reassessed in light of the large investment needs.

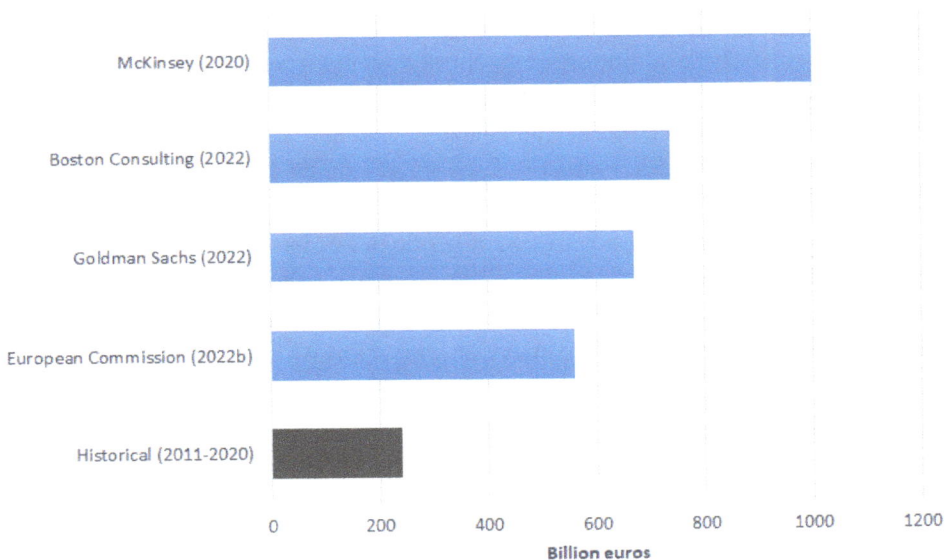

Fig. 8.3 Cumulative investment in power grids in 2022–2030 and historical.
Note: historical investment from European Commission (2021a).

8.1.2 Buildings and District Heating

The decarbonisation of buildings, in particular private and residential, is one of the top challenges in the transition to net-zero emissions. Markets for energy-saving building retrofits across the EU will need to undergo an unprecedented transformation, doubling or tripling the annual rate of renovation of the building stock and shifting towards deep renovations. According to the European Commission, thirty-five million buildings should be retrofitted by 2030 to meet the climate targets and the electrification of heating systems should speed up significantly—soon reaching a 4% annual replacement rate of fossil fuel boilers.

Buildings account for 69% of the non-transport climate investment gap in 2021–2030, according to the Commission's modelling (European Commission 2020b). Both the European Commission (2020b) and McKinsey (2020) estimate that energy-related investments in the building sector should reach 300 billion euros per year between 2021–2030. This figure is 160 billion euros higher than investments in the sector over the last decade, so capital expenditures should more than double rapidly from those levels. A recent study by the Joint Research Centre (Wouter et al. 2021) stated that the renovation of the building envelope and space heating of existing residential buildings alone (excluding new and non-residential constructions) would require 91 billion euros more in annual investment in 2021–2030. Reducing the cost of energy-saving renovation is complicated by a lack of standardisation and serial renovations (BPIE 2020). The heterogeneity of the building stock forces architects and construction companies to adopt customised solutions, a condition that weighs on costs.

The number of homes undergoing energy-saving renovations every year has historically been too low to make a dent in emissions. While spending in home renovations stands at around half a trillion euros annually, most of the spending—60%—is for interventions that do not affect the energy efficiency of the building (European Commission 2019). While 12% of the EU housing stock every year actually undergoes some kind of energy-saving renovations, only one out of ten of those retrofits achieves substantial primary energy savings above 30%. To achieve the EU's 2030 climate targets, the current annual rate of energy renovations will have to double by 2030 and the share of 'deep' renovations, delivering primary energy savings of at least 60%, should rise from 0.2% of dwellings each year to 1.3–1.7% in 2030 (European Commission 2020b).

Private finance will continue to play a key role in financing building renovations, but governments must step up support if they want to increase the rate of retrofitting quickly. The development of instruments such as green mortgages and on-bill financing can unlock the full potential of private capital. However, there are several reasons why public grants and tax incentives will have to cover a significant share of capital expenditures, in order for the emission reduction targets to be achieved:

- the climate externalities from consuming energy and emitting greenhouse gases in the residential and commercial sectors are often insufficiently priced (OECD 2021), and public funding has to fill the incentive gap.

- Other social benefits are not fully internalised in the cost of energy efficiency renovations. Carrying out a deep home renovation can significantly reduce the load on the power grid of switching to a heat pump. But it may not always be attractive for households to pay for the high upfront costs of improving the thermal envelope of the building because of the long payback times (Element Energy 2022). Without the energy efficiency investment, a larger heat pump with higher power demand is installed, leading to higher system costs. Public grants and tax incentives can increase the rate of deep renovations, reducing the effect of heat pump deployment on the power grid.

- Subsidies can be an effective instrument in the short term to quickly scale up the deployment of energy efficiency and clean heating technologies, creating markets for these technologies, attracting talent and inducing further innovation in the sector.

Energy renovation policies and the fraction of costs covered by grants and tax incentives widely vary across EU countries. Economidou et al. (2019) estimated that national governments in the EU were spending around 15 billion euros annually in fiscal support schemes during the 2010s. The most generous scheme currently active is the Italian Superbonus 110% (or Ecobonus), which waives the full cost to the homeowner of renovations delivering an upgrade of two energy classes in the national scale, up to predetermined cost thresholds. Other countries, notably Germany, make a more balanced use of grants and low-interest loans. Building renovation programmes were an important component of the post- COVID-19 recovery plans in Europe, especially those projects financed through the Recovery and Resilience Facility. In the twenty-two plans approved in 2021, energy efficiency programmes for residential buildings received 28.4 billion euros, and 20.2 billion euros were allocated to the renovation of public buildings, in both cases to be spent by the end of 2026 (European Commission 2022a).

Millions of residential buildings housing low-income households will have to be renovated by 2030. Individuals at risk of poverty or social exclusion[4] alone make up 20.9% of the EU population and, even for households in the broader group of low-income earners, the upfront cost of comprehensive energy renovations is not affordable. Moreover, energy expenditures of the lowest income deciles are in absolute value lower than those of richer households,[5] a factor that tends to increase the payback period of home renovations, making them less attractive for low-income households. In countries like the Netherlands, home renovation aid is traditionally provided through social housing, while in Southern and Eastern Europe (and also Germany) subsidised rental housing covers a very small fraction of the housing stock. Governments should create or enhance special programmes to renovate low-income homes. Such policies are becoming increasingly urgent as national and EU regulations

---

4   The 2019 figure is from Eurostat and the indicator is defined as individuals that have an equivalised disposable income below the risk-of-poverty threshold (which is set at 60% of the national median equivalised disposable income) or those that have severe material and social deprivation.

5   See for instance the European Commission's report *Prices and costs of EU energy—Ecofys BV study,* Annex 3.

mandate the renovation of the most energy-consuming buildings by the beginning of the next decade.

Governments of EU countries with lower incomes may have to provide overall higher grants and subsidies for residential renovations, compared to those of richer EU member states. BPIE (2020) argues that more public funding is needed in Southern, Central and Eastern EU countries to mobilise a given amount of investment in home renovations compared to West and North-West Europe (a leverage factor of 1.5 instead of 3). In fact, in lower-income countries, renovation costs tend to account for a higher percentage of GDP. While labour and installation costs are lower in Bulgaria, Greece, Portugal and Romania than in richer EU countries, the price of insulation materials, heat pumps and solar panels should not be significantly different. With the proposed revision of the ETS, European Commission (2021c) estimates that annual residential capital costs in 2030 will increase more as a share of aggregate household consumption in lower-income EU countries (0.97%) than in high-income ones (0.62%).

Non-residential buildings will have to contribute too, and the quite large share of public ownership increases the fiscal costs of renovating this part of the stock. A quarter of the total building area in the EU is used for commercial and public services.[6] Public buildings, i.e. public offices, buildings for public education and health services, make on average around 30% of the non-residential building stock,[7] with stark differences across EU countries. Only 10% of non-residential floorspace was publicly owned in Greece in 2011, whereas the public share was close to 90% in Estonia and Bulgaria (Economidou et al. 2011). Even if time series data on the ownership structure of non-residential buildings in the EU are not available, public shares are thought to have fallen over the last three decades as European governments privatised education and health services and sold buildings to finance the reduction of public debt stocks.

Finally, district heating and cooling is another important component in the decarbonisation of the energy consumption in buildings. Centralised and large-scale heat generators can provide energy efficiency gains compared to individual heating and some EU countries have traditionally invested seriously in this solution. In Poland and Slovakia district heating provides around 20% of the energy consumed in residential buildings, while the figure is somewhere between 30% and 40% in Finland, Estonia, Sweden and Denmark. In Southern and Western Europe the contribution of district heating is instead significantly smaller, at below 10%.[8]

There are therefore sizeable investment needs and opportunities in the district heating and cooling sector across Europe, either to expand the grid and generation infrastructure or to switch existing plants away from fossil fuels. McKinsey (2020) estimates that 500 billion euros are needed up to 2050 to install new district heating networks in the EU, and it considers this technology to have low abatement costs and

---

6   European Commission's *EU buildings factsheet*. Data refer to 2013.
7   Author's calculation based on European Commission's *EU buildings factsheet* data.
8   2017 data from IEA.

to be the best replacement for fossil fuel boilers in densely populated areas and hard-to-retrofit buildings. Similarly, Mathiesen et al. (2019) pin down the spending needs in the sector at 865 billion euros over the same period (of which around 60% is in addition to current trends), with most of the investment carried out before 2040.

8.1.2.1 Industry, Hydrogen and Waste

The industry transition to zero emissions requires a comprehensive policy framework that encompasses the different steps of the value chains. Upstream interventions include the expansion of the zero-emissions hydrogen production capacity, i.e. electrolysers, and the investment in hydrogen and CO_2 pipelines. The production of intermediate goods can be decarbonised with investment in clean technologies supported by capex and opex support. Moreover, measures like a border carbon adjustment may be needed to preserve firms' competitiveness in trade-exposed industries. Currently, these industries receive free allowances in the EU ETS, a subsidy scheme that is worth around 43 billion euros per year with a carbon price of 80 euros per ton of CO_2eq. Final demand can also steer incentives through the value chains when regulation on embedded CO_2 and materials consumption is in place.

Zero-emissions hydrogen will be a key enabler of the industry green transition and it will be used to replace fossil fuels both as fuel and as feedstock in industrial processes. Hydrogen is already used widely, but it is produced with fossil fuels, mostly coal, and must be replaced with green hydrogen. Manufactured with electrolysers and renewable power, green hydrogen is currently more expensive than the "brown" alternatives and it requires a substantial amount of new renewable power capacity. The EU targets the exponential increase of renewable hydrogen production capacity from almost zero today to 40 GW by 2030. RePowerEU plan updated this target to 10 million tons of domestic renewable hydrogen production and 10 million tons of renewable hydrogen imports by 2030. Biomass, biogas and biomethane will also play an important complementary role in decarbonising industry.

The investment needs in industry and hydrogen supply are relatively small compared to other sectors. In a scenario compatible with the Fit for 55 targets and regulation, the European Commission estimates that industrial investment should rise from around 11 billion euros per year in 2011–2020 to 26 billion euros per year in 2021–2030, which is more than double past levels (European Commission 2021a). McKinsey (2020) instead evaluated the green investment gap in the sector at 8 billion euros per year in this decade. These spending needs increased after the war in Ukraine made it urgent to reduce gas consumption. The RePowerEU plan adds 4.5 billion euros per year up to 2030 of investment in industry and around 4 billion euros p.a. in biomethane to eliminate Russian gas imports (European Commission 2022b).

Investment grants for low-carbon industrial projects should absorb the higher capex and cover 20–30% of the investment costs in most cases, with support declining in the technological maturity (Material Economics 2022). Material Economics estimates that scaling up key breakthrough technologies in steel, petrochemicals and cement production in the EU would require 6–11 billion euros in grants up to 2030, to mobilise 31–37 billion euros of green investment. The EU Innovation Fund, which finances innovative low-carbon technologies not only in industry, plays a key role in this area and supports up to 60% of capital expenditures.

The fiscal cost of scaling up green investment in heavy industries will come not only from one-off investment grants but also from recurring subsidy payments. Investments such as energy efficiency improvements and the switch to industrial heat pumps increase productivity and lower the unit costs of production. In other cases, i.e. switching to green hydrogen or capturing and storing emissions, the plant production costs rise. Agora Energiewende (2022a) estimates that decarbonising the production of 11 Mt of steel in Germany before 2030 would increase capital expenditures in the sector by 8 billion euros and operating expenditures by 27 billion euros over ten years (a so called "revenue gap"). While part of these additional production costs may be eliminated in the future with technological progress on the green inputs, i.e. green hydrogen, the rest should be covered either by carbon pricing or public subsidies.

Opex support can take the form of long-term support contracts such as Carbon Contracts for Difference (CCfD). The CCfD commits the public sector to pay a subsidy covering the gap between the actual carbon price and the strike price, for each unit of product manufactured using the green technology. This instrument tracks the realised revenue gaps and reduces the risk of overcompensating investors, contrary to upfront grants. CCfDs have recently gained more and more interest from policymakers. Germany is financing a pilot scheme with 550 million euros under its recovery and resilience plan, and the EU Innovation Fund will also roll out a specific CCfD programme.

Finally, waste management and the efficient use of natural resources (*circular economy*), can make a significant contribution to reducing greenhouse gas emissions. The European economy notably produces a large amount of urban and industrial waste, and the sector generates 3% of EU emissions. Landfills are a main source of methane emissions. Investing in more sustainable waste management systems, shifting to the reuse and recycling of materials, and designing products in a way that minimise waste production, are all essential. The transition to a circular economy also allows the reduction of upstream emissions, as a lower amount of materials is processed in industry (Agora Energiewende 2022c). Circular economy investment also contributes to reducing the material consumption footprint and the extraction of natural resources (e.g. wood, water, minerals). The investment needs in this area are not always included in the assessments of climate mitigation scenarios, because material efficiency is not always modelled directly. For instance, the European Commission (2020a) offers separate estimates of the investment needs for a circular economy.

8.1.3 Transport

Domestic transport generates 22% of the EU greenhouse gas emissions and international aviation and maritime transport contribute to another 7%. Road transport vehicles are notoriously a major source of oil demand and directly consume 48% of the total oil and petroleum products in the EU.[9] While they are the most common type of transport vehicle in circulation, private cars account for only around 44% of domestic and international transport emissions (McKinsey 2020). Light- and heavy-duty trucks release significant amounts of emissions, and account for around 27% of the sectoral total. Transportation is the only sector that has increased greenhouse gas emissions since 1990 (McKinsey 2020) and the demand shift towards heavier cars, i.e. SUVs, has offset fuel economy gains over the last few years (IEA 2021b).

8.1.3.1 Private Transport

Zero-emission vehicles (including fully electric) are still more expensive than their equivalents with internal combustion engines, and subsidies are necessary to ensure a rapid uptake of these technologies. Even if electric cars already offer cost savings while driving in several parts of Europe, their higher price tag and charging infrastructure requirements make them less attractive to most customers. Different forms of subsidies, i.e., purchase discounts and waivers from ownership taxes, are already in place across the EU and should continue as long as price parity is reached. According to BloombergNEF (2021), price parity between battery EVs and ICE cars for the large and medium car segments will be reached significantly earlier than for small cars (2022 and 2023 respectively, instead of 2027 for small cars). However, the timeline is now more uncertain, given the recent sharp increase in the cost of producing batteries and other electric car components.

There are no comprehensive assessments of the fiscal costs of subsidising electric vehicles in the EU, but it is possible to understand the order of magnitude with an example for battery electric cars. There are three components of the total fiscal cost: the subsidy for each car sold (including various tax benefits), the number of annual sales, and the percentage of car models receiving support. In fact, market segments where EVs are already competitive may not be eligible for subsidies going forward. Fig. 8.4 Cost of electric car subsidy programmes and annual sales of BEVs. shows how the cost of the subsidy scheme evolves as support is gradually reduced while the share of EVs rises. We model a 6000-euro subsidy in 2023 that is reduced to 5000 euros in 2025 and to 3000 euros in 2027. The share of supported models also declines over time. Overall, the direct fiscal cost of the car purchase scheme in all EU countries does not exceed 10 billion euros per year, which is less than 0.1% GDP.

---

9   Based on Eurostat data.

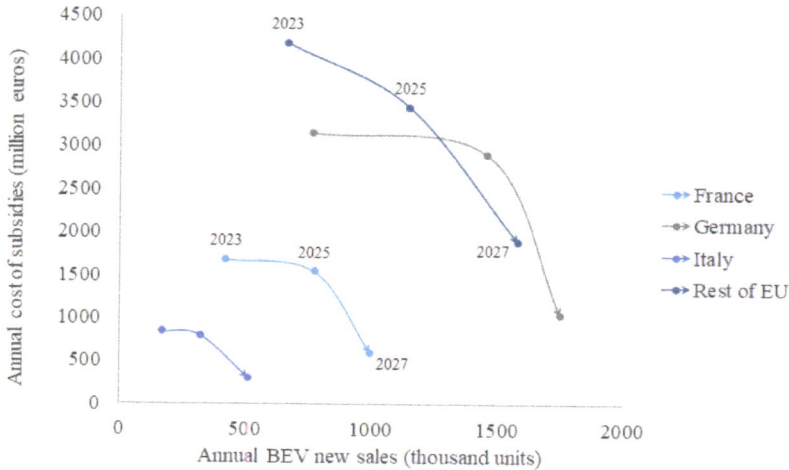

Fig. 8.4 Cost of electric car subsidy programmes and annual sales of BEVs.
Source: author's calculation. Note: the cost for 2023 includes a 2000-euro subsidy for the purchase of new plug-in hybrid electric cars.

Private and public charging stations and other infrastructure for alternative fuels are essential for the rapid diffusion of clean vehicles. Millions of charging points will have to be installed in homes, offices and public areas for shared use. The majority should be slow chargers at home (below 22 kW), which cost less than a couple of thousand euros including installation (BloombergNEF 2021). Ultra-fast and fast chargers are much more expensive, but their cost is expected to drop significantly over the next years and they are needed in lower numbers. In a 2050 net zero emissions scenario, BloombergNEF (2022) estimates annual investment in private and public charging infrastructure in Europe should reach 11 billion US dollars (around 10 billion euros) in the period 2026–2030, of which 4 billion US dollars will be for public charging stations.[10] Deployment subsidies therefore should not put a significant burden on public finances. A back-of-the envelope calculation with a support rate of 50% in 2022–2025 and 30% in 2026–2030, similarly to OBR (2021), gives an estimate of public cost at around 3.1 billion euros per year in 2022–2030.

8.1.3.2 Public Transportation

Modal shift is another way of reducing greenhouse gas emissions and local pollution from road transport and air travel. For climate policy, an increasing use of collective transportation is important to reduce emissions beyond what the switch to alternative zero emissions vehicles can achieve. The share of passenger-kilometres travelled by buses and trains out of the total kilometres travelled within the EU has slightly

---

10   Values refer to the EU, Norway and Switzerland.

declined from 18% in 2000–2002 to 17.2% in 2017–2019. This aggregate figure hides quite stark differences across EU countries, as there has been a general decline in former communist countries, where individuals switched to private transportation, and a small increase in Western Europe (e.g. Italy, France, Austria, Sweden). Panel A of Fig. 8.5 The evolution of public transport use. shows that, over the last twenty years, countries that started with a high usage level of rail and public transportation in the early 2000s have shifted most dramatically to passenger cars. Panel B focuses on Western Europe and rail transport. It displays the relationship between the cumulative investment in rail networks between 1995 and 2015 and the change in the share of trains in inland passenger transport after the year 2000. The shift to rail transport has been limited to a few percentage points even in countries like Austria, Spain and Switzerland that invested quite a lot in their rail networks.

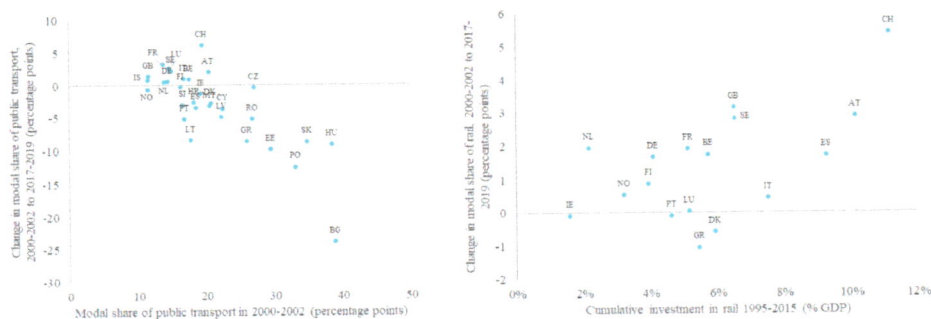

Fig. 8.5 The evolution of public transport use.
Source: author's calculations on Eurostat and OECD data. Note: Cumulative investment in percentage of 2019 GDP.

Grants from central and local governments make up a large fraction of the capital expenditures in rail and local public transport in most EU countries. The European Commission assessment of the TEN-T additional investment needs, which includes cross-country road, rail and other transport infrastructures, evaluates the share of national and EU funding as being at 93% (European Commission 2021b). In Germany, non-repayable public grants contributed to 81% of Deutsche Bahn Group's investment in the rail network and services in 2021 (9 billion out of 11.1 billion euros).[11] In Italy, the Gruppo Ferrovie dello Stato Italiane invested 9.98 billion euros in 2021, 77% of which was financed through public grants.[12] In France, around 50% of the capital expenditures of Groupe SNCF in 2021 and 2020 were subsidised by national and local public budgets.[13] On top of capital expenditures, governments also subsidise the

---

11   https://ir.deutschebahn.com/en/db-group/capital-expenditures/.
12   Relazione finanziaria annuale 2021.
13   See Groupe SNCF's *Rapport financier annuel 2021* and Fipeco's *Le coût de la SNCF pour le contribuable*.

operation and maintenance expenditures to different degrees. This kind of spending will increase, as governments will improve the quality of public transport services while keeping them affordable and convenient *vis à vis* other modes of transport.

8.1.4 Public Spending Needs by 2030 in the EU

Table 8.1 Investment and public spending needs for the EU27 in 2021–2030. shows a selection of investment needs estimates for individual sectors in 2021–2030 and their associated public spending needs. When the fiscal cost is from an investment grant or a similar policy, a coefficient is applied to the investment figure. The coefficients are the share of capital expenditures paid by the public sector, and they are derived from the literature or the observations discussed in the previous sections. In Table 8.2, the assumptions for the base case are compared to those used in a few other studies. When the spending need is a recurring expenditure, like opex support, the amount of public spending is calculated separately. For the case of private transport, namely passenger cars and commercial vehicles (including trucks, tractors, and motor coaches), the public spending figure covers tax incentives and subsidies for vehicle purchases and subsidies to install charging and refuelling points.[14] The public shares are applied to the additional investment needed over this decade, not to the total levels. The results of Table 8.1 Investment and public spending needs for the EU27 in 2021–2030. therefore underestimate the public investment needs if the share of public support will be higher than in the past.

The public spending needs are calculated for a Central scenario and two other scenarios are added to provide nuance to the results. In a low public cost case (L), the policy mix uses less central and local government financing of infrastructures, more carbon pricing and less subsidies, while the high public cost case (H) assumes the opposite. The alternative scenarios show that the size of the climate public spending will depend quite significantly on how policies are designed, in particular in the buildings and transport sectors. It becomes clear that minimising the use of non-repayable grants and subsidies should be a priority, while keeping the decarbonisation incentives of households and firms fixed to the target.

Table 8.2 Public sector shares of additional costs. compares the assumed shares to other studies. EIB (2022) reviews the National Energy and Climate Plans for all EU countries and find an average (unweighted) public share of investment needs equal to 45%. As the plans refer to the old 2030 emission target (40% reduction), the shares are likely to underestimate the public role in achieving the more ambitious current

---

14   The calculation for commercial vehicles is based on Eurostat data. In the Central scenario, around 15% of the fleet of goods vehicles and trailers is replaced with low-carbon alternatives and receives individual subsidies in the range of 10–20 thousand euros on average over the period. 40% of motor coaches and buses are instead replaced and receive an average subsidy of 10 thousand euros. The total cost of such programmes across the EU would be approximately 10 billion euros per year during the period 2021–2030.

Table 8.1 Investment and public spending needs for the EU27 in 2021–2030.

Sector	Annual investment gap (billion euros p.a.) C	Source	Public share (%) C	L	H	Public spending needs (billion euros per year) C	L	H
Power generation (capex)	50	Author's calculation	5%	2%	10%	3	1	5
Power generation (opex)		Author's calculation/Agora Energiewende (2022b)				3	1	5
Power grids	33	European Commission (2022b)	30%	10%	50%	10	3	16
District heating	25	Mathiesen et al. (2019)	40%	20%	60%	10	5	15
Residential and non-residential buildings[15]	165	European Commission (2021a; 2022b)	45%	35%	65%	74	49	120
New fuels production and distribution	7	European Commission (2021a; 2022b)	40%	30%	50%	3	2	3

15   It is assumed that governments support the full cost of home renovations for households earning below 60% of the median equivalised income (18.4%) and for public buildings (30% of non-residential buildings). The public support for home renovations for remaining households is 30% in EU countries with GNI per capita above the EU average and 40% in the others. Grants for the renovation of private non-residential buildings cover 23% of the investment. The investment gap is 141 billion euros in the low public cost scenario and 184 billion euros in the high public cost scenario. See note below table for correspondence with the European Commission scenarios.

Sector	Annual investment gap (billion euros p.a.)	Source	Public share (%)		Public spending needs (billion euros per year)		
Industry (capex)	19	European Commission (2021a; 2022b)	30%	40%	6	4	8
Industry (opex)		Author's calculation/Material Economics (2022)	20%		4	3	5
Waste/Circular economy	42	European Commission (2020a)	50%	60%	21	13	25
Private transport		Author's calculation			20	15	25
Rail and public transport (TEN-T Core)	33	European Commission (2020a)	95%	100%	31	26	33
Rail and public transport (national)	76	European Commission (2020a)	85%	95%	65	46	72
Total (% GDP)	450 (3.2)				249 (1.8)	168 (1.2)	333 (2.4)
Public share capex (excl. private transport)					54%	36%	72%

Note: Monetary values are expressed per year and in billions of euros at 2019 prices. Investment gaps are the difference between the required spending in the periods 2021–2030 and 2011–2020. Columns indicate the alternative scenarios, where (C) is the central case, (L) is the low public cost and (H) is the high public cost scenario. In the European Commission (2021a) modelling, the (L) scenario corresponds to the MIX-CP scenario, whereas (H) corresponds to the REG scenario. The different investment needs for buildings are reported accordingly.

target. While the sectoral assumptions of the Central scenario are similar to those of OBR (2021), the aggregate share (26%, not reported) differs because of the different weights of power and car investment costs in the computation.

Table 8.2 Public sector shares of additional costs.

	Central scenario	OBR (2021)	EIB (2022) / NECPs	IEA (2021)
Expenditure	Capex	Capex and opex	Capex	Capex
Region	EU	UK	EU	AE
Total	54%		45%	
Sectoral details				
Power sector	15%	7%		17%
o/w: Power generation	5%	-		
o/w: Power grids	30%	10%		
District heating	30%	90%		
Residential buildings	45%	44%		
Non-residential buildings	45%	43%		
Industry	30/50%	50%		
Private transport		20%		
Rail and public transport	95/90%	85/50%		

The estimate of the total climate public spending that is needed in 2021–2030 in the EU is 1.8% of 2019 GDP. Additionally, there are other fiscal costs that should not be neglected but are harder to quantify, such as spending to protect the most vulnerable parts of the economy from policy-induced unemployment and higher living costs. Low-income households facing carbon pricing and other costly regulations will have to be supported financially. One way to assess the cost of such social support is to consider the recycling of carbon pricing revenues. According to Held et al. (2022), compensating households in the lower two income quintiles in all MS requires 23.4% of revenues from the proposed EU ETS for road transport and buildings. These resources therefore would not contribute to closing the climate investment gap, unless the aid were in the form of investment grants. At the same time, a new green workforce will have to be trained and workers displaced from shrinking industries will need help to transition to new jobs. Krebs and Steitz (2021) estimate Germany's spending needs in climate-related education and reskilling by 2030 at 20 billion euros. Finally, the decline in consumption of fossil fuels will erode energy tax revenues, especially from motor fuels. However, the effect is likely to be small before 2030 (OBR 2021).

8.2 Conclusion

The transition to climate neutrality by 2050 will be achieved only if green investment in the EU is scaled up quickly within the next few years. Closing the climate and energy security investment gap of 450 billion euros per year in 2021–2030 will require governments to strengthen environmental regulation and make more funds available to support the transition. The analysis presented in this paper suggests that the annual public spending needs to support green investment stand at around 250 billion euros (1.8% of 2019 GDP) over this decade. Without public transport investment, the figure stands at 153 billion euros (1.1% of GDP). Almost three quarters of these spending needs are in the buildings and transport sectors. The necessary public expenditures could be significantly higher or lower, depending on how policies are designed with respect to the use of carbon pricing and instruments to leverage private capital. Moreover, the impact of this spending on public debt and budget balances will depend on the multiplier effects on economic activity and tax receipts. This is a key component in the assessment of the fiscal implications of climate change policies.

The EU average of public spending needs is however not representative for all countries. Reviewing the results from the NECPs, which refer to the old 2030 target (-40%), EIB (2022) shows significant country variation not only with respect to investment needs, but also to expected public share of climate expenditure. Krebs and Steitz (2021) estimate a public spending gap of 1.3% of GDP in 2021–2030 for Germany. Agora Energiewende (2022d) derives national estimates of the public spending gaps and shows how they compare with the EU funds that each member state is expected to receive in the current EU budget period. The higher investment needs, as a percentage of GDP, in Central and Eastern Europe are in general well-matched by EU funding. In Southern Europe, the significant EU support of climate action through the EU Budget and RRF still leaves national climate spending gaps of around 1% of GDP annually. To ensure all EU countries deliver on the 2030 climate goals, without excessive political and social costs, the EU economic and fiscal governance should monitor the green spending and remaining gaps in the evaluation of the necessary fiscal adjustments. As most of these expenditures are in a few sectors, i.e. buildings and transport, even narrowly defined green spending exemptions to fiscal rules could help. In the long term, the EU will need an instrument like the RRF to continue sharing some of the cost of decarbonisation, and to provide fiscal support to those countries most in need.

References

ACEA (2022) "Share of Alternatively-powered Vehicles in the EU Fleet, per Segment", *ACEA*, https://www.acea.auto/figure/share-of-alternatively-powered-vehicles-in-the-eu-fleet-per-segment/.

Agora Energiewende (2021) 10 Benchmarks for a Successful July Fit for 55 Package. Berlin: Agora Energiewende, https://www.agora-energiewende.de/en/publications/10-benchmarks-for-a-successful-july-fit-for-55-package/.

Agora Energiewende (2022a) *Klimaschutzverträge für die Industrie transformation: Kurzfristige Schritte auf dem Pfad zur Klima-neutralität der deutschen Grundstoffindustrie.* Berlin: Agora Energiewende, https://www.agora-energiewende.de/veroeffentlichungen/klimaschutzvertraege-fuer-die-industrietransformation-gesamtstudie/.

Agora Energiewende (2022b) *Regaining Europe's Energy Sovereignty.* Berlin: Agora Energiewende, https://www.agora-energiewende.de/en/publications/regaining-europes-energy-sovereignty/.

Agora Energiewende (2022c) *Mobilising the Circular Economy for Energy-intensive Materials.* Berlin: Agora Energiewende, https://www.agora-energiewende.de/en/publications/mobilising-the-circular-economy-for-energy-intensive-materials-study/.

Agora Energiewende (2022d) *Delivering RePowerEU: A Solidarity-based Financing Proposal.* Berlin: Agora Energiewende, https://www.agora-energiewende.de/en/publications/delivering-repowereu/.

BloombergNEF (2021) "Long-Term Electric Vehicle Outlook 2021", *Bloomberg New Energy Finance*.

BloombergNEF (2022) "EV Charging Infrastructure Outlook 2022", *Bloomberg New Energy Finance*.

BPIE (2020) *Covid-19 Recovery: Investment Opportunities in Deep Renovation in Europe.* BPIE, https://www.bpie.eu/publication/covid-19-recovery-investment-opportunities-in-deep-renovation-in-europe/.

Bódis K., Ioannis Kougias, Arnulf Jäger-Waldau, Nigel Taylor, Sándor Szabó (2019) "A High-resolution Geospatial Assessment of the Rooftop Solar Photovoltaic Potential in the European Union", *Renewable and Sustainable Energy Reviews* 114, October 2019, 109309, https://doi.org/10.1016/j.rser.2019.109309.

Boston Consulting Group (2022) "Achieving Energy Security in the EU", Boston Consulting Group, https://www.bcg.com/publications/2022/achieving-energy-security-in-the-eu.

CEER (2021) *Status Review of Renewable Support Schemes in Europe for 2018 and 2019.* Council of European Energy Regulators, https://www.ceer.eu/res-status-review#.

CEER (2022) *Report on Regulatory Frameworks for European Energy Networks 2021.* Council of European Energy Regulators, https://www.ceer.eu/documents/104400/-/-/ae4ccaa5-796d-f233-bfa4-37a328e3b2f5.

Economidou, M., B. Atanasiu, C. Despret, J. Maio, I. Nolte, O. Rapf, and S. Zinetti (2011) *Europe's Buildings under the Microscope. A Country-by-Country Review of the Energy Performance of Buildings*, Brussels: BPIE.

Economidou, M., V. Todeschi, and P. Bertoldi (2019) *Accelerating Energy Renovation Investments in Buildings*. Luxembourg: Publications Office of the European Union, http://dx.doi.org/10.2760/086805.

Element Energy (2022) *The Consumer Costs of Decarbonised Heat*. Cambridge: The European Consumer Organization, https://www.beuc.eu/sites/default/files/publications/beuc-x-2021-111_consumer_cost_of_heat_decarbonisation_-_report.pdf.

Energy Transitions Commission (2020) *Making Mission Possible—Delivering a Net-Zero Economy*, Energy Transitions Commission, https://www.energy-transitions.org/publications/making-mission-possible/.

European Commission (2019) *Comprehensive Study of Building Energy Renovation Activities and the Uptake of Nearly Zero-energy Buildings in the EU*. Luxembourg: Publications Office of the European Union, https://doi.org/10.2833/14675.

European Commission (2020a) *Commission Staff Working Document—Identifying Europe's Recovery Needs*, SWD (2020) 98, CELEX: 52020SC0098(01).

European Commission (2020b) *Commission Staff Working Document—2030 Climate Target Plan Impact Assessment*, SWD (2020) 176, CELEX: 52020SC0176.

European Commission (2021a) *Revision of the Renewable Energy Directive (REDII)—Impact Assessment*, COM (2021) 557, CELEX: 52021PC0557.

European Commission (2021b) *Revision of the TEN-T Regulation—Impact Assessment Report*, COM (2021) 812, CELEX: 52021PC0812.

European Commission (2021c) *Revision of the ETS Regulation*, COM (2021) 551, CELEX: 52021PC0551.

European Commission (2022a), *Report on the Implementation of the Recovery and Resilience Facility*, COM (2022) 75, https://op.europa.eu/en/publication-detail/-/publication/854d575a-9959-11ec-83e1-01aa75ed71a1.

European Commission (2022b) *RePowerEU plan—Staff working paper*, SWD (2022) 230, https://op.europa.eu/en/publication-detail/-/publication/12cf59a5-d7af-11ec-a95f-01aa75ed71a1.

European Investment Bank (2022) *EIB Investment Report 2021/2022: Recovery as a Springboard for Change*, Luxembourg: European Investment Bank, http://dx.doi.org/10.2867/82061.

Goldman Sachs (2022) *Electrify Now: The Rise of Power in European Economies*, https://www.goldmansachs.com/insights/pages/electrify-now-the-rise-of-power-in-european-economies.html.

Held, B., C. Leisinger, M. Runkel, G. CAN-Europe, Deutschland eVKA, and WWF Deutschland (2022) *Criteria for an Effective and Socially Just EU ETS 2, Report 1/2022*, https://www.germanwatch.org/sites/default/files/criteria_for_an_effective_and_socially_just_eu_ets_2.pdf.

ICCT (2021) *A Global Comparison of the Life-cycle Greenhouse Gas Emissions of Combustion Engine and Electric Passenger Cars*, https://theicct.org/publication/a-global-comparison-of-the-life-cycle-greenhouse-gas-emissions-of-combustion-engine-and-electric-passenger-cars/.

IEA (2021a) *Financing Clean Energy Transitions in EMDEs*. Paris: IEA Publications, International Energy Agency, https://www.iea.org/reports/financing-clean-energy-transitions-in-emerging-and-developing-economies.

IEA (2021b) *Global SUV Sales Set Another Record in 2021, Setting back Efforts to Reduce Emissions.* Paris: IEA Publications, International Energy Agency, https://www.iea.org/commentaries/global-suv-sales-set-another-record-in-2021-setting-back-efforts-to-reduce-emissions.

IEA (2021c) *World Energy Outlook 2021.* Paris: IEA Publications, International Energy Agency, https://www.iea.org/reports/world-energy-outlook-2021.

IEA (2022) *Renewable Energy Market Update—May 2022.* Paris: IEA Publications, International Energy Agency, https://www.iea.org/reports/renewable-energy-market-update-may-2022.

IRENA (2021) *Renewable Power Generation Costs in 2020.* Abu Dhabi: International Renewable Energy Agency, https://www.irena.org/publications/2021/Jun/Renewable-Power-Costs-in-2020.

IRENA and CPI (2018) *Global Landscape of Renewable Energy Finance 2018.* Abu Dhabi: International Renewable Energy Agency, https://www.irena.org/publications/2018/jan/global-landscape-of-renewable-energy-finance.

IRENA and CPI (2020) *Global Landscape of Renewable Energy Finance 2020.* Abu Dhabi: International Renewable Energy Agency, https://www.irena.org/publications/2020/Nov/Global-Landscape-of-Renewable-Energy-Finance-2020.

Linden, A. J., F. Kalantzis, E. Maincent, and J. Pienkowski (2014) *Electricity Tariff Deficit: Temporary or Permanent Problem in the EU?* (No. 534), Directorate General Economic and Financial Affairs (DG ECFIN), European Commission Publications Office, https://data.europa.eu/doi/10.2765/71426.

Krebs, T. and J. Steitz (2021) "Öffentliche Finanzbedarfe für Klimainvestitionen im Zeitraum 2021–2030", *Forum for a New Economy Working Papers* 3–2021, https://www.agora-energiewende.de/veroeffentlichungen/oeffentliche-finanzbedarfe-fuer-klimainvestitionen-2021-2030/.

Material Economics (2022) "Scaling Up Europe, Bringing Low-CO2 Materials from Demonstration to Industrial Scale", https://materialeconomics.com/publications/scaling-up-europe.

Mathiesen, B. V., N. Bertelsen, N. C. A. Schneider, L. S. García, S. Paardekooper, J. Z. Thellufsen, and S. R. Djørup (2019) *Towards a Decarbonised Heating and Cooling Sector in Europe: Unlocking the Potential of Energy Efficiency and District Energy.* Aalborg: Aalborg Universitet, https://vbn.aau.dk/en/publications/towards-a-decarbonised-heating-and-cooling-sector-in-europe-unloc.

McKinsey (2020) *Net Zero Europe: How the European Union could achieve net-zero emissions at net-zero cost,* https://www.mckinsey.com/capabilities/sustainability/our-insights/How-the-European-Union-could-achieve-net-zero-emissions-at-net-zero-cost.

OECD (2021) Effective Carbon Rates 2021: Pricing Carbon Emissions through Taxes and Emissions Trading. Paris: OECD Publishing, https://doi.org/10.1787/0e8e24f5-en.

OBR (2021) *Fiscal Risk Report—July 2021.* London: Office for Budget Responsibility, https://obr.uk/frs/fiscal-risks-report-july-2021/.

Trommsdorff, M., S. Gruber, T. Keinath, M. Hopf, C. Hermann, and F. Schönberger (2020) *Agrivoltaics: Opportunities for Agriculture and the Energy Transition-A Guideline for Germany.* Freiburg: Fraunhofer ISE, https://www.ise.fraunhofer.de/content/dam/ise/en/documents/publications/studies/APV-Guideline.pdf.

Wouter Nijs, Dalius Tarvydas, and Agne Toleikyte (2021) *EU Challenges of Reducing Fossil Fuel Use in Buildings—The Role of Building Insulation and Low-carbon Heating Systems in 2030 and 2050.* Luxembourg: Publications Office of the European Union, https://doi.org/10.2760/85088.

9. The Investment Needs for REPowerEU

Miguel Gil Tertre and Bert Saveyn

Introduction

On 18 May 2022, the European Commission presented REPowerEU (European Commission, 2022a, b), the concrete EU plan to reduce dependency on Russian fossil fuels. This plan details how to achieve the objectives laid out by the Commission in March (European Commission 2022c) that were endorsed by the heads of state and governments at Versailles (European Council, 2022).

The plan provides a clear identification of the required investment needs (including infrastructure bottlenecks) and policy actions on both the demand and supply sides. Reducing dependence on Russian fossil fuels will on the one hand require a faster reduction of our dependence on fossil fuels more broadly, and, on the other hand, a diversification of gas supplies. Both of these actions will require investments to boost energy efficiency gains, increase the share of renewables, address infrastructure bottlenecks, increase LNG imports and pipeline imports from non-Russian suppliers, and increase the levels of renewable hydrogen and bio-methane. In the immediate term, this requires a diversification of supply sources and a reduction in demand. In the longer term, this will call for the deployment of alternative sources of energy.

This article provides an estimate of the investment needs and additional costs of reducing our fossil fuel dependence on Russia to zero by 2027, with a specific focus on the use of natural gas. This analysis was instrumental in preparing the REPowerEU plan as presented by the Commission on the 18 May 2022. The decoupling of the EU and fossil fuel imports from Russia has already started and will pass through different stages, affecting both the demand and supply sides. Taking into account the above elements, this analysis indicates that reducing our dependence to zero (310 billion cubic metres, or bcm) would require €300bn[1]

---

1   All monetary values are in EUR 2022 with HICP index (March 2022) being 115.88 (compared to 2015).

https://doi.org/10.11647/OBP.0328.09

cumulatively from now until 2030, in addition to the Fit for 55 proposals.[2] By the end of 2027, this transition corresponds to approximately €210bn of investments (and 235 bcm). These REPowerEU investments correspond to about 5% of the total Fit for 55 investments until 2030, and are in addition to them. The Commission analysis estimates that with the Fit for 55 and REPowerEU measures combined, the EU can save €80bn on gas import expenditures, €12bn on oil import expenditures and €1.7bn on coal import expenditures per year.

Full implementation of our Fit for 55 proposals would lower our gas consumption by 30%, which is equivalent to 116 billion cubic meters (bcm), by 2030. Along with additional gas diversification and accelerated gas decarbonisation, frontloaded energy savings and electrification have the potential to jointly deliver at least the equivalent of the 155 bcm imports of Russian gas by 2027.

The REPowerEU plan proposed higher targets for renewables (-45%) and energy efficiency (-13%, final energy consumption) by 2030, thereby strengthening the Fit–for–55 package. This article explores how these higher renewables and energy efficiency levels contribute to the REPowerEU objectives.

Achieving the objectives of REPowerEU relies notably on scaling up renewable hydrogen and bio-methane and will make a crucial contribution to efforts to reduce EU dependence on Russian gas.[3]

The scaling up of the deployment of renewable hydrogen will reduce our dependence on natural gas, coal and oil imports from Russia, and will help to accelerate the EU energy transition. For this reason, the REPowerEU report of 8 March mentioned the Hydrogen Accelerator in relation to the ambition to use 20 million tons of renewable hydrogen in 2030 in the EU.

The proposed measures would not only facilitate an increase in the production of biogas, but would also boost its subsequent conversion into bio-methane,

---

2   The additional investments beyond the Fit for 55 proposals reflect both the impact of the REPowerEU measures and that of the higher (see Annex 1) fossil fuel price context. The analysis excludes:
- Transport
- The possibility to increase intra-EU sources of fossil fuels (e.g Groningen in the Netherlands)
- The investments and infrastructure needed outside of the EU (e.g. LNG terminals or tankers outside the EU removing bottlenecks to increase supply from Third Countries).

3   The European Commission (2022b) explores how the development of hydrogen can be accelerated and the bio-methane targets achieved. In particular, the Staff Working Document develops the Hydrogen Accelerator by identifying activities to support the implementation of these accelerated ambitions. It describes in which priority sectors the increased amount of renewable hydrogen can be used and what measures would enable this uptake, identifies possible activities and support for the rapid development of the required hydrogen infrastructure, including pipelines, storages and terminal facilities, and sets out how the EU could step up its international engagement and coordinate its actions to facilitate the import of 10 million tons of renewable hydrogen, while ensuring respect for the EU's international trade obligations. Further, the Staff Working Document presents a number of possible actions to boost biomethane production to 35 bcm by 2030. The actions cover four key areas and could unlock the full biogas and bio-methane potential that exists across all EU member states.

respecting strict environmental criteria agreed in the REDII. Recognising existing barriers to entry, the actions also target the facilitation of biomethane integration into the EU internal gas market. Further co-ordination of support for biogas and bio-methane at the EU, national and regional levels is needed if we collectively want to achieve the 35 bcm target. Challenges include improving infrastructure deployment, improving access to finance, and supporting research, development and innovation.

9.1 Drivers of Natural Gas Demand Reduction in REPowerEU

The March REPowerEU Communication states that the full implementation of the Fit for 55 proposals would **lower our gas consumption by 30%**, which is equivalent to 116 bcm, by 2030. The higher long-term gas and oil price paths will reduce natural gas demand further by about 40 bcm before 2030, whereas the implementation of the REPowerEU measures will complete the process with an additional almost 100 bcm reduction by 2030.

Together with additional gas diversification and renewable gases, frontloaded energy savings and electrification have the potential to jointly deliver **at least the equivalent of the 155 bcm** imports of Russian gas by 2027.

While there is currently an ongoing shift from gas to coal and oil, under the Fit for 55 proposal, demand for oil and coal is projected to decrease by 28% and 50% respectively between 2019 and 2030. Under REPowerEU, demand for coal is expected to decrease by 36% (by 2030 vs 2020). The demand for oil will be comparable in 2030 to the Fit for 55 projections (since the focus of this analysis is on gas). The reduction in the demand for coal suggests that we will fully replace Russian coal imports by 2027.

Three main drivers will change the energy system beyond the Fit for 55 proposals:

1. The decoupling from Russian gas imports, leading to the need for alternative suppliers and entry points into the EU, alternative intra-EU pipeline routes and other infrastructure. Regarding natural gas, additional imports from alternative sources can reach Europe either by pipeline or in the form of LNG. In the short term, i.e. by using only existing infrastructure, an additional 10 bcm can be imported by pipeline and a further 50 bcm using existing LNG infrastructure.

2. The REPowerEU plan further increases the ambition level beyond the Fit for 55 Package for gas alternatives (bio-methane, renewable hydrogen), deployment of renewables, and structural demand measures such as energy efficiency;

○ The renewables reach a 45% share in 2030;[4]

○ Energy efficiency reaches a 13% share in 2030;

○ Bio-methane production reaches 35 bcm in 2030;

○ Renewable hydrogen use[5] reaches 20 Mt by 2030 (of which about 4 Mt as ammonia);

○ Ensuring that the minimum -55% GHG objective of the Fit for 55 package is achieved.

3. Prices are expected to be persistently higher than the reference (but lower than the peak prices observed in 2021 and 2022). Experts expect that current events will temporarily fragment oil and coal markets resulting in higher prices, while these markets will rebalance in the medium term. The fuel price trajectories used in the REPowerEU and Fit for 55 scenarios are provided in Figure 9.1 in Annex A.

9.2. Investment Needs

Reduction of Gas Demand and Investments by Technology

Achieving the objectives of the REPowerEU communication to reduce the dependence of Russian fossil fuels will require significant investments to:

- **Reduce our dependence on fossil fuels faster** at the levels of homes, buildings, transport, industry and the power system by boosting energy efficiency gains, increasing the share of renewables and addressing infrastructure bottlenecks.

- **Diversify gas supplies**, via higher LNG imports and pipeline imports from non-Russian suppliers, and higher levels of bio-methane (domestically produced) and renewable hydrogen (domestically produced and imported).

Full implementation of our Fit for 55 proposals would lower our gas consumption by 30%, which is equivalent to 116 bcm, by 2030. Along with additional gas diversification and more renewable gases, frontloaded energy savings and electrification have the potential to jointly deliver at least the equivalent of the 155 bcm imports of Russian gas by 2027.

For the purpose of this analysis, fossil fuels considered are coal, oil and refined petroleum products (e.g. diesel) and, in particular, natural gas.

The analysis considered three dimensions for the menu of options:

---

4   Using the definition in RED III.
5   Including the use of e-fuels derived from hydrogen.

1. How fast can these measures be deployed?

2. How cost-efficient are these measures (contribution to reducing the dependency, number of bcm saved in the case of gas)?

3. How green? The measures should not lead to stranded assets and should be future-proof, as far as possible.

Several policy actions can be considered both from the supply and demand sides:

- In the short term
  - Diversification of gas pipeline routes (including higher load factor of existing pipelines)
  - Limited additional LNG under current infrastructure or floating storage regasification units (e.g. import terminals and pipeline network)
  - Demand-side behavioural measures
  - Energy efficiency investments (including heat pumps)
  - Industry gas prioritisation (emergency measure)
  - As a response to high prices, users switch to other fuels. With existing capacities, this can be achieved with relatively little additional investments (e.g., when coal and nuclear power plants increase operating hours)

- In the medium term:
  - Further energy efficiency investments and innovation (including heat pumps, retrofitting and energy-efficient industrial processes)
  - Development of bio-methane production and infrastructure
  - Additional photovoltaic (PV), on-shore and off-shore wind deployment and energy system integration
  - Additional investment in the power grid and storage
  - Limited new LNG and gas pipeline infrastructure and adapting the existing gas networks to bio-methane and renewable hydrogen

- In the longer term
  - Development of renewable hydrogen production and hydrogen infrastructure

The analysis looks at the investments needed to build a structurally new energy system that is independent from Russia as a fossil fuel producer. Taking into account the above elements, the up-front additional investment needs, complementing the Fit for 55 package, to reduce the dependence to zero would amount to €300bn from now until 2030 (or, approximately €210bn by the end of 2027).

Table 9.1 below focuses on a gradual decoupling from Russian gas and assesses the options for additional gas demand reduction and associated investment needs compared to the Fit for 55 scenario. It is based on comparing results of modelling scenarios of REPowerEU and implementation of the Fit for 55 package[6] using the PRIMES model.[7] The modelling implements the REPowerEU drivers as described in Section 2. More particularly, the investments listed in the table below notably cover the implementation of all the measures in the REPowerEU Communication and the specific needs for gradual gas decoupling from Russia by 2027, new LNG infrastructure and gas pipeline corridors, and production, transmission and demand sides of the transition outlined in the REPowerEU Communication including energy efficiency, renewables, heat pumps, renewable hydrogen including electrolysers, biomethane. Those investments do not cover the impacts of sanctions, oil savings, oil production or demand measures, curtailment of oil, natural gas or coal, nor investments in existing infrastructures related to the diversification of gas supply. As the focus of the analysis is on gas, Table 9.1 does not include transport, and investments in transport are similar in the REPowerEU and Fit for 55 projections.

---

6   The additional investments beyond the Fit for 55 proposals reflect both the impact of the REPowerEU measures and that of the higher fossil fuels prices.
7   https://web.jrc.ec.europa.eu/policy-model-inventory/explore/models/model-primes.

Table 9.1 Potential measures and investments to reduce dependence on Russian gas via technology, in addition to the Fit for 55 package.

Timing	Measure	bcm (in 2030)	€bn invest-ments (2022-2030)	Justification/ explanation of the bcm figure	Eligibility under EU financial programmes
Ff55 savings by 2030	Total of all Fit for 55 measures	116		Fit for 55 modelling estimates 30% natural gas savings	-
Short-term prepared-ness	Diversification (additional LNG using existing infrastructure)	50		REPowerEU Communication COM(2022) 108 final	-
	Diversification of pipeline imports using existing infrastructure	10	-	In 2030, long term contracts account for about 110 bcm (of which about 55 bcm are take-or-pay contracts) Using existing capacity.	
	Delayed phase-out and more operating hours for coal	24	2	The investment refers to CAPEX. The fuel cost (coal) is not included (OPEX). The total expenditure of the switch from gas to coal is the sum of CAPEX and OPEX.	-
	Abandoned phase-out nuclear plants	7	-8	Recent political decisions in BE and FR	-
	Fuel switch in the residential and service sectors EU Save:	9		Fuel switch driven by price changes	
	Demand measures (behaviour) EU Save:	(10)	-	Measure 9 of the IEA plan on gas in the EU (gas saving counted under energy efficiency)	-
	Industry curtailment	-	-	Emergency measure	-

---

8   Investments for nuclear long-term operation are included in investments for other power technologies and infrastructure.

Timing	Measure	bcm (in 2030)	€ bn invest-ments (2022-2030)	Justification/ explanation of the bcm figure	Eligibility under EU financial programmes
Mid-term (until 2027)	New LNG infrastructure and pipeline corridors	-	10	These infrastructure and pipelines facilitate the full effect of the diversification. Compared to average EU LNG imports of 7 bcm/month (in 2019–2021), the EU system could absorb an additional 3.8 bcm/month (45.6 bcm/year) of LNG if bottlenecks are removed. oe However, there are currently only 8 to 10 available Floating Storage Regassification Units LNG terminals in the world.[9]	Modernisation Fund,[10] RRF,[11] CEF,[12] ERDF and CF, for projects on the 5th PCI list
	Additional investments in the power grid and storage	-	39	The storage is about 10bn.	CEF, InvestEU,[13] HE,[14] ERDF,[15] CF,[16] JTF,[17] RRF, ETF Funds[18]

9   As an example, the Wilhelmshaven LNG Import Terminal, scheduled to enter service by 2023, once completed could deal with 10 bcm of additional gas per year. The cost of the project is around €672m.

10 Natural gas transmission (and distribution as well as gas-fired energy generation) are capped at a maximum of 30% of the overall Modernisation Fund allocation.

11 Recovery and Resilience Facility.

12 Connecting Europe Facility.

13 InvestEU Programme.

14 Horizon Europe.

15 European Regional Development Fund.

16 Cohesion Fund.

17 Just Transition Fund.

18 Refers to two funds established under the ETS Directive: the Innovation Fund and the Modernisation Fund. The Modernisation Fund is available to ten MS: Bulgaria, Croatia, Czech Republic, Estonia, Hungary, Latvia, Lithuania, Poland, Romania, and Slovakia.

Timing	Measure	bcm (in 2030)	€bn invest-ments (2022-2030)	Justification / explanation of the bcm figure	Eligibility under EU financial programmes
	Biomass in power generation	1	2	In line with the sustainability criteria of the Renewable Energy Directive.	HE, InvestEU, LIFE, ERDF, CF, JTF, RRF, ETS Funds, RES EU FM, EAFRD[19]
	Energy Efficiency and Heat Pumps	37	56	Including energy efficiency in buildings; Lower final electricity demand;	HE,[20] InvestEU, LIFE, ERDF, CF, JTF, RRF, ETS Funds
	PV	-	See Hydrogen	In this scenario, all additional PV and wind power is used to produce the additional hydrogen. Alternatively, direct use of PV electricity to replace natural gas requires approximately €1.6bn of investment per bcm saved.	HE, InvestEU, CEF[21] LIFE, ERDF, CF, JTF, RRF, ETS Funds, RES EU FM[22]
	Onshore wind; Offshore wind	-	See Hydrogen	Due to the long lead times and higher costs, in the short term, there is little additional deployment of offshore wind power. In this scenario, all additional PV and wind power is used to produce the additional hydrogen. Alternatively, direct use of wind electricity to replace natural gas requires approximately €1.6bn of investment per bcm saved.	HE, InvestEU, CEF[23] LIFE, ERDF, CF, JTF, RRF, ETS Funds, RES EU FM

---

19 European Agricultural Fund for Rural Development.
20 Horizon Europe.
21 Here, eligibility would be possible under the CEF-Energy cross-border RES envelope.
22 RES EU financing mechanism.
23 Here, eligibility would be possible under CEF-Energy cross-border RES envelope.

Timing	Measure	bcm (in 2030)	€bn invest-ments (2022-2030)	Justification/ explanation of the bcm figure	Eligibility under EU financial programmes
	Sustainable bio-methane	17	37	Increased use in households, industry and agriculture. The total (with Fit for 55) adds up to 35 bcm in 2030. Including electrification, energy efficiency, and fuel substitution (including hydrogen);	InvestEU,ERDF,[24] CF,[25] JTF,[26] CEF,[27] ETS Funds,[28] EAFRD
	Reduced use in industry	12	41	Excluding the cost of production of hydrogen and biogas/bio-methane; Excluding refineries.	HE, ETS Funds, InvestEU, ERDF, CF, RRF

24 European Regional Development Fund.
25 Cohesion Fund.
26 Just Transition Fund.
27 Connecting Europe Facility.
28 Refers to two funds established under the ETS Directive: the Innovation Fund and the Modernisation Fund. The Modernisation Fund is available to ten MS: Bulgaria, Croatia, Czech Republic, Estonia, Hungary, Latvia, Lithuania, Poland, Romania, and Slovakia.

Timing	Measure	bcm (in 2030)	€bn invest-ments (2022-2030)	Justification/ explanation of the bcm figure	Eligibility under EU financial programmes
				About 6.6 Mt is produced domestically and included in the Fit for 55 scenario.	
				REPowerEU increases the domestic production by 3.4 Mt while 6 Mt of renewable hydrogen and approximately 4 Mt of ammonia are imported.	
	Renewable hydrogen	27	113	Out of the approximately additional 10 Mt hydrogen, 8 Mt replace 27 bcm of gas, whereas the remaining 2 Mt replace oil (4 Mt) and coal (1.4 Mt of which 156 kt are from Russia[29]).	CEF, InvestEU, HE, ETS Funds, RRF, ERDF, CF, JTF[30]
				Out of €113bn, €27bn corresponds to the direct production and distribution of hydrogen.	
				€37bn covers the related investment for PV and €49bn is for related investment in wind electricity capacity.	
Total		310	300		

Infrastructure

Note: bcm figures in brackets are provided for information but not included in the total.

---

29 In 2020, 12% of coking coal consumed in the EU was imported from Russia.
30 Concerning the ERDF, Cohesion Fund, and JTF, the eligibility refers to RES hydrogen as "promoting renewable energy in accordance with Directive (EU) 2018/2001" according to Regulation (EU) 2021/1058 on the ERDF/CF.

The measures proposed for decoupling the energy supply from Russia constitute a significant change to the energy system in terms of quantities, prices, and directions of energy flows. As a result, the infrastructure needs for electricity, hydrogen and natural gas should also adapt. These infrastructure investments should solve the future needs in a coordinated manner, avoiding creating stranded assets as far as possible, and facilitating the long-term transition to a carbon-neutral economy.

Diversification of suppliers is essential for eliminating natural gas imports from Russia. In particular, it will be necessary to import sufficient additional natural gas from other pipeline suppliers and LNG ports. These new import routes and new intra-EU gas flows will require about €10bn of investment (e.g. LNG terminals, pipelines, reverse flows) by 2030, in order to guarantee a sufficient supply and a fluid distribution of natural gas across all member states.

Simultaneously, REPowerEU proposes an ambitious level of renewable hydrogen deployment, which also requires an acceleration of the development of renewable hydrogen infrastructure. These gas and hydrogen infrastructure investments should make use of synergies in order to be future-proof investments. Hydrogen networks should enable a pan-European integration of hydrogen supply and demand. This is closely related to the deployment of renewable energy (reaching a 45% share with REPowerEU), the location of electrolysers producing renewable hydrogen, and the form in which hydrogen is to be transported or imported (e.g. including ammonia).

The further increase and integration of renewable energy requires an efficient and adapted electricity network. REPowerEU increases and frontloads the renewable capacities compared to the Fit for 55 package, and the electricity network should adapt accordingly, including both offshore and onshore grids. By 2030, €39bn of additional investments in the power grid will be needed (including transmission, distribution and storage plants), compared to the Fit for 55 scenario, in line with the higher deployment of renewables.

9.3 Why Should the Potential for Natural Gas Reduction Be Higher than 155 bcm?

The combined effect of the Fit for 55 proposals—the measures announced in the March Communication, a higher price trajectory for natural gas, and the LNG and pipeline diversification—all have the potential to lead to a cumulative demand reduction of 310 bcm of natural gas by 2030 compared to 2020 (Table 9.1 Potential measures and investments to reduce dependence on Russian gas via technology, in addition to the Fit for 55 package.). By 2027, this will correspond to 235 bcm (including 60 bcm of diversification measures).[31] REPowerEU aims to improve energy security in the EU,

---

31   The 60 bcm of diversification measures can be achieved entirely by 2027; the remainder is multiplied by 70% (to bring 2030 figures to 2027). Arithmetically, 235 = 60 + 70% * (310–60).

while respecting cost-efficiency and the decarbonisation pathway. Therefore, it is in the interest of the EU to have a broad range of options to allow for sufficient flexibility and to prepare for other unforeseen events. The objective should go beyond 155 bcm, which is the quantity of Russian natural gas imports in 2021.

1. In previous years, the Russian imports have been significantly higher (e.g. 195 bcm in 2019[32]). Further, domestic natural gas production continues to decrease by several bcm every year in the EU and its surroundings. Not all reductions in natural gas consumption will directly translate to fewer imports from Russia (e.g. in the Western part of the EU).

2. Another uncertainty is the price trajectories of natural gas and the other fossil fuels. Higher gas prices than usual, as shown in the price trajectory (see Annex), will drive about 40 bcm out of the EU energy system by 2030 (e.g. by switching to coal). While lower gas prices are beneficial for the EU economy, the price signal to use less gas will evaporate, possibly compromising the decoupling from Russia, and putting the energy security of the EU at risk in the longer term.

3. The REPowerEU measures and the Fit for 55 proposals rely heavily on a quick and ambitious deployment of fossil-free technologies. Various bottlenecks may delay this deployment, such as the dependence on rare-earth elements, supply chain constraints, skilled labour shortages, higher than average price inflation, financing, and the development of new production capacities and transport infrastructures (e.g. for renewable hydrogen).

Finally, the greater potential for gas reduction may allow the EU member states to roll back the temporary measures before 2027, including (i) measures to reduce the temperature in buildings by one degree (10 bcm), (ii) more operating hours and a delayed phase-out of coal power plants (24 bcm), and (iii) a delayed phase-out of nuclear plants (7 bcm).

9.4 Conclusion

The REPowerEU communication presents an ambitious but credible plan to reduce the EU's dependence on Russian fossil fuels, identifying critical actions and specific investment needs.

Its implementation will depend on the ambition and ability to coordinate of member states in a very unstable context. In this sense, the EU would have to be ready to further develop its solidarity arrangements in case of supply disruptions and to coordinate demand reduction measures, complementing the current diversification efforts (particularly in the context of the EU energy platform). It would be advisable

---

32   Total of 178 bcm of pipeline and 17 bcm LNG (ENTSOG).

to strengthen solidarity requirements and tools so as to be better prepared in case emergencies arise.

With REPowerEU, the EU's gas consumption will reduce at a faster pace, limiting the role of gas as a transitional fuel in the energy transition. REPowerEU solidly builds on the full implementation of the Fit for 55 package and proposes higher ambitions for renewables and energy efficiency. REPowerEU, combined with the Fit for 55 package, has the potential to reduce the EU's natural gas use by up to 310 bcm by 2030.

Moving away from Russian fossil fuels will also require targeted investments for security of supply in gas and (very limited) oil infrastructure alongside large-scale investments in the electricity grid and an EU-wide hydrogen backbone. These investments are estimated to amount to €210bn by 2027 and require initiatives related to demand and supply, involving industry, buildings, infrastructure and the energy sector.

References

European Commission (2022a) *REPower Plan*, COM/2022/230 final, https://eur-lex.europa.eu/resource.html?uri=cellar:fc930f14-d7ae-11ec-a95f-01aa75ed71a1.0001.02/DOC_1&format=PDF.

European Commission (2022b) *Commission Staff Working Document Implementing the REPower EU Action Plan: Investment Needs, Hydrogen Accelerator and Achieving the Bio-Methane Targets*, SWD/2022/230 final, https://eur-lex.europa.eu/legal-content/EN/TXT/PDF/?uri=CELEX:52022SC0230&from=EN.

European Commission (2022c) *Joint European Action for More Affordable, Secure and Sustainable Energy*, COM/2022/108 final, https://energy.ec.europa.eu/system/files/2022-03/Communication_Security_of_supply_and_affordable_energy_prices.pdf.

European Council (2022) Informal meetIng of the Heads of States or Government. The Versailles Declaration, 10 and 11 March 2022, https://www.consilium.europa.eu/en/press/press-releases/2022/03/11/the-versailles-declaration-10-11-03-2022.

Annex on Price Trajectories between 2020 and 2050 for Gas, Oil and Coal

Figure 9.1 shows the price trajectories between 2020 and 2050 for gas, oil and coal. Oil and coal prices are based on historical data for 2020–2021, combined with estimates of prices in 2022 and complemented by a linear interpolation to the long-term trajectory assumed in the EU Reference Scenario 2020 for the following years. The same approach is followed for gas prices, except that these are expected to remain higher than in the Fit for 55 scenario in the long run.

Gas Prices

Oil Prices

Coal Prices

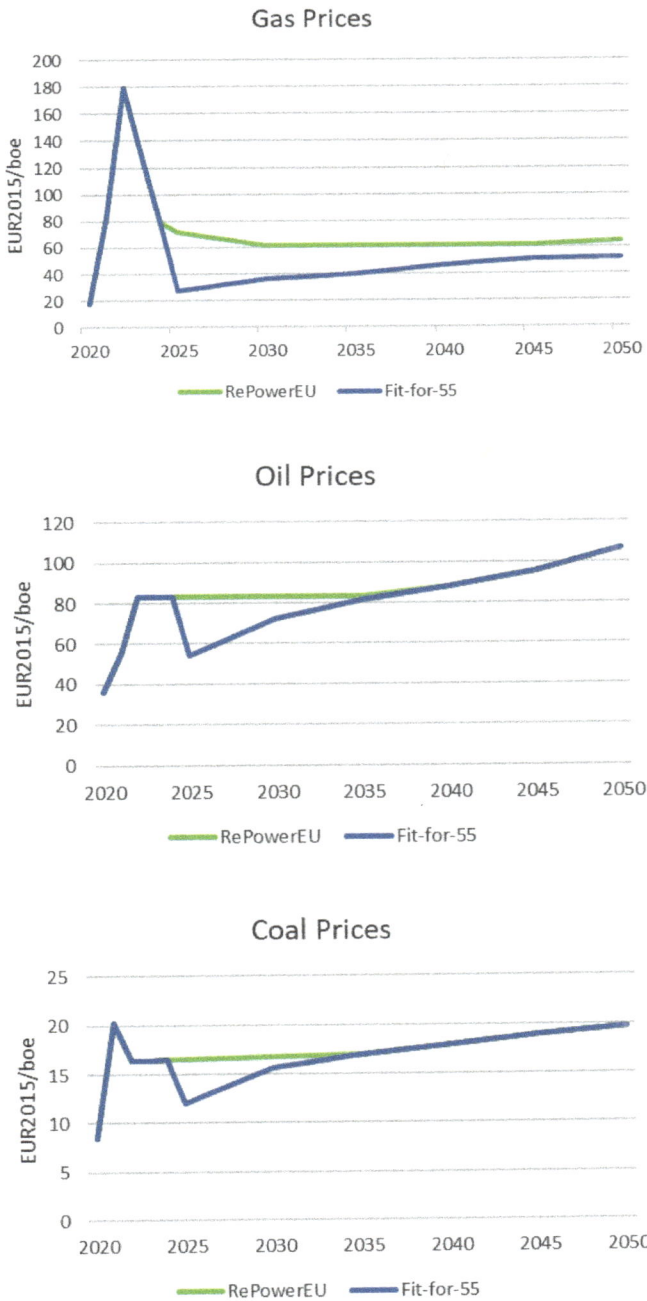

Fig. 9.1 Fuel price trajectories used for REPowerEU and Fit for 55 analysis.

10. Public Spending for Future Generations

Recent Trends in EU Countries[1]

Lorenzo Ferrari and Valentina Meliciani

Introduction

Public investment, traditionally measured using the so-called *gross fixed capital formation* (hereinafter GFCF) of the public sector, decreased dramatically in the European Union (hereinafter EU) between 2010 and 2016, both as a percentage of GDP and in relation to the population, passing respectively from 3.7% to 2.7% of GDP and from approximately 1,000 to 800 euros per capita. The contraction of this category of expenditure, traditionally considered discretionary and more compressible by governments, is mainly due to the measures implemented to contain public expenditure (austerity) imposed in Europe following the global financial crisis and has therefore mainly affected the Mediterranean countries, which are traditionally characterised by high levels of public debt and low growth rates. As explained in Cerniglia and Saraceno (2021), there is only a partial recovery of public investment, which in 2019 reached 3% of GDP and approximately 890 euros per capita respectively, starting from 2017.

The use of the public sector GFCF (the so-called gross fixed investment) for the evaluation of government expenditure policies and the measurement of the latter's impact not only on economic growth but also on the level of a country's development and social and environmental prosperity, however, have been the subject of extensive institutional and academic discussions over the past few years. An example is the UN System of National Accounts, whose 2008 revision (UN 2009) expresses the need to consider the entire expenditure on Research and Development (hereinafter R&D) and Education in the GFCF.[2] In the academic field, for example, Streeck and

---

1   This work has benefited from a postdoctoral grant provided by the Territorial Public Accounts (CPT) of the Agency for Territorial Cohesion.
2   A similar need is expressed by the Italian Territorial Cohesion Agency (CPT 2020).

   https://doi.org/10.11647/OBP.0328.10

Mertens (2011) also include in the scope of their evaluation of public investment policies the so-called "soft investment", i.e., public expenditure not accounted for as GFCF in R&D, Education, Active Labour Policies, and transfers to households. In fact, public sector GFCF expenditure is limited to the construction and maintenance of a country's physical infrastructure (roads, railways, canals and bridges, machines used by the public sector). It can be easily noted that, first of all, the comparison of national policies carried out exclusively on the basis of this variable is made extremely complex by the latter's dependence on both the geographical characteristics and the level of infrastructural development of each country.[3] Secondly (and above all), we believe that the public sector GFCF does not include some items of expenditure which, although formally accounted for as "current" expenditure, decisively determine the public sector's contribution to economic and social development and to the protection of a country's environmental heritage, and must therefore be included in the evaluation of public expenditure policies and in the measurement of their effects on economic, social, and environmental indicators.[4] The analysis of these categories of public expenditure is also motivated by some objectives and policies introduced at the European level such as, for example, the Next Generation EU, which require EU countries to spend a certain percentage of resources in projects aimed at promoting digital transition, scientific research, the green transition and social cohesion.

This chapter has two main objectives. First, we intend to contribute to the aforementioned debate by defining an innovative expenditure aggregate, which we have chosen to call Expenditure for Future Generations (hereinafter EFG) and which includes, in addition to the public sector GFCF, public contributions to investment by private companies (which, although they actually contribute to the creation and maintenance of a country's private fixed capital stock, are not traditionally included in the GFCF), as well as primary current expenditure (hereinafter PCE) in some key sectors of public intervention, namely (i) Research and Development, (ii) Education, (iii) Environmental Protection, and (iv) General Economic, Commercial and Labour Affairs. In fact, it appears evident that (i) and (ii) contribute both to innovation in the industrial field and to the formation of human capital, which in turn have a positive impact on productivity and therefore on long-term economic growth (UN 2009). The PCE in Environmental Protection is mainly divided, within the European System of National Accounts, into the sub-functions management of solid and liquid waste, reduction of pollution, and protection of biodiversity and the landscape and, in our opinion, improves the quality of life of individuals. Finally, (iv) is linked to

---

3   For example, a low expense for the construction of new highways in a country like Germany could be justified by the presence of an already highly developed motorway infrastructure.

4   As specified in Streeck and Mertens (2011), "it would be necessary to focus attention on a different kind of public investment that is more important for post-industrial societies: the so-called 'light investment' which can be defined as those types of public expenditure that have as their objective that of creating the conditions for increasing the prosperity and sustainability of a post-industrial knowledge society."

active employment policies, which increase employability prospects and therefore social inclusion (see, for example, Vooren et al. 2019). The dynamics of this innovative aggregate in the EU and for a group of "representative" countries of the geo-economic groups present within it will then be analysed and compared with those of the public sector GFCF. The second objective is to provide both European and national policymakers with innovative tools that allow them to evaluate (and, if necessary, modify) expenditure policies in European countries in relation to the EFG and economic categories (such as the GFCF) and the sectors comprising it. To this end we have defined three further variables, which we have called Comparative Advantage, Absolute Advantage, and Absolute Advantage Per Capita, which will make it possible to evaluate not only the performance in absolute terms (as a percentage of GDP and per capita) of the different countries of the EU in relation to the EFG and its components, but also in terms of the composition of public expenditure and therefore of expenditure priorities within the countries themselves. In particular, the analysis of these variables will allow us (i) to verify whether the EFG in the various countries is higher or lower than the EU as a whole (ii) to create a ranking of EU countries based on these variables and (iii) to look at trends in expenditure in EFG.

10.1 GFCF and EFG in the EU

10.1.1 From the GFCF to the EFG

The data relating to public expenditure used in our analysis are presented by the "Classification of the Functions of the Government" dataset (hereinafter COFOG), made available by Eurostat (and originally by OECD), which reports the public expenditure classified in functions[5] (and sub-functions) of the government, the public entity that supports the expenditure (central and local administrations, and social security funds), as well as the economic category of expenditure (for example, GFCF, wages and salaries, interest on debt, intermediate and final consumption of the public sector). The data are presented in three main formats, namely in millions of euros, as a percentage of GDP, and as a percentage of total public expenditure. The geographical coverage includes all EU countries from 1995 to 2019.[6] We define the EFG as the sum of the following economic categories of expenditure:

- GFCF in all functions of the state, generally defined as expenditure for (i) the construction of the physical infrastructure of a country; (ii) the purchase of

---

5   The intervention sectors defined in COFOG are General Public Services, Defence, Economic Affairs, Environmental Protection, Construction and Community Services, Healthcare, Recreation, Culture and Religion, Education, and Social Protection. Each sector is divided into a series of specific subsectors.

6   It should be noted that the time series for the United Kingdom is no longer present in the Eurostat dataset starting from 2021. Furthermore, some of the entries in the COFOG dataset are only available starting from 2001.

capital goods used by the government; and (iii) to improve and maintain the existing capital stock (OECD 2009).

- Public Contributions to Investment: capital transfers in cash or in kind made by governments to other resident or non-resident institutional units in order to finance all or part of the costs of acquiring fixed assets (OECD 2009).

- PCE in the sectors of R&D, Education, Environmental Protection, and General Economic, Commercial and Labour Affairs.[7] PCE is defined as the sum of (i) employee wages, (ii) intermediate consumption, (iii) subsidies, (iv) other current transfers, (v) social benefits other than social transfers in kind, and (vi) transfers that are social in nature—purchased market production (Lenzi and Zoppè 2020).

Finally, we define the Residual Primary Current Expenditure (hereinafter RPCE) as the PCE in the sectors not included in the EFG perimeter. It should be noted that the GDP deflator has been applied to the absolute values of all the variables in order to ensure the comparability of the series over time for the various countries.[8]

10.2 Trends in the EFG in the EU and Comparisons with the GFCF

In this section we focus on the temporal evolution of the EFG and the comparison of its dynamics with those of the GFCF. Figure 10.1 shows, respectively in the left and right columns, the GFCF and the EFG in relation to GDP (top) and per capita (bottom) for a subgroup of "representative" countries of the geo-economic subgroups that are part of (or were part of, in the case of the United Kingdom) the EU, or two "Mediterranean" countries (Italy and Spain), two Central European founding countries (France and Germany), a country belonging to the group of "new entrants" to the EU (Poland), a "Nordic" country (Sweden), the United Kingdom, and overall for the EU28 in the 2001–2019 period.[9] Figure 10.2 shows, for the same countries and the same time interval, the GFCF (left) and EFG (right) as a percentage of the PCE and the RPCE, respectively. First of all, it can be noted that in some countries, namely Italy, Spain, Sweden, the United Kingdom, the EU as a whole and, to a lesser extent, Germany, GFCF and EFG

---

7   This sub-function of the "Economic Affairs" function is made up of the sub-items "General Economic and Commercial Affairs" and "General Labour Affairs". The first sub-item includes, among other functions, the formulation and implementation of general economic and commercial policies, as well as the management and support of institutions that deal with patents, trademarks, and copyrights. The second includes general labour policies and policies aimed at increasing employability and reducing the unemployment rate.

8   In order to ensure series comparability between GFCF and EFG we have chosen not to use the deflator of the GFCF.

9   The choice of the 2001–2019 time interval for the analysis carried out derives from the lack of data on public expenditure on research and development from 1995 to 2000.

follow rather similar dynamics. The only exceptions are France and, partially, Poland, where instead we observe at least a partial divergence between the two series. This result seems to indicate the existence of a shift between policies relating to gross fixed investment and other expenditure components included in the EFG.[10] In particular, while the governments of the countries most affected by the measures implemented to contain public expenditure have contracted both the GFCF and the other components of the EFG following the imposition of austerity policies in response to the global financial crisis, those not affected by these measures did not reduce either of them (or even increased them, as in the case of Sweden).

It should be noted that Sweden is the country with the highest ratio of EFG to GDP and also to population, followed by France. Moreover, both countries show an increasing trend. The two countries also perform well in terms of GFCF. On the other hand, Poland, which is at the top of the ranking when we consider the ratio of GFCF to GDP, probably due to the EU funding for investment policies, does not show the same performance in terms of EFG. It is worth observing that Italy has a declining trend in the ratio of EFG to GDP reaching the last position at the end of the period.

With regards to the temporal dynamics of the variables relating to the EFG, it should first be noted that the EU value of the ratio between EFG and GDP first gradually increased, reaching a peak of 11.1% in 2009, and then gradually decreasing until 2018 (9.4%) and growing slightly in 2019. It should also be noted that, while the EFG per capita remains roughly constant during the analysis period, the ratio with the RPCE steadily decreases starting from 2006, reaching a minimum of 30.1% in 2018 and only partially recovering in 2019.

The EFG follows profoundly different dynamics in the representative countries of the geo-economic groups identified above, which mainly depend on the austerity constraints introduced by the EU which have led, in some of them, to a substantial decrease in public expenditure on GFCF, traditionally considered more compressible with respect to current expenditure, and the other components of the EFG that, as explained above, are strongly correlated:

- Italy and Spain: in these countries, which are part of the group of the "Mediterranean" countries most affected by the measures to contain public spending, there is a substantial contraction in both the EFG and GDP ratio, which passes respectively from 10.4% and 13% in 2009 to 7.5% and 8.2% in 2017, and of the EFG per capita, which decreases from about 3,000 to just over 2,000 euros in 2017 and then begins to increase again only slightly. Furthermore, it can be noted that the relationship between EFG and RPCE is strongly reduced in both countries, respectively from 28.7% and 41.5% in 2009

---

10   The correlation between FLCF and the sum of the other components of the SGF is positive for Italy (0.77), Spain (0.66), Sweden (0.69), the United Kingdom (0.65), Germany (0.12), and the EU 28 as a whole (0.52). This correlation is instead strongly negative for France (-0.7) and partially for Poland (-0.31).

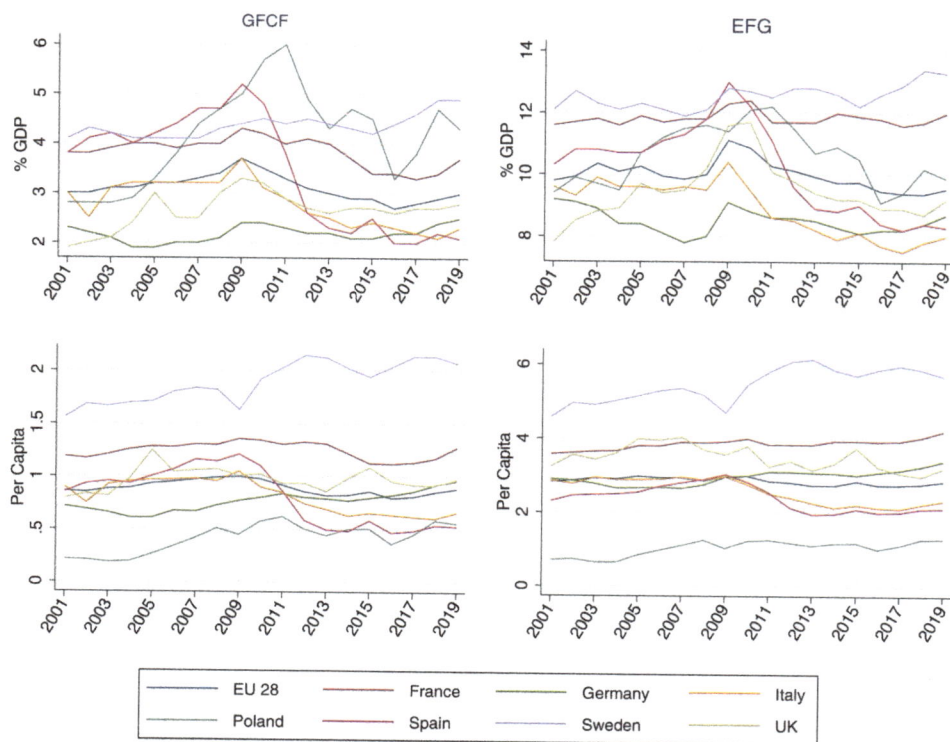

Fig. 10.1 GFCF (left) and EFG (right) as a percentage of GDP (top) and per capita (bottom) in thousands of euros, 2001–2019. *Source*: elaboration by the authors from Eurostat COFOG data.

to 20.4% and 27% in 2017, suggesting a recalibration of public expenditure at the expense of investment spending, which is traditionally considered more easily compressible and whose effects are observed with more delay by the voters (Cerniglia and Saraceno 2021).

- France and Germany: France is characterised by similar dynamics to those of the Mediterranean countries in terms of GFCF on GDP and as a percentage of the PCR (but not of GFCF per capita), although much less pronounced, but the same cannot be said of EFG, which remains almost constant (if not slightly increasing) during the analysis period, and in any case always above the EU value. Nevertheless, it is possible to note a reduction in the ratio between EFG and RPCE, which goes from a maximum of 31% in 2010 to 27.5% in 2017. Germany, similarly to Italy, is characterised by an EFG decidedly below the EU value both in terms of GDP and RPCE in all the years analysed. First of all, it should be noted that the series for the two countries follow substantially similar trends up to 2009, with Germany characterised

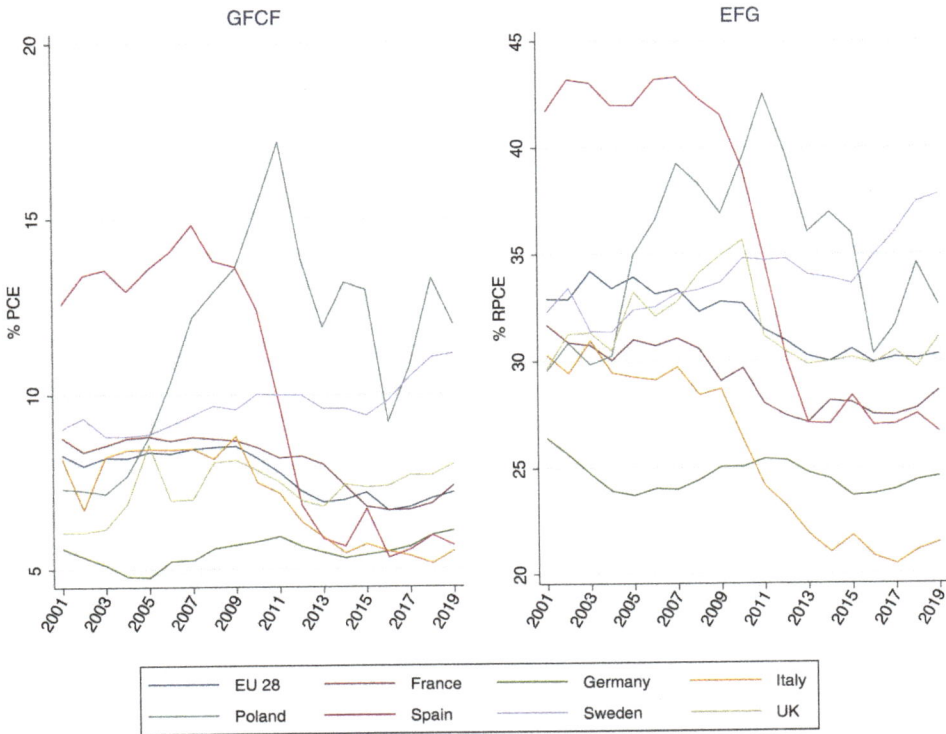

Fig. 10.2 GFCF (left) and EFG (right) as a percentage of public sector PCE and RPCE, 2001–2019. *Source*: elaboration by the authors from Eurostat COFOG data.

by an EFG that is lower than that of Italy both in terms of GDP and in relation to the RPCE. However, while in Italy the EFG has registered a very evident decline since 2010, the two ratios remain more or less constant in Germany. The problem of the low ratio of public investment to GDP in recent decades in Germany is analysed in Bardt et al. (2019). The authors identify as the main cause of these dynamics the erroneous forecasts of a decrease in the German working-age population and the consequent decrease in potential GDP growth, which then led to the fiscal consolidation measures introduced in 2009, in particular the "almost" breakeven budget ("Schuldenbremse") introduced in the German constitution that limits the structural deficit of the public sector to 0.35% of GDP each year. Furthermore, some social reforms have shifted the tax burden of unemployment policies to municipalities, which in Germany also have the task of maintaining a whole series of infrastructures, such as roads and local public transport and schools. This further reduced the public investment rate of local authorities. As regards the EFG per capita, it is interesting to note once again how the historical series of Italy and Germany follow almost the same trends up to 2009, the year in which they start to diverge considerably. In particular, there is a slight increase in the EFG per capita in Germany, which reaches 3,400 euros in 2019.

- Poland: representative of the "New Entrants" countries in the EU in 2004, is characterised by an increase in all three relationships, also following the large amount of funds relating to the Cohesion Policy received after joining the EU. In particular, the ratios between EFG and GDP and between EFG and PCE reach their maximum, respectively 12.2% and 42.5%, in 2011, then decrease but remain stably above the EU value in 2019 (respectively 9.9% and 32.6%). Furthermore, the EFG per capita experiences a slow but almost constant growth trend. It is interesting to observe how, once the other components of the EFG are introduced into the analysis, the difference between per capita expenditure in Poland and in the Mediterranean countries increases (although it has been decreasing over the years), suggesting a lower priority of these sectors in the public expenditure policies of this country. The high ratio of EFG to GDP, accompanied by a low EFG per capita suggests, on the one hand, that Poland started in 2001 with a GDP per capita significantly lower than the EU value and, on the other hand, that the process of adjusting infrastructure of the country to European standards has been gradual but constant also in terms of per capita expenditure.

- Sweden: as in the other northern European countries not affected by the public debt containment measures introduced by austerity policies and traditionally characterised by efficient management of public resources, no decline is observed in the three ratios defined above, but rather an increase of the same during the analysis period. In particular, the ratios between EFG and GDP and between EFG and PCE rise respectively from 12.1% and 32.3% in 2001 to 13.3% and 37.8% in 2019, while the GFCF per capita, much higher than the EU as a whole for the whole period of analysis, increased from about 4,600 to 5,700 euros between 2001 and 2019.

- The United Kingdom: the ratio between EFG and GDP is below that of the EU for all the years analysed except those between 2008 and 2011. A similar trend can be observed for the relationship between EFG and PCE, although the latter converges at the EU value starting from 2011. Finally, the EFG per capita is always greater than the total EU value, although it approaches the latter towards the end of the period considered.

Figure 10.3 shows, for the selected countries and for the EU as a whole, the sum of public expenditure in relation to GDP for the different items that make up the EFG and the RPCE as an average for the years 2001–2007, 2008–2013, and 2014–2019. In particular, the EFG is divided into *GFCF, Contributions to investments, Total Expenditure on Research and Development (GFLF and PCE), and PCE in the sectors of General Economic,*

Commercial, and Labour, Education, and Environmental Protection.[11] An analysis of this graph allows us not only to analyse the composition of public expenditure (EFG or RPCE), but also to understand the weight of each component within EFG in the selected countries. Predictably, it can be seen that the RPCE represents the generally most relevant spending category in all countries, with a value in the EU in the three periods of respectively 30%, 32.7%, and 31.7% of GDP. It can be noted that the RPCE is higher than that of the EU overall in all three periods in France, Sweden, Germany, and Italy. The total EFG fluctuates between 9% and 10% in the EU in the three periods considered, and is, as already observed in Figure 10.1, higher than the EU figure for Sweden, France, and Poland.

Let us now move on to analyse the EFG components individually. First of all, it should be noted that, in addition to the GFCF, the PCE in Education represents (as widely expected) a very significant component of the EFG, equal to 4.73%, 4.75%, and 4.48% of EU GDP in the three periods analysed. It can also be observed that this ratio is lower in Spain, Germany, and Italy, which is the only country among the three in which the gap with the EU has widened over time. Regarding the total expenditure on Research and Development[12] and the PCE on Environmental Protection, these two items represent a smaller percentage of the EFG in the countries analysed. In particular, EU expenditure on R&D is equal to 0.77% of GDP in the 2001–2007 period, and then grows to about 1% in the following two periods. It should be noted that the weight of this component is decidedly lower in the United Kingdom (although growing), Poland, Germany (which nevertheless reaches the EU value in the 2014–2019 period) and Italy, which, once again, sees the gap widening with the other countries over time. Similarly, the PCE in Environmental Protection grows from 0.46% to 0.5% between the first and last period overall in the EU, and is higher in Spain, Italy, France, and the United Kingdom. A similar argument applies *to Public Contributions to Investments* and to *PCE in General Economic, Commercial and Labour Affairs*, which represent residual categories in which the EU as a whole has spent between 0.5% and 0.7% of GDP respectively in the three periods analysed. It is interesting to note that, while the first item tends to decrease over time at the EU level and in most of the selected countries, an opposite trend is seen in France, where it increases from 0.55% to 0.8% of GDP between the first and the last period. Finally, as regards the PCE in *General Economic, Commercial and Labour Affairs*, the latter represents a substantial and growing component of the EFG

---

11   Note that R&D expenditure, presented separately, has been subtracted from the GFCF and PCE in key areas.

12   Note that the data for R&D expenditure present in the COFOG dataset are not perfectly superimposable on those of the two datasets traditionally used for the analysis of this expenditure, namely GERD and GBARD, as explained in OECD (2015). While COFOG and GERD expenditure data are based on the national accounts principle, GBARD data are recorded on a budgetary basis. In addition, GERD data are reported along the "R&D performance sectors" and separately for the government sector and higher education. Finally, the GBARD data for some countries do not include local government expenditure. In any case, the correlation between COFOG and GERD/GBARD data is very high, 0.84 and 0.79 respectively. It is also important to underline that R&D spending does not constitute a separate sector in COFOG but is present as a sub-item in every function of the state.

especially for Sweden and France, where it reaches 1.45% of GDP between 2014 and 2019.

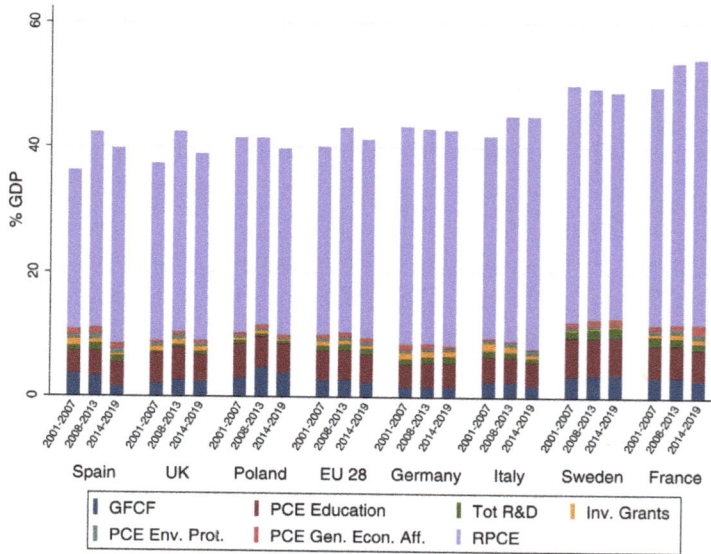

Fig. 10.3 Components of the EFG and RPCE, averages over the years 2001–2007, 2008–2013, and 2014–2019.
Source: elaborations by the authors from Eurostat COFOG data.

Finally, Figures 10.4 and 10.5 respectively show for all countries of EU 28 a scatterplot of the GFCF over GDP ratio on the PCE over GDP ratio (the two components of EFG) after the financial crisis (2010–2019) and a scatterplot of the change in the EFG over GDP ratio on the RPCE over GDP ratio from 2001–2009 to 2010–2019. The horizontal and vertical red lines in the figures represent the value of these two variables for EU 28 as a whole. From Figure 10.4 it can be observed that all Mediterranean countries (but Greece) plus Germany, Ireland and the UK are below the EU value in both components of the EFG, while all Nordic countries plus France, Netherlands, Luxembourg, and a few new entrants are above. It is also interesting to observe that most new entrants and Greece are above the European value in GFCF but not in PCE, probably due to the use of cohesion funds that focus especially on public investment.

When looking at Figure 10.5 it becomes apparent that all Mediterranean countries after the financial crisis have decreased the share of EFG over GDP while increasing the share of the other components of current expenditure. This is a concern to the extent that they seem to sacrifice expenditure for future generations probably due to the short-run attitude of their governments. Conversely, all Nordic countries and most European continental countries have increased (or maintained at an even level) the EFG over GDP ratio. Finally, many new entrants have decreased the EFG while increasing RPCE shares (although less than the EU average), probably also due to the convergence of their stock of physical capital to European standards.

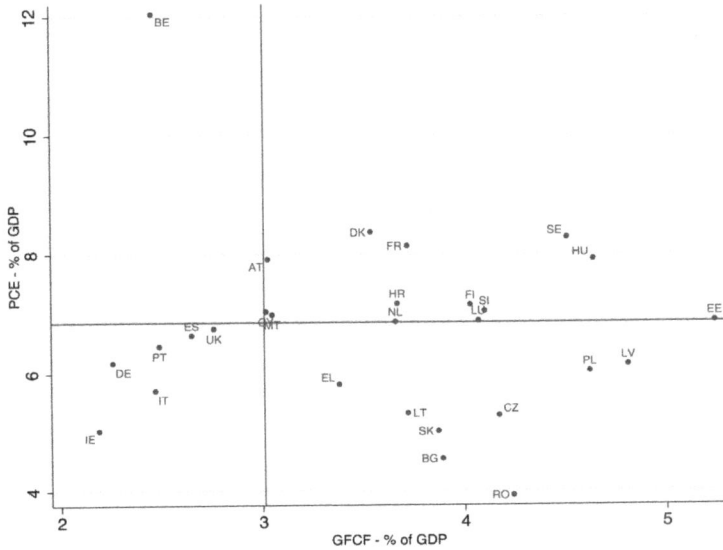

Fig. 10.4 PCE over GDP ratio and GFCF over GDP ratio for EU countries averages over the years 2010–2019.
Source: elaborations by the authors from Eurostat COFOG data.

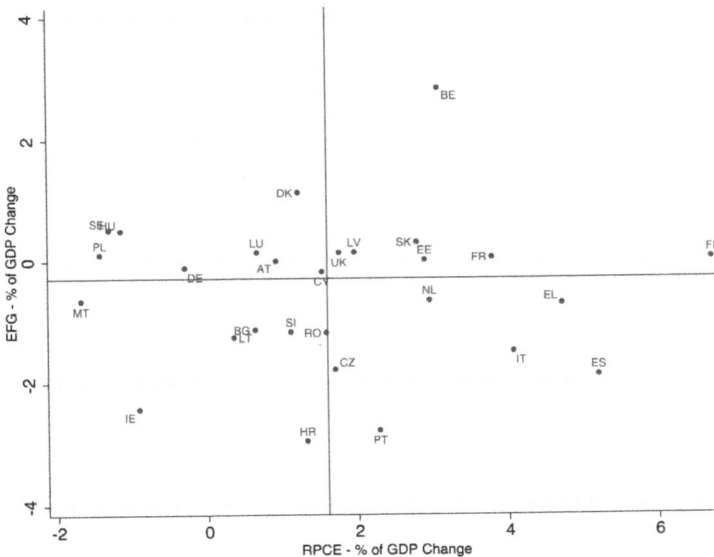

Fig. 10.5 Change in EFG over GDP and change in RPCE over GDP between 2001–2009 and 2010–2019.
Source: elaborations by the authors from Eurostat COFOG data.

10.3. Comparative and Absolute Advantage: International Comparisons

10.3.1 Definition of Variables

In the previous paragraph we defined a new aggregate, the EFG, which we believe more accurately captures the vast range of national public expenditure policies aimed at economic and social development and progress, and at the environmental protection of a country. We now focus on the definition of some "advantage" indicators that we believe can be of support to policymakers in evaluating and, if necessary, adjusting these expenditure policies. In order to compare the EFG of the various European countries we introduce, in particular, three indices, called (i) Comparative Advantage (hereinafter CA), (ii) Absolute Advantage (hereinafter AA), and (ii) Absolute Advantage Per Capita (hereinafter AA per capita). While indices (ii) and (iii) allow us to verify whether each of the EU countries in a given year has experienced a ratio between EFG and, respectively, GDP and population that is lower or higher than the EU as a whole, (i) is a measure of the country's specialisation in this expenditure component with respect to the other components.

In particular, the CA, similar to the index developed by Balassa (1965; 1989), which measures the export specialisation of countries, is defined as the ratio between (i) the EFG divided by the total expenditure of the public sector in the generic country i in the considered year t and (ii) the EU EFG as a whole divided by total public sector expenditure in the EU in considered year t. Note how this index, which allows us to analyse the expenditure priorities of EU countries in terms of its composition, is greater (less) than 1, and therefore takes the form of a comparative advantage (disadvantage) for a country if the percentage of EFG expenditure compared to the total in the year considered is greater (less) than that of the EU as a whole:

We define AA as the difference between the EFG on GDP in generic country i in considered year t minus the EFG on overall EU GDP in the same year. Obviously, if this difference is greater (less) than zero, country i will have an absolute advantage (disadvantage) in the year considered:

Finally, the AA per capita is defined in a similar way as the difference between the EFG on the population residing in generic country i in year t minus the EFG on the total EU population (in thousands of euros) in the same year. Again, a positive (negative) value implies that generic country i has a higher (lower) EFG than the EU as a whole in the year. Formally:

10.3.2 Indicators of Advantage in the EU: Evolution

First of all, note that there is a decidedly positive correlation between AA and CA and, although lower, between AA and AA per capita (0.57 and 0.29 respectively). The correlation between AA per capita and CA is instead extremely close to zero (0.002), suggesting that the two variables are not correlated when we consider the whole sample. The latter result seems to indicate that the specialisation of countries in the EFG does not necessarily coincide with a high EFG per capita.

Figures 10.6, 10.7, and 10.8 show the evolution, respectively, of the CA, AA, and AA per capita in all EU28 countries in the 2001 to 2019 period. It is useful to divide the countries again into the groups already identified above:

- "Mediterranean" countries: Italy is characterised by CA below 1 and negative AA and AA per capita in all the years analysed. It should be noted that these disadvantages tend to worsen significantly during the period analysed, with a particularly evident collapse starting from 2010 and, subsequently, substantial stability. A similar dynamic can be observed for Greece, although the latter starts in 2001 in line with the EU in terms of CA and AA and, after experiencing a sharp decline in spending following the austerity measures, returns to pre-crisis levels in 2018. It should also be noted that Greece is characterised by a constant negative AA per capita and affected by a marked decrease starting from 2009. Spain and Portugal instead have a very positive CA and AA (although decreasing for Portugal) until 2009, the year from which the aforementioned cost containment measures come into force. However, it should be noted that Portugal, and for almost all the years of analysis, Spain, are affected by an EFG per capita that is lower than that of the EU as a whole. Ireland, one of the countries most exposed to the European sovereign debt crisis and subjected to severe austerity measures, follows partially comparable dynamics. In particular, a decidedly increasing absolute disadvantage can be observed starting from 2009, accompanied by a substantial decrease in the CA between 2008 and 2010. The latter returns in any case greater than 1 in 2015 (and increasing), while the AA per capita is always positive between 2001 and 2019.

- "Nordic" countries: it can be noted that Denmark, Finland, and Sweden have a generally positive and increasing AA and AA per capita in the analysis period. Note, however, that while Sweden is characterised by a consistently positive and strongly increasing CA, Denmark experiences a slight comparative disadvantage until 2011 and then follows the same dynamics as Sweden. Finally, in Finland, the CA is only initially positive, but then converges to 1 and becomes even slightly lower starting from 2015. Belgium, France, and Austria, even if not strictly belonging to this geographical aggregation, are affected by similar dynamics. Belgium, in particular, is characterised by a very strong increase in all three variables analysed starting from 2006, while France and Austria have a CA around unity for the entire analysis period, accompanied by positive and growing AA and AA per capita. Finally, the Netherlands, although experiencing substantial advantages in relation to EFG, is affected by a slight but steady decrease in CA and AA over the years.

- "New Entrants": the countries that entered the EU after 2004, i.e. the Baltic republics (Estonia, Latvia, and Lithuania), the Czech Republic, Poland, Romania, Slovenia, Slovakia, Bulgaria, and Croatia, are characterised in most cases by strong comparative and absolute advantages. However, they are generally accompanied by negative AA per capita in all the years analysed. It is interesting to note that Romania, the Czech Republic, and Lithuania have comparative advantages even in the face of absolute negative AAs, suggesting that countries pay particular attention to the EFG, probably also thanks to cohesion policies.

- Germany and the UK: both countries have negative AA (apart from the UK between 2008 and 2010) throughout the analysis period. However, the United Kingdom has a slightly positive AA per capita in this time interval, while the latter is negative for Germany until 2008. Furthermore, Germany is characterised by a significant comparative disadvantage, although the latter tends to decrease over time.

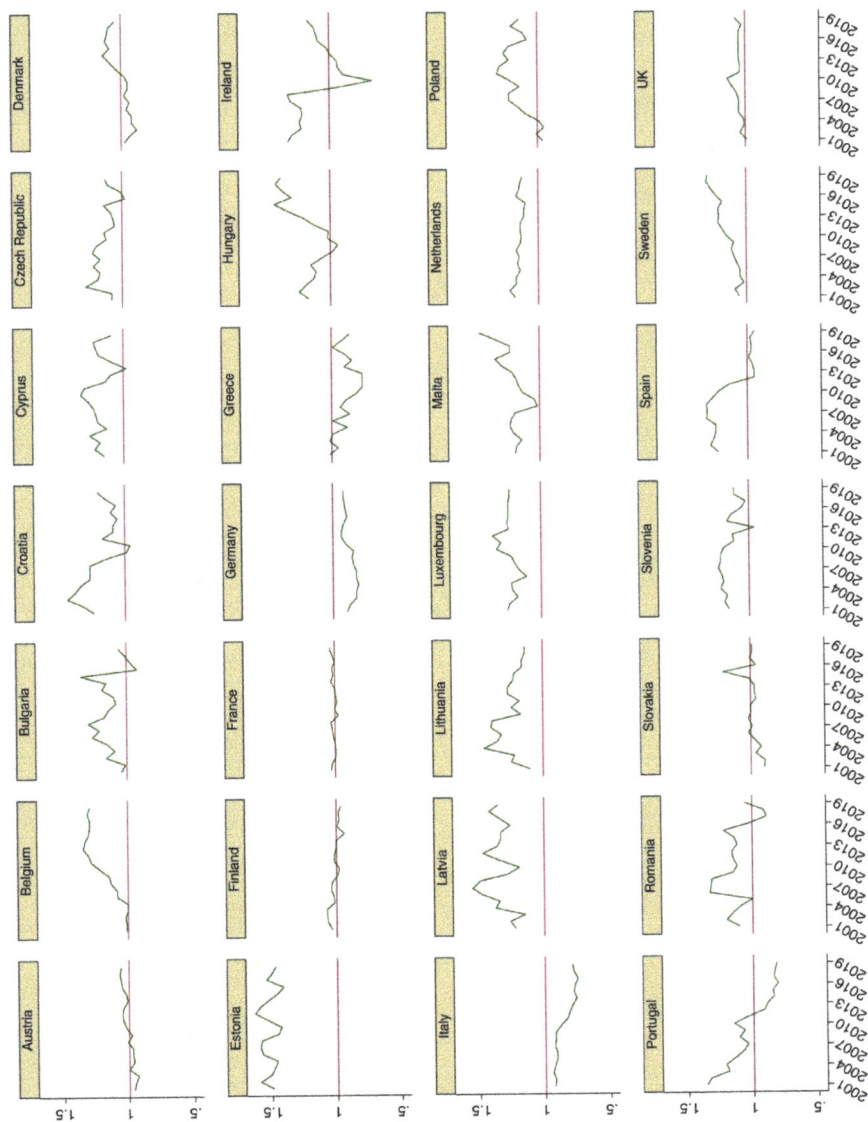

Fig. 10.6: CA in EU28 countries in the EFG, 2001–2019.
Source: elaborations by the authors from Eurostat COFOG data.

Greening Europe

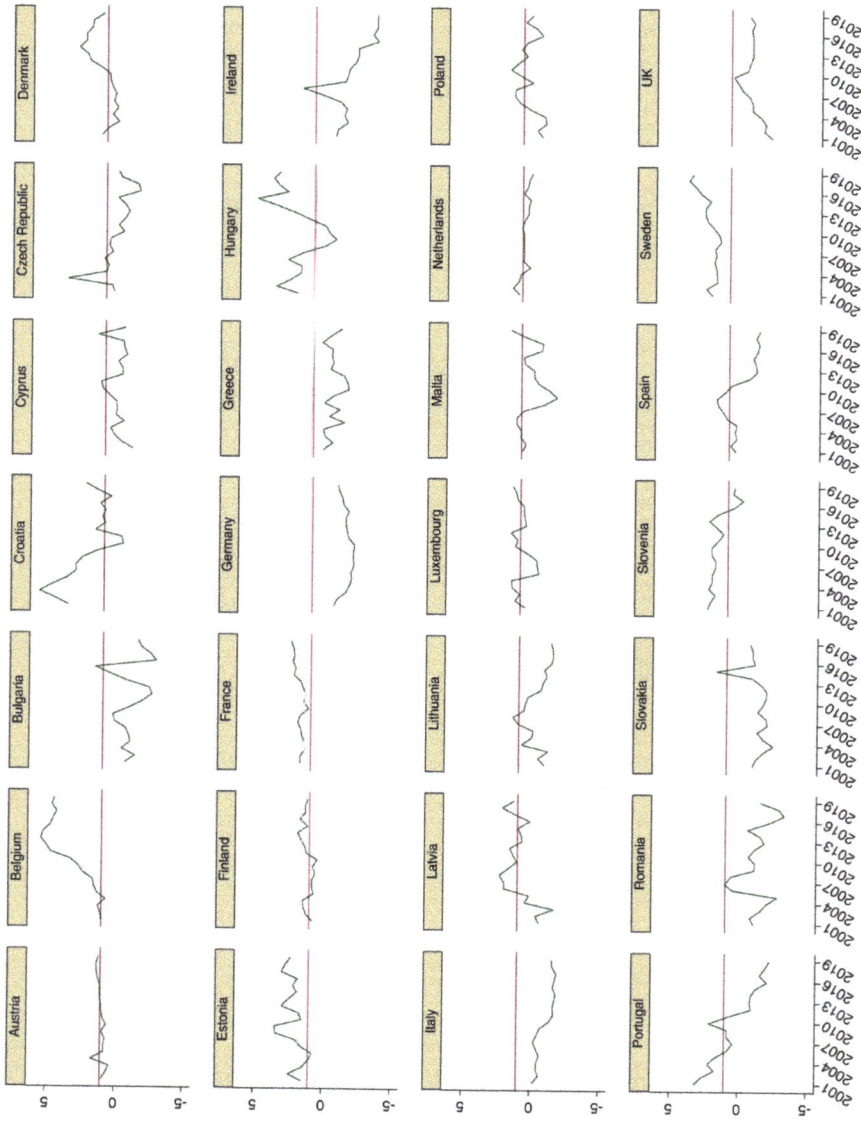

Fig. 10.7: AA in EU28 countries in the EFG, 2001–2019.
Source: elaborations by the authors from Eurostat COFOG data.

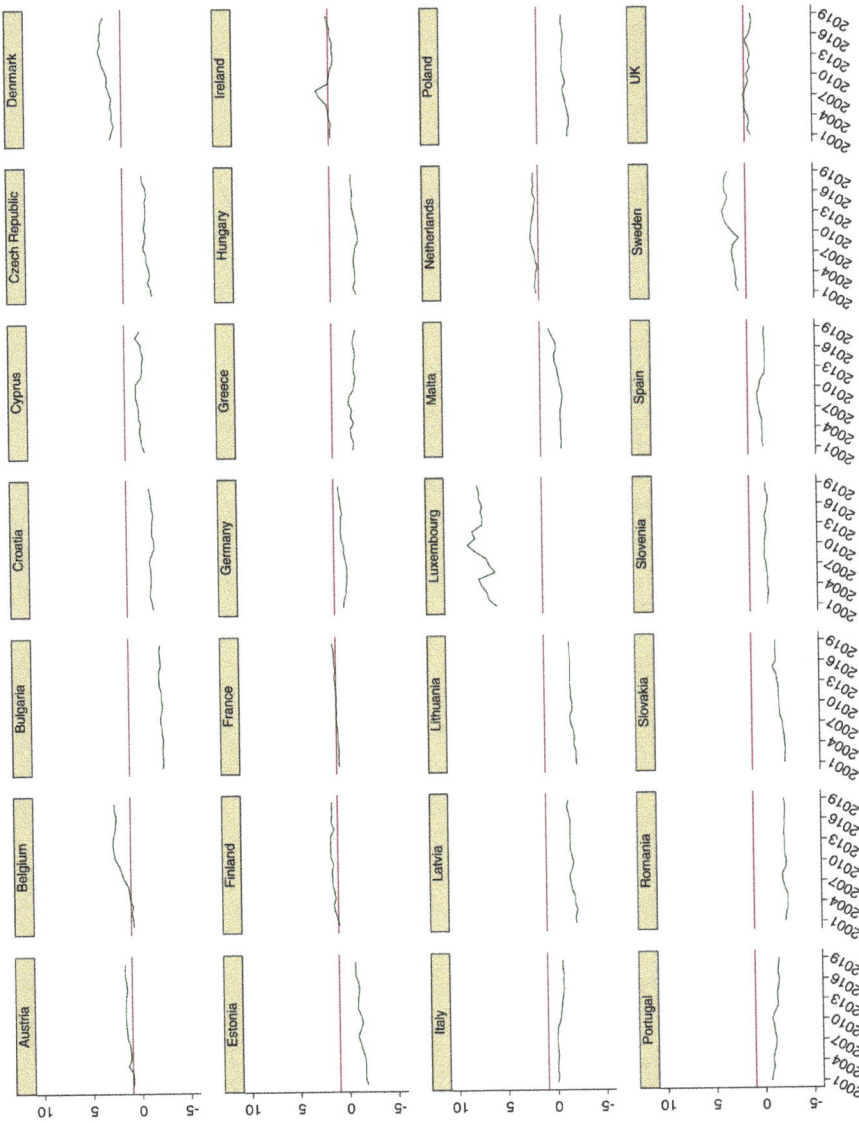

Fig. 10.8: AA per capita in EU28 countries in the EFG, 2001–2019.
Source: elaborations by the authors from Eurostat COFOG data.

Finally, Table 10.1 shows the CA, AA, and AA per capita of the countries selected in the 2001–2019 period (for the sake of brevity) in relation to the aggregates that make up the EFG , or GFCF , *Current Expenditure on General Economic, Commercial, and Labour Affairs, Education, Environmental Protection, Total Expenditure on Research and Development, and Public Contributions to Investment*. A synthetic index is also presented for the *Primary Current Expenditure* in all the key sectors that make up the EFG (thus excluding the *Public Contributions to Investment*).

We believe that the use of these metrics, taken both individually and as a whole, can provide a valid guide to public decision-makers at the national level in order to verify the past performance of national public policies, but also to modify them, if deemed appropriate and possible, given the domestic and European political constraints on expenditure in the future. The CA, in particular, provides an extremely useful indicator even in the presence of constraints on public expenditure, and provides an incentive to rebalance the latter in favour of expenditure items aimed more at a country's economic and social development.

10.4 Conclusions and Policy Considerations

In this chapter we have proposed a new aggregate for comparing the "quality" of public expenditure across countries. While there is a large literature emphasising the importance of public investment with respect to public current expenditure, with the first considered to be more conducive to economic growth than the latter, we believe that public investment alone does not capture the contribution of the public sector to economic and social development and to the protection of the environment. We have therefore considered a larger aggregate which we have defined as Expenditure for Future Generations (EFG) and which includes, in addition to the public sector GFCF, public contributions to investment by private companies as well as primary current expenditure in some key sectors of public intervention, namely (i) Research and Development, (ii) Education, (iii) Environmental Protection, and (iv) General Economic, Commercial and Labour Affairs. The analysis of this aggregate is more in line with the objectives and policies introduced at the European level in the Next Generation EU, which include among its priorities sustainable development and social cohesion. We have shown that, particularly after the financial crisis, countries with high levels of debt have also strongly reduced this component of overall public expenditure when they have not cut the overall share of public expenditure over GDP.

Overall, we are convinced that governments should focus on indicators of public expenditure that are consistent with the long-term objectives of sustainable development. Since this does not seem to have been the case in many countries (Italy is a typical example), such an approach could be taken at the European level. While this may require an extended "golden rule", the difficulty faced so far in following this path suggests that it is unlikely that it will be adopted in the future. Alternative policies might include a larger flexibility in the application of the European fiscal rules for these types of expenditures and/or even just a monitoring of the evolution of EFG

Table 10.1 Absolute advantage, absolute advantage per capita (in thousands of euros) and comparative advantage for the selected EU28 countries in the components of the EFG, averages over the years 2001–2019.

Country	Index	GFCF (R&D included)	PCE Key sectors	PCE General Economic, Commercial, and Labor Affairs	PCE Environmental Protection	PCE Education	Total expenditure in R&D	Public Contributions to Investment
France	CA	1.05	0.98	1.21	1.1	0.94	1.18	1.01
	AA	0.73	0.88	0.27	0.14	0.47	0.35	0.11
	AA PC	0.33	0.33	0.1	0.05	0.18	0.13	0.04
Germany	CA	0.72	0.87	1.03	0.94	0.84	1.04	1.62
	AA	-0.93	-0.91	0	-0.04	-0.87	0.01	0.35
	AA PC	-0.14	-0.36	0	-0.02	-0.34	0	0.14
Italy	CA	0.86	0.79	0.26	1.14	0.83	0.88	1.55
	AA	-0.32	-1.03	-0.47	0.09	-0.65	-0.08	0.37
	AA PC	0.04	-0.36	-0.16	0.03	-0.23	-0.03	0.13
Poland	CA	1.44	1.09	0.86	0.59	1.17	0.59	0.71
	AA	1.03	0.05	-0.13	-0.22	0.4	-0.41	-0.21
	AA PC	-0.64	0.01	-0.02	-0.03	0.05	-0.05	-0.03
Spain	CA	1.24	1.07	1.62	1.63	0.93	1.16	1.39
	AA	0.35	-0.24	0.29	0.23	-0.76	0.04	0.15
	AA PC	-0.01	-0.07	0.08	0.07	-0.22	0.01	0.04
Sweden	CA	1.29	1.17	1.22	0.7	1.21	1.41	0.29
	AA	1.25	1.57	0.21	-0.12	1.48	0.48	-0.42
	AA PC	0.7	0.8	0.11	-0.06	0.75	0.24	-0.21
The UK	CA	0.95	1.12	0.71	1.36	1.15	0.46	1.46
	AA	-0.46	0.05	-0.23	0.11	0.17	-0.53	-0.21
	AA PC	-0.07	0.02	-0.1	0.05	0.08	-0.24	0.09

Source: elaborations by the authors from Eurostat COFOG data.

across countries and over time, since indicators on their own have the merit of raising the attention towards the variables that they capture.

We are aware that the indicator we propose is very tentative and can certainly be improved, but we think that we should go beyond the simple distinction between GFCF and current government expenditure consistently with a shift in the focus from GDP to broader concepts of sustainable development. Future studies may try to test whether EFG and/or their sub-components positively impact GDP and/or multidimensional measures of sustainable development.

References

Balassa, B. (1965) "Trade Liberalization and 'Revealed' Comparative Advantage", *The Manchester School of Economic and Social Studies* 33: 92–123.

Balassa, B. (1989) "'Revealed' Comparative Advantage Revisited", in B. Balassa (ed.), *Comparative Advantage, Trade Policy and Economic Development*, New York: New York University Press, pp. 63–79.

Cerniglia, F. and F. Saraceno (2020) *A European Public Investment Outlook*, Cambridge: Open Book Publishers, https://doi.org/10.11647/OBP.0222.

Agenzia per la Coesione Territoriale, Nucleo di Verifica e Controllo, Area 3 Monitoraggio dell'attuazione della politica di coesione e Sistema Conti Pubblici Territoriali (2020) *Analisi degli Investimenti Pubblici. Dati, Indagine Diretta ai Responsabili Unici del Procedimento e Casi di Studio.* Roma: CPT Temi, https://www.agenziacoesione.gov.it/wp-content/uploads/2021/03/CPT_InvestimentiPubblici-1.pdf.

Eurostat (2019) *Manual on Sources and Methods for the Compilation of COFOG Statistics*. Luxembourg: Publications Office of the European Union, https://ec.europa.eu/eurostat/documents/3859598/10142242/KS-GQ-19-010-EN-N.pdf/ed64a194-81db-112b-074b-b7a9eb946c32?t=1569418084000.

European Commission (2022) *Cohesion in Europe towards 2050—Eighth Report on Economic, Social and Territorial Cohesion*. Luxembourg: Publications Office of the European Union, https://ec.europa.eu/regional_policy/sources/docoffic/official/reports/cohesion8/8cr.pdf.

Lenzi, F. S. and A. Zoppé (2020) *Composition of Public Expenditures in the EU*. Brussels: European Parliamentary Research Service (EPRS), https://www.europarl.europa.eu/RegData/etudes/BRIE/2019/634371/IPOL_BRI(2019)634371_EN.pdf.

OECD (2015) *Frascati Manual 2015: Guidelines for Collecting and Reporting Data on Research and Experimental Development*. Paris: OECD Publishing, https://www.oecd-ilibrary.org/science-and-technology/frascati-manual-2015_9789264239012-en.

OECD (2010), *National Accounts at a Glance 2009*. Paris: OECD Publishing, https://doi.org/10.1787/9789264067981-en.

Streeck, W. and Mertens, D. (2011) "Fiscal Austerity and Public Investment: Is the Possible the Enemy of the Necessary?" *MPIfG Discussion Paper 11/12*, Max Planck Institute for the Study of Societies, https://papers.ssrn.com/sol3/papers.cfm?abstract_id=1894657.

United Nations et al. (2009) *System of National Accounts 2008*. New York: United Nations, https://unstats.un.org/unsd/nationalaccount/docs/SNA2008.pdf.

Vooren, M., Haelermans, C., Groot, W, Maassen van den Brink, H. (2019), "The Effectiveness of Active Labor Market Policies: A Meta-Analysis", *Journal of Economic Surveys* 33(1): 125–49, https://onlinelibrary.wiley.com/doi/epdf/10.1111/joes.12269.

11. Assessing the Quality of Green Finance Standards

Xi Liang and Hannah Gao

Green finance is a rapidly growing mechanism for facilitating investment in sustainable transition. This chapter reviews the generic process in labelling green finance products governed by different green finance standards. The key differences in green finance standards are assessed, including governance, scope, and definition of green. Although the EU has been widely considered as the global leader in green finance, the recent inclusion of nuclear and natural gas in the sustainable finance category has generated controversy. This chapter also identifies current green finance standards whose added value is not clear. In other words, it is uncertain whether green finance is purely a statistical exercise or could bring additional sustainable benefits for the community.

Climate change is one of the greatest challenge humans face in this century. Mobilising investment and finance to address climate change is key for unlocking actions on climate change across countries. The estimated investment required to achieve the climate mitigation goal set up by the Paris Agreement range from US\$1.6 trillion to US\$3.8 trillion annually between 2016 and 2050, while the tracked annual flow of climate finance was US\$579 billion on average, based on data in 2017 and 2018, as illustrated in Figure 11.1 (in the following text). Despite a significant growth in climate finance flow, the gap remains quite substantial. In response to the vast financing gap, the effectiveness of climate investment and finance must urgently be maximised.

Developing green finance, such as green bonds, green funds, or green loans, has given hope as a potential solution for bridging the funding gap for climate change. Since the first green bond was issued in 2007 by the European Investment Bank (EIB), the green finance market has been growing rapidly in both scale and market coverage. Green bonds remain the dominant asset in terms of the green finance market share. In 2021, green, social, sustainability, sustainability-linked and transition themed debt reached USD\$1 trillion with growth spearheaded by green bond issuance. This represents a twenty-fold increase from 2015, and accounts for 10% of global debt markets.

In spite of the rapid growth of the green bond market, there are concerns of "greenwashing". For example, Tariq Fancy, former chief investment officer of the

 https://doi.org/10.11647/OBP.0328.11

largest asset management firm Blackrock, which has US$ 8.7 trillion assets under management (AUM), has suggested that "Wall Street is greenwashing the economic system and, in the process, creating a deadly distraction.". In response to concerns, the US Securities and Exchange Commission (SEC) created a Climate and ESG Taskforce to "proactively identify ESG-related misconduct" in March 2021.

The EU has always led the development of green investment practices in the world. In May 2022, MEPs passed a text seeking to better regulate the green bond market, improve its supervision, reduce greenwashing, and add clarity when money goes to gas or nuclear energy. This chapter will review how green finance standards have been defined and applied, identify the current problems, and propose measures the EU could adopt in establishing a future-proof green finance standard system.

11.1 What Are Green Finance Standards?

The green finance standards system generally refers to a series of classification methods and measurement indexes that are established to identify, confirm and track green assets and green investment with the orientation of international, regional or national green development strategic goals. A variety of international and national green credits, green bonds, green stock indexes, green development funds, green insurance and other related financial products and services have been widely established, and various green finance standards systems with different connotations and extensions have been adopted. In general, a green finance standards system includes the following six elements:

1. Sectoral Taxonomy/Classification;
2. Identification and Standards;
3. Proceeds Requirements;
4. Incentives;
5. Verification and Labelling; and
6. Post Investment Monitoring

Currently, there are three major types of widely recognised green finance standards systems. The first type is a series of voluntary principles issued by financial institutions or organisations, including the Green Bond Principles (GBP), the Equator Principles (EPs) and the Climate Bonds Standard (CBS), the World Bank's Green Bond Process Implementation Guidelines and the Asian Development Bank's (ADB) Green Bond Framework. The European Commission is issuing its Green Bond Standard and ISO 14100 is developing its Guidance on Environmental Criteria to Support Green Finance. The second type is assessment systems introduced by financial services institutions, mainly developed by assessment and rating agencies, such as Moody's Green Bond Assessment System and Standard & Poor's Green Evaluation System. The third type is systems issued by the relevant regional or national departments, including the European UnionGreen Bond Standard that the EU is pushing for, and China's *Green Credit Guidelines, Green Bonds Issue Guidelines, Green Bonds Supporting Project Directory* (2015 edition), and *Green Industry Guidance Catalogue* (2019 edition).

The **industry category** assessment of green finance standards is the first step in identifying green financial assets and industry categories, including primary and secondary catalogues. The green finance standard catalogue has a high degree of convergence, covering areas such as renewables, energy efficiency, pollution prevention and control, water management, clean and low-carbon transportation, and green and low-carbon buildings. There are two significant differences in the industry classification of green finance—China's green finance standards generally do not include climate change adaptation. In contrast, international green finance standards include climate mitigation and adaptation-related fields. The question of whether coal, nuclear power and rail transit should be included in the green finance category is still controversial. International green standards generally explicitly exclude fossil fuels except for the use of CCUS technology. The Green Credit Guidelines issued by the China Banking Regulatory Commission (now the CBIRC) in 2012 also did not cover the coal sector. However, the Green Industry Guidance Catalogue released by NDRC in 2019 still includes clean coal use. Nonetheless, the categories related to coal use are removed in the 2021 Green Bond Guideline released jointly by NDRC and PBOC.

Compared to the simple filtering criteria of the fields in the international standards, some of China's green finance standards are more targeted for technology application. For instance, the Green Industry Guidance Catalogue of the NDRC sets the scale or the technical threshold for the industry green finance project. These are, for example, minimum capacity for coal-fired thermal power units; the industry standard for energy-saving technological transformation projects; and clear, quantified indicators of the photoelectric conversion efficiency and the attenuation rate of polysilicon components (monocrystalline silicon components, high concentrated photovoltaic modules, membrane cells components) of photovoltaic power generation projects. Establishing industry thresholds complicates the certification process but avoids the outdated capacities of industries being identified as green assets.

There are different ways to **identify green assets**, including sector identification, sector plus threshold identification, negative list/exclusion identification and a scoring system. The scoring system can be further extended into two types, a qualitative evaluation system (according to expert opinions) and a quantitative evaluation system (according to quantitative data). The GBP, CBS and EU's forthcoming classification schemes are identified by sector. For example, under these three principles, all wind power assets are simply classified as green assets. The operation cost of sector identification is low, but it is difficult to exclude the critical influencing factors beyond the green attribute, such as social influence and backward production capacity. The NDRC's Green Industry Guidance Catalogue adopts thresholds of technology and scale, which are conducive to eliminating outdated production capacity and projects in which governments do not encourage investment. Moody's and Standard & Poor's, the world's leading credit rating agencies, use a scoring system that includes disclosure and other factors, in addition to green attributes.

Capital requirements include requirements for the use and management of green capital raised, referred to as capital requirements, including the field or project invested in, the time of investment, reinvestment requirements, whether it can be used to repay corporate debt, and other factors. CBS requires companies to invest in green assets with raised capital within two years. Currently, most green finance standards require that all, or a certain percentage, of green funds, raised be invested in approved green assets. For corporate green bonds issued under the NDRC's Green Industry Guidance Catalogue, raised capital can be used to repay the existing liabilities of the enterprise. If the enterprise involves both green and non-green assets, it is difficult to supervise the use of funds. Reinvestment of the capital obtained by enterprises through green finance is often not restricted by green finance standards.

The essential factor that distinguishes green finance from traditional finance is **incentive policy**, which directly affects the rate of return of green financial products and non-green financial products. Incentive policies include pre-issuance incentives, in-issuance incentives and post-issuance incentives, including public sector interest discounts and tax relief policies, low-interest loans from policy-based financial institutions, and grants from multilateral institutions. The implementation of incentive policies is conducive to encouraging enterprises to increase investment in green assets. However, due to the large scale of assets involved in green finance, the cost of screening and auditing needs to be urgently reduced, and the difficulty of fiscal subsidies (such as interest discounts on green bonds) is significant. At present, the support policies of governments for green finance have not had a substantial impact on the income of green financial products worldwide. However, Singapore has adopted a policy of subsidising the assessment fees for green bond issues.

The **certification** of green financial products mainly refers to the evaluation and verification of the issuer's internal processes, including screening of projects and assets, and tracking of projects, assets, internal processes, and expenditure of capital raised. The verification bodies adopt procedures to assess the readiness of the issuer and the compliance of the proposed bonds with the standards and employ general procedures (or lists) to assess the compliance of the proposed bonds with the pre-issuance requirements of the climate bond standard. Specifically, this includes the following steps: confirmation of green asset investment, certification application, second opinion or third-party review (if any), green asset labelling, and green asset issuance, as shown in Figure 11.1.

Confirmation of green asset investment refers to the preliminary review of whether the green financing application submitted (green credit, bonds, etc.) meets the definition and requirements of "green" classification for financial institutions. For the

Confirmation of green asset investment	Request certification	External audit (if any)	Green asset labeling	Issue green asset
Confirmation of whether the applied assets meet the basic green requirements of the certification body	sumbit application materials to certification authority	- Second Party Opinion - Third Party Assessment	The certification body decides whether to label and allow the applicant to publicise after verification	

Fig. 11.1 The flow chart of the certification process of green financial products.

identified projects, the applicant must formally submit the certification application to the financial institution, including the project application and issuance qualification, capital use, monitoring and reporting methods. During this period, the financial institution may require the applicant to submit a second opinion or a third-party review. The largest second-party opinion service on green bonds is an assessment conducted by the Centre for International Climate and Environmental Research at the University of Oslo in Norway (CICERO), which has innovatively further subdivided approved green bonds into dark, medium and light green categories.

The second opinion is usually a general summary of a project carried out in the form of consultation; therefore, it is likely to lack credibility. Third-party review is a comprehensive assessment of the industry standard, capital use, capital management and monitoring and reporting of the product carried out by an independent institution hired by the issuer, according to the recognised green financial standards system. Whether it is a second opinion or a third-party verification, the existing market model is evaluated by the organisation hired by the issuer, and consequently, there will be potential conflicts of interest that are difficult to resolve.

The financial institution decides whether to label and issue the green asset after considering all of the application materials. In practice, the primary international assessment and certification standards are GBP and CBS, with China mainly adopting the Green Bond Supporting Project Catalogue released by the GFC.

Post-issuance monitoring is an essential but complicated part of the application of green finance standards. This is mainly due to the additional costs and strict monitoring system involved. Post-issueance monitoring will restrict the investment opportunities of financing institutions, which may reduce enterprises' enthusiasm to issue green financial products. Post-issuance monitoring and tracking includes reporting the use of funds and proceeds, regularly disclosing the environmental and social impacts of the project, and post-release verification and assessment by third-party agencies. CBS strictly sets out the specific requirements and revocation of green bond issuance certification. The Equator Principles (EP4) requires that direct GHS emissions (Scope 1) and indirect GHGs from thermal or thermal use (Scope 2) must be publicly disclosed annually for projects with total annual CO_2 emissions of more than 100,000 metric tons. The above standards, issued by mainstream international organisations, institutions and governments, are highly authoritative and influential. They provide a practical basis for developing green and climate financial products worldwide. However, there are certain differences in details, which reflect their different backgrounds and development demands.

11.2 What Are the Differences between Green Finance Standards?

Firstly, the definition of "green" differs. The definition of green varies from country to country due to the differences in stage, key concerns and operating institution of socio-economic development. The EU and institutions such as the CBI, the World Bank and the ADB have gradually focused on climate change mitigation and adaptation in recent years. On this basis, the Green Bond Principle also pays much attention to biodiversity conservation and other fields. China's green finance standards had focused more on energy conservation, clean energy, pollution control, green infrastructure, clean transportation and ecological protection. A more noticeable difference is all parties' attitude to the utilisation and upgrading of coal fossil energy. For example, the updating of old coal plants is generally judged as a "brown project" by international standards, which is not supported. However, in countries like India and China, the primary energy would rely on coal and clean coal or coal with carbon capture, utilisation and storage are usually considered as a green finance option.

Secondly, the scope and degree of refinement of the standards differ. From the perspective of range, the CBS, the GBP, the rating agency systems and the current green standards in China fail to include social benefits in the scope of screening and monitoring. The EP4, the World Bank and the ADB cover environmental, social and governance (ESG) indicators in their standards. The directory level and technical details of standards vary significantly. Both the Climate Bond Standard (CBS) and China's Green Industry Guidance Catalogue subdivide the industry into three categories and specify the threshold of industry technology. GBP and the World Bank set the first-class directory, and the standard is relatively broad, with a lack of operability. The EP4 are mostly descriptive in principle and impose conceptual requirements on environmental risks. Other criteria should refer to the ADB's basic theoretical specifications. China's *Green Bond Supporting Project Catalogue* (2021 edition) and the *Green Industry Guidance Catalogue* (2021 edition) both stipulate specific projects and quantitative standards for loan use and separately explain the standards, which are of great guiding significance for the selection and evaluation of actual projects.

Thirdly, nature and implementation effectiveness differ. International standards are mostly voluntary in terms of adoption and compliance, and not mandatory. The green project or financial institution can obtain the labelling or certification after the voluntary application and verification by the standard-setting institution or third party. Moreover, after issuance, the reporting and disclosure requirements are relatively loose, and the role of the government is unclear. China's green finance standards are issued by the government regulatory departments, which have executive force for the involved industries and participants. Besides, relevant departments are also responsible for examining, approving and supervising green investment and financing activities, thereby tangibly standardising and promoting the orderly development of green finance.

We note that with the increase of cross-border finance and international environmental cooperation, global green finance standards are gradually converging. Meanwhile, as global awareness of the environment and climate change issues deepens, more and more governments and organisations are realising that the current traditional green finance system is unable to effectively support the strong financial and institutional needs for countries to achieve their NDCs in the Paris Agreement and the UN 2030 Sustainable Development Goals (SDGs). In the discussion and practice of green finance, due to the particularity of its nature, purpose and methodology, the concept and development demands of "climate finance" have become increasingly prominent, and climate effect is often the most crucial consideration of the international green finance system.

11.3 Nuclear and Natural Gas as Green Investments?

In Feb 2022, the EU's executive proposed to extend green finance criteria (EU Sustainable Finance Taxonomy) to natural gas-fired power and nuclear energy despite objections from NGOs, investors, a few member states, and members of its own expert group. Under the act approved by commissioners, private investment in natural gas-fired power generation will be classified as "transitional" if the plants use an increasing share of cleaner fuels like biogas or hydrogen.

The inclusion of gas-fired power, which emits mostly NOx and CO_2 as well as methane via the natural gas supply chain, has drawn abundant criticisms. The decision was fiercely contested by EU member states. While Germany and some of Central and Eastern Europe had supported the inclusion of gas, nations like Sweden, the Netherlands, Denmark, Luxembourg and Austria had opposed it and called for parliament to reject the proposal or risk its being challenged in court.

The inclusion of nuclear power in the sustainable taxonomy also drew criticism from Germany, Spain and Belgium, countries which had committed to phasing out nuclear power after the 2011 Fukushima nuclear disaster. In fact, a new, large-scale nuclear power plant is too expensive to construct in Europe in the last decade. However, France is supporting the inclusion of nuclear power in the taxonomy, and generates 69% of its total power from nuclear.

The green taxonomy will provide a strong signal for private investment decisions in the EU and potentially create a template for other jurisdictions. Most countries have been cautious about including fossil fuel and nuclear power in a green or sustainable taxonomy. For example, China removed clean coal and natural gas from its green taxonomy in 2021. Even though coal and gas will have strong roles to play in China over the next decade, the taxonomy needs to be strategic about facilitating finance for long-term green growth.

11.4 Does Green Finance Product Deserve Public Financial Incentive?

The 2019 EU Green Bond Standard proposal encourages member states and financial institutions to link the standard directly with the future standards of the financial industry. Central banks will step up their participation to enhance the market's acceptance and recognition of green finance. At the same time, it is advised that all member states implement preferential tax policies, including adopting an "accelerated depreciation method" for green assets and investment and improving the competitiveness of green assets. Similarly in China, the city of Huzhou in Zhejiang Province has taken the lead in formulating local standards for green finance. It is building a green finance reform and innovation pilot zone, promoting financial institutions to carry out green rating, labelling and information disclosure, as well as promoting the greening of the construction industry and the marketisation of environmental rights and interests, thereby comprehensively supporting the development of green finance.

It is noteworthy that the ability to generate additional green benefits should be the basis for policy support from governments and multilateral institutions. If a green investment and financing project is successfully carried out without being labelled as green (i.e., without additionality), the preferential policies provided by the government and multilateral institutions are likely to lead to wastage of resources and to squeeze the commercial investment and financing. It is a great pity that many green finance standard-setting organisations are aware of this problem (e.g., section 2.1 of the EU Green Bond), but do not encourage green bond issuers to disclose the additionality, which may mislead climate-friendly investors and policymakers. The authors reviewed the policy and marketing documents of the following green finance standards and found that none of them actually assessed and disclosed additionality (Table 11.1).

We reviewed seven major green bond standards in the world launched by International Capital Market Association (ICMA), Climate Bond Initiative (CBI), EU Technical Expert Group on Sustainable Finance (TEG), People's Bank of China (PBOC), National Development and Reform Commission of China (NDRC), Moody, S&P, and Fitch. Only ICMA, CBI, and EU have been reported to discuss the additionality issue explicitly (as illustrated in Table 11.1 beneath). ICMA, in their working group research in 2018/2019, suggested "additionality in sustainable finance" as a discussion topic for consideration, while the EU Green Bond Standard report acknowledged the missing additionality issue in the current green bond market but argued there were other benefits in classifying bonds as green bonds, such as improving information transparency in green asset refinancing and developing policy debates in green finance. The discussion on additionality by CBI is rather vague and an "additionality assessment" is not needed for green bond certification in their frequently asked questions page on the carbon market. As shown in Table 11.1, none of these eight existing green bond standards have assessed or disclosed additionality issues.

Table 11.1 Review of whether "Additionality" is Discussed, Assessed and Disclosed in Major Green Bond Related Standards.

Major Green Bond Standards in the World	Discussed	Assessed	Disclosed
ICAM Green Bond Principle	Yes	No	No
CBI"s Climate Bonds Standard	Yes	No	No
Proposal for EU Green Bond Standard, EU-GBS	Yes	No	No
PBOC Green Bond Guidance, China	No	No	No
NDRC Green Bond Guidance, China	No	No	No
Moody Green Bond Assessment	No	No	No
S&P Green Evaluations	No	No	No
Fitch Green Bond Rating	No	No	No

A future-proof green finance standard should provide more accurate disclosure requirement, i.e. investors of green bonds should notice that green bond investment does not create additional climate benefits and that the emission reduction of green assets is not attributed to such investment. Additional assessments of green finance should be introduced. We recommend a process illustrated in Figure 11.2 in the following text. Policymakers should meet the urgent need to create an investment environment that facilitates additional green assets, rather than simply making green statistics the baseline case. To generate additionality for a green asset, at least one of the following four investment environment scenarios needs to be created, in addition to a green additionality and financial additionality assessment.

1. Willingness of the issuers to accept a lower rate of return, i.e. environment- or climate-friendly firms would accept a lower required rate of return if the underlying project is certified with additionality. The condition may be possible if the additionality certificate generates significant reputational benefits to the issuer.

2. Climate-friendly concessional investors (either equity or debt investors) are willing to accept a lower required rate of return if the underlying project is certified with additionality. The climate finance commitments by MDBs shown in Figure 11.1 are likely meeting this condition. There are other climate-friendly family foundations or charities which may meet the condition as well.

3. Return increased: the return of the underlying project certified with additionality is increased to above the threshold level through either policy support or higher market price driven by additionality certification of the underlying asset.

4. Risk mitigation: the required rate of return (e.g. required IRR or discount rate) of the underlying project is decreased to below the project rate of return (e.g., IRR) through risk mitigation by additionality certification of the underlying asset.

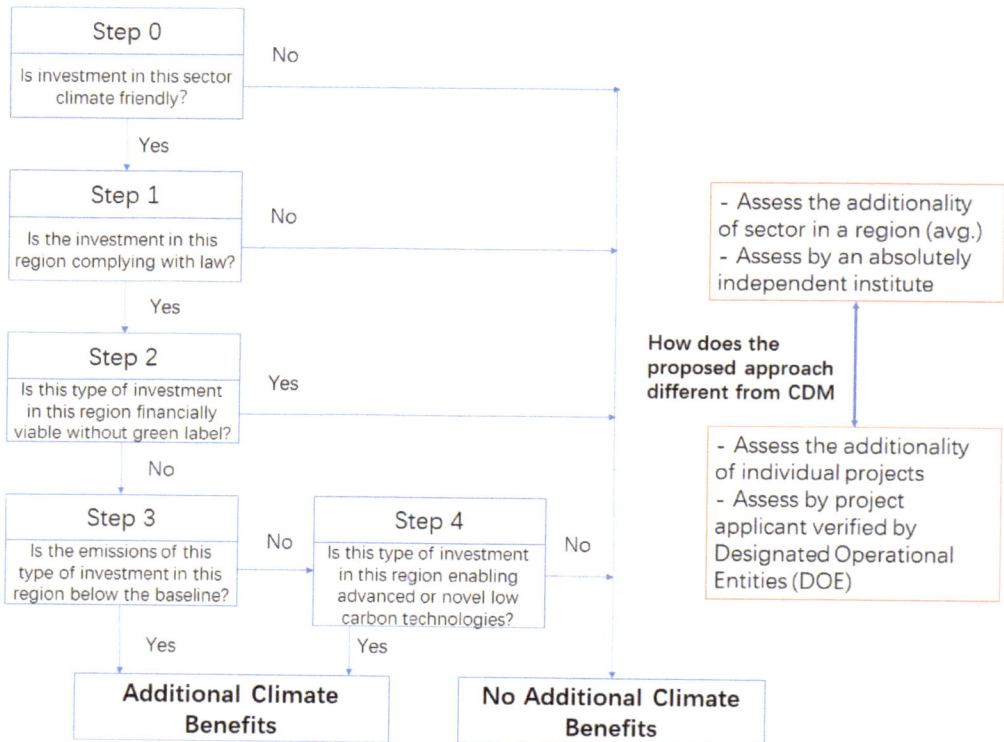

Fig. 11.2 Proposed Approach for Assessing Climate Mitigation Additionality.

To maximise the efficiency of utilising climate funding and green finance, we make the following four recommendations:

1. We recommend classifying new green finance products into two categories. Products without verified additionality could be defined **as "green statistics financial products"** and products with additionality could be defined as **'green impact financial products'**.

2. We recommend that all existing green finance products, if possible, **disclose whether additionality is assessed** and, if assessed, disclose whether additionality is verified. This disclosure would avoid limited public resources and climate-friendly concessional investors mistakenly investing in projects without generating additional green or climate benefits.

3. For potential green-impact financial products, further research is needed to understand how to maximise the effectiveness of grants, public finance, and concessional finance, **to avoid generating significant windfall profit for projects with additionality**.

4. We recommend that **green finance standards be updated with mandatory additionality disclosure**. For standards currently at the development stage, such as the European Green Bond Standard, these should be more rigorous and transparent, and the additionality issue should be taken into account in the standard development process.

References

ADB (2015) *Green Bond Framework*. Manila: Asian Development Bank, https://www.adb.org/sites/default/files/adb-green-bonds-framework.pdf.

Buchner, B., A. Clarke, A. Falconer, R. Macquarie, C. Meattle, R. Tolentino, and C. Wetherbee (2019) *Global Landscape of Climate Finance 2019*. London: Climate Policy Initiative, https://climatepolicyinitiative.org/wp-content/uploads/2019/11/2019-Global-Landscape-of-Climate-Finance.pdf.

CBRC (now CBIRC) (2012) *CBRC's Notice on the Issuance of Green Credit Guidelines (CBRC (2012) No.4)*. https://www.cbirc.gov.cn/en/view/pages/ItemDetail.html?docId=68035&ite.

China Financial News (2018) *Huzhou Released the First National Green Finance Local Standards* (湖州发布全国首批绿色金融地方标准). Tonghuashun Finance, http://field.10jqka.com.cn/20180904/c606935597.shtml.

CICERO (2020) *Shades of Green*. https://www.cicero.green/our-approach.

Climate Bonds Initiative (2019) *Climate Bonds Standard Version 3.0*. CBI, https://www.climatebonds.net/files/files/climate-bonds-standard-v3-20191210.pdf.

Climate Bonds Standard (2019) https://www.climatebonds.net/standard/faqs.

de Coninck, H., A. Revi, M. Babiker, P. Bertoldi, M. Buckeridge, A. Cartwright, W. Dong, J. Ford, S. Fuss, J.-C. Hourcade, D. Ley, R. Mechler, P. Newman, A. Revokatova, S. Schultz, L. Steg, and T. Sugiyama (2018) "Strengthening and Implementing the Global Response", in *Global Warming of 1.5°C. An IPCC Special Report on the Impacts of Global Warming of 1.5°C above Pre-industrial Levels and Related Global Greenhouse Gas Emission Pathways, in the Context of Strengthening the Global Response to the Threat of Climate Change, Sustainable Development, and Efforts to Eradicate Poverty*, ed. by V. Masson Delmotte, P. Zhai, H.-O. Pörtner, et al., IPCC, pp. 313–444, https://www.ipcc.ch/site/assets/uploads/sites/2/2019/06/SR15_Full_Report_High_Res.pdf.

Equator Principles (2020) *The Equator Principles (EP4): A Financial Industry Benchmark for Determining, Assessing and Managing Environmental and Social Risk in Projects*. Equator Principles, https://equator-principles.com/wp-content/uploads/2020/01/The-Equator-Principles-July-2020.pdf.

EU Technical Expert Group on Sustainable Finance (2019) *Report on EU Green Bond Standard*. EU, https://ec.europa.eu/info/publications/sustainable-finance-teg-green-bond-standard_en.

Fu, Y., Y. Wu and Y. Shi (2019) (2018) Practice Analysis of China's Green Bond Appraisal and Certification (2018中国绿色债券评估认证实践分析), *IIGF*, http://www.tanjiaoyi.com/article-28329-1.html.

ICMA (2018) *2018/2019 Working Group Research.* https://www.icmagroup.org/assets/documents/Regulatory/Green-Bonds/WG-Research-ToR-_-2018-2019-251018.pdf.

IRS (2019) *How to Depreciate Property (Publication 946).* https://www.irs.gov/publications/p946.

ISO (2021) *Green and Sustainable Finance.* Geneva: International Organization for Standardization, https://www.iso.org/files/live/sites/isoorg/files/store/en/PUB100458.pdf.

Jia, F., J. He, J. Yang et al. (2019) *2019 Climate Investment and Finance Case Study* (2019气候投融资典型案例研究报告). Beijing: Publicity and Education Centre of the Ministry of Ecology and Environment.

Jiang, N. (2019) "Huzhou, Zhejiang Province, Has Embarked on a New Journey of Green Finance Reform and Innovation Pilot Zone Construction" (浙江省湖州市全面开启绿色金融改革创新试验区建设新征程), *China Financial Information Network*, http://greenfinance.xinhua08.com/a/20190308/1802593.shtml.

Moody's Investors Service (2016) *Green Bond Assessment (GBA).* Moody's, https://www.amwa.net/sites/default/files/GBA%20Methodology-final-30march2016.pdf.

NDRC (2015) *Notice on the Issuance of Guidelines on the Issuance of Green Bonds (NDRC (2015) No. 3504).* https://www.ndrc.gov.cn/xxgk/zcfb/tz/201601/t20160108_963561.html?code=&state=123.

Refinitiv (2022) "Sustainable Finance Continues Surge in 2021", *Refinitiv.com*, 2 February, https://www.refinitiv.com/perspectives/market-insights/sustainable-finance-continues-surge-in-2021/.

S&P Global Ratings (2018) *Green Evaluation: Time to Turn over a New Leaf?*, S&P Global Ratings, https://www.spratings.com/documents/20184/1481001/Green+Evaluation/bbcd37ba-7b4f-4bf9-a980-d04aceeffa6b.

The World Bank (2017) *Green Bond Process Implementation Guidelines*, The World Bank, http://pubdocs.worldbank.org/en/217301525116707964/Green-Bond-Implementation-Guidelines.pdf.

12. Green Investments

Two Possible Interpretations of the "Do No Significant Harm" Principle

Claudio De Vincenti

Introduction

With the Delegated Act draft approved by the European Commission on February 2, 2022—which includes, albeit under restrictive conditions, gas and nuclear power generation plants within the taxonomy of eligible investments for the purposes of the green transition—a decisive issue, on which the actual achievement of the Green Deal sustainable growth objectives depends, has come to a head: the question of what is really meant by the "do no significant harm" (DNSH) principle.

The Commission's proposal—and the following 18 May 2022 REPowerEU Communication adopted in the light of Russia's invasion of Ukraine[1]—are, in fact, trying to overcome some of the consequences of the rigidity with which that principle was interpreted in the previous application documents of the taxonomy launched in the regulation of 18 June 2020.[2] In those previous documents, the principle was formulated in an extreme fashion, that actually risks compromising both the decarbonisation roadmap (reduction of emissions by 2030 and the achievement of net zero by 2050) and the diversification of energy sources.

In this chapter I propose an alternative interpretation of the "do no significant harm" principle, so that it becomes an effective lever, as opposed to an obstacle, for the fundamental investments of a sustainable development strategy and for the quickest possible achievement of the European energy security.

12.1 The DNSH Principle in the EU Documents

The "do no significant harm" principle was set out as a qualifying element of the eligibility of an investment for the purpose of accessing financial instruments more

---

1   COM (2022) 231 final.
2   (EU) Regulation 2020/852

    https://doi.org/10.11647/OBP.0328.12

favourable in terms of conditionality and cost, by Regulation 2020/852 of the European Parliament and of the Council.

In Article 3, the regulation specifies that "an economic activity shall qualify as environmentally sustainable where that economic activity: (a) contributes substantially to one or more of the environmental objectives" and "(b) does not significantly harm any" of them. The objectives are indicated in the following Article 9: "(a) climate change mitigation; (b) climate change adaptation; (c) the sustainable use and protection of water and marine resources; (d) the transition to a circular economy; (e) pollution prevention and control; (f) the protection and restoration of biodiversity and ecosystems."

The regulation entrusted the establishment of the criteria for the technical screening of sustainable economic activities pursuant to the taxonomy to a European Commission act. The Commission thus launched the 4 June 2021 Delegated Regulation which establishes those criteria in detail for the first two environmental objectives.[3] For the purposes of this paper, I would like to recall that: in the energy section of the Delegated Regulation there is neither electricity generation from natural gas nor from nuclear energy, while the natural gas transport and distribution networks are present insofar as the investment relates to their conversion or upgrading for the transmission of renewable and low-carbon gases or for the transport of hydrogen;[4] in the section concerning the management of the waste cycle, incineration activity is not considered.[5]

In parallel to this taxonomy elaboration, the Recovery and Resilience Facility (RRF) was developed with the Regulation of the European Parliament and of the Council of 12 February 2021,[6] which specifies in Article 5 that "the Facility shall only support measures respecting the principle 'do no significant harm'."

The RRF Regulation was accompanied by a communication with which, also on 12 February 2021, the Commission provided the technical guidelines for the application of the DNSH principle in the context of the RRF.[7] I recall here two particularly significant prescriptions from this communication. The first indicates that "Member States need to provide an *individual* DNSH assessment (Commission's italics) for each measure" of the National Recovery and Resilience Plan (NRRP), so that "the DNSH assessment is not to be carried out at the level of the Plan or of individual components of the Plan, but at measure level."[8] The second provides that "the assessment of the negative environmental impact of each measure should be carried out against a 'no intervention' scenario by taking into account the environmental effect of the measure *in absolute terms* [my italics]). This approach consists of considering the environmental impact of the measure, compared to a situation with no negative environmental impact,"

---

3   Commission Delegated Regulation (EU) 2021/2139.
4   Ibid., Annex I, para. 4.14.
5   Ibid., para. 5.
6   (EU) Regulation 2021/241.
7   COM (2021) 1054 final.
8   Ibid., pp. 2–3.

and therefore it "is not assessed in comparison to the impact of another existing or envisaged activity that the measure in question may be replacing."[9]

Here I point out two of the examples that are given in the text and in the annexes: "measures related to power and/or heat generation using fossil fuels (including natural gas, my notation), as well as related transmission and distribution infrastructures as a general rule should not be deemed compliant under DNSH for the purposes of the RRF;"[10] an investment which supports the construction of new waste-to-energy plants, "while it aims to divert [...] combustible non-recyclable waste from landfills", would still violate the DNSH principle as it "leads to a significant increase in incineration of waste."[11]

Compared to this very restrictive approach referenced in the guidelines, a somewhat different perspective is introduced by the late February draft of the Commission's Delegated Act,[12] which amends the Delegated Regulation of 4 June 2021 on the technical application criteria of the taxonomy. The new Delegated Act supplements the original one with reference to two activities that were not previously included, namely the production of electricity from natural gas and through nuclear energy.

For nuclear energy—which is considered capable of giving "a substantial contribution to the climate change mitigation objective"[13]—the draft provides a series of prescriptions regarding the safety of the plants and their location, the treatment of waste, and the monitoring of activities so that the DNSH criterion can be considered satisfied with reference to the other environmental objectives.[14]

For electricity generation starting from natural gas—which is considered capable of making a substantial contribution to the climate change mitigation objective as a "transitional activity as referred to in Article 10 (2) of Regulation (EU) 2020/852" on Taxonomy[15]—the draft provides the threshold values for permissible greenhouse gas emissions, the capacity limits related to the capacity of the coal or oil plants that are replaced, compatibility with the use of renewable and low-emission gases, and the existence of an integrated energy-climate plan in which the member state has committed itself to abandoning coal-fired generation.[16]

12.2 An Evaluation: The Need to Get out of an Impasse

It is clear that with the new Delegated Act the European Commission is trying to overcome some of the rigidity with which the "do no significant harm" principle was applied in previous documents.

---

9   Ibid., p. 7.
10   Ibid., p. 8.
11   Ibid., Annexes 1–4, p. 12.
12   The draft dated 2 February 2022, already mentioned at the beginning of this paper.
13   Ibid., p. 3.
14   Ibid., Annex 1, para. 4.26–4.28.
15   Ibid., p. 28.
16   Ibid., para 4.29–4.31.

In particular, the substantial exclusion of natural gas from Delegated Regulation 2021/2139, added to the restrictions in the eligibility criteria of the possible technological transformations in road and sea transport vehicles, seriously risks hindering the achievement of the emission reduction targets that the Union has set for 2030.[17] Indeed, if in order to achieve the 55% reduction in emissions by 2030 it is absolutely necessary to accelerate the development of renewable sources and progress in energy efficiency—as well as the development of biofuels and hydrogen research and experimentation—it also appears necessary to safeguard the possibilities of replacing oil and coal with gas in all uses where this can lead to the reduction of emissions more rapidly. Failure to achieve the 55% target by 2030 would not only have effects on the current level of emissions, but also significant carry-over effects on achieving the goal of net zero in 2050, making it much more difficult and expensive. Faced with the evidence—supported by the working materials and the conclusions of COP26 in Glasgow—that the current trajectory in the world (but also in Europe) of greenhouse emissions is incompatible with the goal of containment in 1.5°C of global warming compared to the pre-industrial level, we cannot afford delays in adopting all measures necessary to change that trajectory.[18]

It would instead be necessary for the amending scope of the new Delegated Act to go beyond the still partial and restrictive indications contained at the moment in the draft, and to pave the way for the consideration of the role that the entirety of the possible processes of replacing oil and coal with gas can and must play in the transition, both in electricity generation and in the transport system and industrial production processes.

But how did we end up in the impasse that the draft of the new Delegated Act is trying in some way to unblock? Provided that the "do no significant harm" principle is in itself a positive novelty that ensures the internal consistency of the green transition strategy—and avoiding the pursuit of environmental objectives at the expense of others—the cause of the impasse lies in the very particular way in which the principle has been formulated in the acts launched up to now.

In this regard, the approach adopted in the Communication on the Guidelines for the technical screening of investments in the RRF is particularly significant.[19] The

---

17   Note that the same Commission forecasts contained in SWD (2020) 176 final, Annexes, p. 50, Fig. 36 and p. 61, Fig. 49, indicate a still significant use of natural gas in 2030; and that these forecasts—p. 62, Fig. 50 and pp. 75–76, Figs 62–63—seem to count only modest processes of replacing oil and coal with gas in sectors, such as heavy transport and some industrial processes, which could instead benefit from new gas-based technologies while, at the moment, they appear difficult to convert to electricity. On a global level, the International Energy Agency estimates that, on the path towards zero emissions by 2050, the very substantial increase in renewables in the mix of sources for electricity production will need to be complemented in 2030 by a gas usage not lower in absolute terms than current levels, and the same will happen for the industrial sector; cf. IEA, World Energy Outlook 2021: p. 125, Fig. 3.12; p. 133, Fig. 3.16; p. 213, Fig. 5.2.
18   Cf. also IEA, World Energy Outlook 2021, p. 34, Fig. 1.5.
19   See above COM 2021/1054.

two prescriptions mentioned above are decisive in determining the "bottleneck" that risks blocking the transition to projects of great value for the success of the European roadmap.

The first, as we have seen, provides that for the purposes of the DNSH assessment the impact of a given measure must be considered "*in absolute terms,*" that is, "compared to a situation with no negative environmental impact," and not "in comparison to the impact of another existing or envisaged activity that the measure in question may be replacing."[20] Since in absolute terms gas produces CO_2 emissions, albeit much lower than those produced by oil and coal that it could replace, its use in electricity generation, in the transport system, and in manufacturing activities can only violate the criterion as formulated in the Communication.

Yet, looking at the overall path of decarbonisation, we know that in some sectors the alternatives to coal and oil other than gas (electricity generation from renewables, heavy transport by road or sea, as well as industrial processes, powered only by electricity or hydrogen or fuels with zero emissions) need investments in plants and further technological innovations that are unlikely to reach the scale necessary to reduce emissions by 55% by 2030. It would be quite logical, then, to consider natural gas as an energy source to be used during the transition phase, until those alternatives are fully developed: curbing the replacement of oil and coal with gas would mean slowing down the path of decarbonisation.

But this logical conclusion is prevented by the second DNSH assessment prescription which, together with the one considered above, precisely determines the "bottleneck" I was talking about. I refer to the provision that imposes "an *individual* DNSH assessment for each measure" of the NRRP, without reference to the plan or its components.[21] In this way, the single measure is analysed by removal from its role in the path of reducing emissions and pollution. Therefore—abstracted from the timeframes, methods and conditions for the adequate scale implementation of alternatives to natural gas in electricity generation, in heavy or maritime transport, and in industrial processes—the conclusion to which the guidelines lead is to consider natural gas *per se* as not compliant with the DNSH principle.

The results of such a way of interpreting the "do no significant harm" principle are paradoxical. Firstly, because, as mentioned, the technologies that use gas to replace oil and coal and therefore accelerate the abatement of CO_2 emissions, as well as other pollutants, are penalised. Secondly, because, even beyond the energy sector, the introduction and diffusion of "cleaner" technologies in a number of other sectors may be slowed down. The most striking example, in this regard, is that of incinerators.

As we have seen, the DNSH non-compliance of an investment aimed at supporting the construction of new waste-to-energy plants is made explicit in the guidelines. It is recognised that it would help to divert "combustible non-recyclable waste from

---

20   Ibid., p. 7.
21   Ibid., p. 2.

landfills", but it is reiterated that it would violate the DNSH principle as it "leads to a significant increase in incineration of waste."[22] Such a conclusion of DNSH non-compliance always refers to the evaluation criterion "in absolute terms" combined with specific consideration of the single measure outside any reference to a coherent plan for the management and closure of the waste cycle that makes use of all the best available technologies. The paradoxical result is that this decision ends up endorsing the choice made up to now by certain local government authorities—for example in a part of Italy—to rely on landfill until the extreme exhaustion of available space and, for the remainder, to resort to the export of waste to waste-to-energy plants located in other territories. This is a striking contradiction of the European principles of "proximity" in the treatment of waste and of overcoming landfilling!

12.3 An Open Mind Approach to the DNSH Principle

For the sake of the green transition, it is necessary and urgent to correct at the root the very particular way in which the "do no significant harm" principle has been applied in the acts launched up to now, in order to interpret it in a form that supports—and does not hinder—the set of strategic choices that the Green Deal needs. The analysis conducted in the previous paragraph highlights the key steps of a new, more advanced and comprehensive interpretation of the DNSH principle.

The first consists in adopting a *comparative*, not absolute, environmental impact assessment criterion: what matters to accelerate the abatement of emissions or pollution is the net environmental benefit of the investment. A project must therefore be assessed not with respect to a hypothetical state of nature but comparatively to the activities that are concretely replaced with that investment and that are already in place or would be realised in the future if the investment in question were not made: with respect to them the project must produce a positive net benefit.

The second step consists in the fact that this assessment in comparative terms must be carried out by considering the investment in the *framework of the green transition strategy* that the member state is required to adopt and which must be consistent in its temporal development with the objectives set at the European level. The individual investment, therefore, must be assessed with reference to the role it plays within the path of increasing the share of energy produced from renewable sources, of progress in terms of energy efficiency, of reduction of polluting sources, of protection of natural resources and of biodiversity. Therefore, the project must be compared with those alternatives that can be concretely—not abstractly—implemented with an equivalent timing and scale in order to achieve the planned transition targets.

It is only in this context—thus carrying out the assessment in comparative and strategic terms—that it becomes possible to address two further issues that will have decisive relevance in the concrete choices that the authorities will be called upon to make.

---

22   Ibid., Annexes 1–4, pp. 12.

The first concerns the assessment of the possible "lock-in" effects created by an investment: an assessment which in itself requires taking into account the realisation times and useful life as well as any future alternative uses of the infrastructure created, so as to make the intervention adopted for the transition consistent with the final objectives. The issue is relevant, for example, precisely for the supply and transport infrastructures of natural gas, for their role in the transition and for their future usability in the transport of gas from renewable sources and hopefully of hydrogen.

The second question concerns the trade-offs that may arise between the different objectives established by the taxonomy. This is an issue that has so far been substantially "avoided," as if it were possible to consider only interventions that do not cause any harm to one or more environmental objectives compliant with the DNSH principle: a way to reduce "do no significant harm" to "do no harm." Concrete situations are often more complex, with benefits for one objective but possible harm for another. These trade-offs cannot be exorcised and will require a weighing of the costs and benefits of an investment by the authorities that clarify the degree of "significance" of any harm and therefore the net environmental benefit of the intervention for the purposes of the path towards an environmentally compatible economy. It is with this in mind that the issue of waste-to-energy plants as a tool for closing the waste cycle, complementary to recovery/recycling processes and alternative to landfill, must be addressed. The nuclear issue also cannot be addressed except by weighing the benefits (lower emissions) and costs (waste problem) and arriving at a positive or negative assessment of the net benefit.

In conclusion, the two assessment criteria indicated—comparative and strategic— would allow us to define a general framework for the application of the "do no significant harm" principle without paradoxes that risk causing serious harm to the green transition.

12.4 The War, REPowerEU and Taxo4

The European Commission Communication of 18 May 2022 on REPowerEU strategy opens by noting that "unprecedented geopolitical and economic events have drastically impacted the Union's society and economy".[23] The invasion of Ukraine by Russia has brought back to the foreground the issue of energy security, and REPowerEU is aimed at giving the tools to member states and the EU in order to address this issue. In particular, the National Recovery and Resilience Plans "shall contain a REPowerEU chapter", with reforms, investments and other measures aiming to "improving energy infrastructures and facilities to meet immediate security of supply needs for oil and gas, notably to enable diversification", and "boosting energy efficiency in buildings, decarbonizing industry, [...] and increasing the share of renewable energy".[24]

---

23   COM (2022) 231, p. 1.
24   Ibid., p. 15.

The Communication does not question the way the DNSH principle has been interpreted up to now, and prefers to take a shortcut: "a targeted exemption from the obligation to apply the do no significant harm principle [...] for reforms and investments improving energy infrastructure to meet immediate security" and "to enable diversification" of supply.[25]

Of course, the solution adopted in REPowerEU Communication has the advantage of avoiding lengthy discussions and immediately unlocking necessary and urgent infastructures. But it leaves in the shadows the role of gas infrastructures not only for energy security but also, as emphasised before, for the green transition itself.

A timid—very timid—step towards a more open way of interpreting the DNSH principle can be found in some passages of the latest document published by the Technical Working Group of the Platform on Sustainable Finance.[26] The document is called Taxo4, because it provides recommendations for the four environmental objectives other than climate change mitigation and climate change adaptation, addressed by Regulation 2021/2139.

Taxo4 does little to deal with the DNSH principle: in a short paragraph, the document hints that it would be useful "to undertake a review of the DNSH criteria [...] to improve consistency and usability of the Taxonomy",[27] but does not give more than some very generic, methodological indications.

Later, in dealing with air transport, the document introduces a criterion that in fact abandons the absolute and specific approach to the DNSH evaluation in favour of a comparative and strategic one. The Commission's strategy proceeds from the awareness that the "so-called zero emission aircraft, electric or powered by green hydrogen" will become ready for market no earlier than 2035; "until then, incremental efficiency improvements of airframes and engines in combination with the use of sustainable aviation fuels (SAF) producing less CO_2 over their life cycle than conventional jet fuel are the main mitigation options available to the sector", so that "aviation can be included in the taxonomy as a transition activity" and "the replacement of old, less efficient aircrafts with new, more efficient ones" can satisfy screening criteria.[28]

This is, however, one of the very few cases in which a comparative and strategic criterion is adopted in the document. The same, for instance, does not happen for the incinerators, which in the Annex dedicated to waste management continue to be excluded by the taxonomy.[29] It is also significant that the Annex dedicated to manufacturing does not deal with the most energy-intensive sectors.[30]

---

25   Ibid., p. 7.
26   See Platform on Sustainable Finance: Technical Working Group, Part A and Part B, March 2022.
27   Ibid., Part A, p. 73.
28   Ibid., Part B, pp. 525–26.
29   See Part B, Chapter 11.
30   Ibid., Chapter 2.

12.5 We Need a Flapping of Wings

Even after the REPowerEU and Taxo4 documents, the DNSH interpretation remains essentially the extreme one, which *per se* hinders investments that are fundamental for green transition and energy security: Taxo4 contains only timid steps towards a more open interpretation of the principle, and REPowerEU simply uses the shortcut of exemptions from the application of DNSH, which is like saying that the principle must be circumvented if you do not want to compromise the European energy security objectives.

It is time to free ourselves from the straitjacket of a rigid and short-sighted approach, and to adopt the open-minded interpretation of the DNSH principle presented above in Section 3 and based on:

- a *comparative*, not absolute, environmental impact assessment criterion: what matters in the acceleration of the abatement of emissions or pollution is the net environmental benefit of the investment; a project must therefore be assessed not with respect to a hypothetical state of nature but comparatively to the activities that are concretely replaced with that investment;

- an assessment which considers the investment in the *framework of the green transition strategy* that the member state is required to adopt; a project must be compared with those alternatives that can be concretely—not abstractly—implemented with an equivalent timing and scale in order to achieve the planned transition targets.

It is only with an assessment in comparative and strategic terms that it becomes possible to address two further issues—the possible "lock-in" effects and the trade-offs arising between different environmental objectives—which will have decisive relevance in the concrete choices that the authorities will be called upon to make.

In conclusion, we need a flapping of wings: building an economy that has the protection of the environment as its guiding star requires looking with an open mind at ways of realising the fundamental goal of a society that finally achieves a balanced, organic exchange between mankind and nature.

References

European Commission Staff Working Document (2020) *SWD (2020) 176 final, Impact Assessment Accompanying Communication Stepping up Europe's 2030 Climate Ambition*, https://www.eea.europa.eu/policy-documents/swd-2020-176-final-part.

European Commission (2021a) *C (2021) 1054 final, Technical Guidance on the Application of "Do No Significant Harm" under the Recovery and Resilience Facility Regulation*, https://ec.europa.eu/info/sites/default/files/c_2021_1054_en.pdf.

European Commission (2021b) *Commission Delegated Regulation (EU) 2021/2139 Supplementing Regulation (EU) 2020/852*, https://eur-lex.europa.eu/legal-content/IT/TXT/?uri=CELEX%3A32021R2139.

European Commission (2022a) *Draft of 2 February 2022 of the Commission Delegated Regulation Amending Delegated Regulation (EU) 2021/2139*, https://ec.europa.eu/finance/docs/level-2-measures/taxonomy-regulation-delegated-act-2022-631_en.pdf.

European Commission (2022b) *COM (2022) 231 final, Proposal for a Regulation of the European Parliament and of the Council Amending Regulation (EU) 2021/241*, https://ec.europa.eu/info/system/files/com-2022-231_en.pdf.

European Union (2020) *Regulation EU 2020/852 of the European Parliament and of the Council on the Establishment of a Framework to Facilitate Sustainable Investment*, https://eur-lex.europa.eu/legal-content/IT/TXT/?uri=CELEX:32020R0852.

European Union (2021) *Regulation EU 2021/241 of the European Parliament and of the Council Establishing the Recovery and Resilience Facility*, https://eur-lex.europa.eu/legal-content/IT/TXT/?uri=CELEX%3A32021R0241.

European Union (2022) *Platform on Sustainable Finance: Technical Working Group, Report on Environmental Taxonomy Extension*, https://ec.europa.eu/info/sites/default/files/business_economy_euro/banking_and_finance/documents/220330-sustainable-finance-platform-finance-report-remaining-environmental-objectives-taxonomy_en.pdf.

International Energy Agency (2021) *World Energy Outlook 2021*, https://iea.blob.core.windows.net/assets/4ed140c1-c3f3-4fd9-acae-789a4e14a23c/WorldEnergyOutlook2021.pdf.

13. Towards a Socially Just Green Transition

The Role of Welfare States and Public Finances

Cinzia Alcidi, Francesco Corti, Daniel Gros, and Alessandro Liscai

Introduction

Finding a balance between the objectives of economic growth, environmental sustainability and social fairness has been one of the key priorities of the EU agenda of the last years. While the link between economic growth and social and ecological objectives has historically received much attention, a focus on the socio-environmental nexus is far more recent (Mandelli 2021). On the one hand, social logics may determine environmental damage (Laurent 2015) and the welfare state entails an "ecological footprint" (Matthies 2017). On the other hand, environmental protection is critical to long-term social welfare, and ecological degradation implies significant social costs (Sabato et al. 2021). Along with this thinking, some scholars have recently attempted to identify the possible functions that the welfare state could perform to accompany the green transition. Based on this recent literature, we identify two main functions:[1]

- *Activating:* Welfare states actively support the green transition, by providing workers with the right skills and competences needed for the new jobs that are created. The focus is on activating policies such as education and training, re-skilling, and active labour market policies.

- *Buffering:* Welfare states put in place traditional social protection policies which compensate for the social costs (e.g. unemployment, inequalities) of the green transition.

---

[1] Here we take inspiration from Sabato et al. (2021). The authors, however, identify two further functions of the welfare state in the green transition: 1) Welfare states as a benchmark for the green transition; and 2) Welfare states as consensus-builders or conflict-management tools of the green transition.

                    https://doi.org/10.11647/OBP.0328.13

These functions are not mutually exclusive, but they can coexist. Welfare states can indeed at the same time actively support the green transition by upskilling and reskilling workers and protecting those negatively affected by the transition. Conversely, they can pursue one of the above-mentioned functions or none of them. An important distinction to be made here concerns the logic under which the welfare intervention is carried. Two different logics can underpin eco-social policies:

- The *compensatory logic*, i.e. social policy objectives and tools are linked to environmental objectives and tools only by the extent to which the latter produce negative externalities. A compensatory logic can be applied both to the first and second functions. As an example, workers dismissed in brown sectors can both be compensated for the income loss and re-trained, re-skilled and accompanied in their search for a new occupation.

- The *integrated logic*, i.e. social policies and goals are designed together with ecological objectives and goals. Welfare policies do not only compensate for the social costs of the green transition, but they are also conceived as a necessary pre-condition to facilitate the ecological transition.

An integrated approach to social and environmental policies seems to be the most suitable solution to achieve green and social outcomes. A recent work by Zimmermann and Graziano (2020), for instance, shows that among European countries the best performers in environmental protection are the ones (notably the Nordic countries) with a high performing welfare state, both in terms of buffers and in terms of activating policies. In September 2015, the United Nations (UN) adopted the '2030 Agenda for Sustainable Development', which explicitly promoted the three dimensions of sustainable development: social, environmental and economic, and supported a balanced approach to achieve them simultaneously.

As mentioned above, the European Union has placed itself in the driving seat of the green transition and has since 2019 put in place a new reference framework for a socio-ecological transformation. While national welfare states are still meant to play a key role in making the green transition socially fair, it should be recognised that the shift towards such an approach was largely led by the EU. Against this background, the purpose of this chapter is twofold. As a first step, we illustrate the existing EU reference framework for a socio-ecological transition, zooming in on two of the most recent initiatives: the European Green Deal (EGD) and the Recovery and Resilience Facility (RRF). The aim is to briefly identify the approach followed to link environmental, economic, and social concerns, the function to be performed by welfare states, and the logic of interaction between social and environmental policies. As a second step, since the EU financial support to pay for the cost of the eco-social transition is not sufficient, we advance and compare two concrete proposals that can help national governments in building an activating welfare state, devoted to supporting a socially inclusive transition: a social golden rule and the amortisation of public investment.

13.1 The EU Initiatives to Address the Socio-Ecological Transition

The EGD adopted in December 2019 addresses the economic-ecological nexus by promoting the transition towards an economic model decoupled from its ecological footprint, and explicitly tackles socio-ecological challenges, in particular those that pertain to the social implications of environmental issues and policies. In so doing, the EGD calls for a "socially just" transition that aims to leave "no one behind". The EGD indeed specifies that "the most vulnerable are the most exposed to the harmful effects of climate change and environmental degradation" (European Commission 2019) and that "citizens, depending on their social and geographic circumstances, will be affected in different ways" (ibid.). In particular, the identified socio-ecological challenges are divided by the EGD into issues affecting vulnerable energy consumers or people at risk of energy poverty and those impacting the labour market, with a focus on sectors and territories which would face "the greatest challenges" (European Commission 2019). Overall, the underlying logic of the socio-ecological dimension of the European Green Deal is compensatory of the social costs triggered by the green transition.

Such logic is reflected in the key policy instruments for delivering the EGD, namely the Just Transition Mechanism (JTM) and the Just Transition Fund (JTF), that were launched as part of the Sustainable Europe Investment Plan. The purpose of the JTM consists in addressing the socio-economic impact of decarbonisation by spurring virtuous social investment policies and setting the conditions for the promotion of public and private funding. Within the JTM, the Just Transition Fund was established to reduce regional disparities, improve economic diversification, upskill and reskill workers, and increase assistance and active inclusion of jobseekers. All in all, the policies seek to meet the needs of two main targets: 1) vulnerable energy consumers and people at risk of energy poverty;[2] and 2) redundant workers employed in greenhouse gas-intensive sectors and their communities (e.g., JTM, JTF).

If the EGD promotes a *compensatory logic* where social policies intervene *ex-post* to buffer the cost and accompany life-course transition (with a focus on vulnerable groups and affected sectors), the socio-ecological dimension of the RRF marks a further step forward towards an *integrated understanding* of eco-social policies. The social dimension of the post-pandemic recovery is given a particular prominence in the RRF, which explicitly aims at "*contributing to the upward economic and social convergence, restoring and promoting sustainable growth and the integration of the economies of the Union, fostering high quality employment creation*" (RRF Regulation, Art. 4). Stronger activating and inclusive welfare states are explicitly acknowledged as a pre-condition for a socially sustainable green transition. In defining their responses to the crisis, the member states should "factor in", across green policy areas, the need to ensure a just and socially fair transition. A clear call to adopt measures ensuring equal opportunities,

---

2   Two examples of these policies include the 2016 proposal for a Clean Energy for All package and the 2020 Communication "A Renovation Wave for Europe".

inclusive education, fair working conditions and adequate social protection, in light of the European Pillar of Social Rights, was made by EU institutions and is explicitly linked to the green transition. Contrary to the JTF, which is targeted to support the social consequences of the green transition, the RRF explicitly recognises the need to address interlinkages between environmental and social policies and aims to promote a "balanced recovery" in the EU. This translates into combining green growth with the promotion of a just transition based on a guarantee of high social standards. As stressed by Sabato et al. (2021) *"in a just transition perspective, the recovery and resilience plans will be crucial to ensure workers' protection, representing a sort of buffer in the green transition"* (ibid., p. 46).

13.2 How to Tackle the Persisting Social Infrastructural Gap in the EU

In a report published in 2018 by the High-Level Task Force on Investing in Social Infrastructure in Europe, the need for social infrastructure investment to cope with the challenges of the twin green and digital transitions, an ageing population and globalisation, has been estimated for EU countries to be around €142 billion per year, and around €1.5 trillion over the period 2018 to 2030 in the sole areas of healthcare, education, and housing (Fransen et al. 2018). Preliminary evidence from the plans submitted so far shows that the total social envelope amounts to around €150 billion, i.e., about 30% of the total RRF, to be spent over five years, between 2021 and 2026, so on average €30 billion per year.

Even though the comparison is a bit forced, we might say that the entire RRF envelope, hence EU common funds, covers only one year of the social public infrastructure investments gap. This crude comparison suggests that the individual member states will have to take care of the remaining gap. This raises the question about how member states, and their public finances, can cope with the need for public investment to support and strengthen their welfare systems to face the challenges of the twin transition. One proposal that has been discussed to address such a significant investment gap is the introduction of a qualified treatment for public social investment under a revisited fiscal framework (see among others Corti et al. 2022).

In practice, one possible option is the inclusion of a golden rule in the EU fiscal framework. The general argument for a golden rule is that governments should be allowed to incur debt if it creates new capital and hence produces value (in principle not only economic) for future generations. Indeed, public investment increases the public and/or social capital stock, thereby creating growth to the benefit of future generations, that contribute to financing those investments via the debt service (Truger 2016). Reuter (2020) reinforces Truger's argument by showing that debt-financed productive expenditure can improve fiscal sustainability in the medium to long term if it increases potential growth, since exempted investment expenditure can generate additional assets that counteract debt increases. In the specific EU context, this would imply exempting certain investment expenditures from the calculation of the SGP-relevant variables. A second argument used in favour of a golden rule is that it could help to avoid underinvestment in times of crisis. In this respect, evidence shows that public investments tend to be pro-cyclical in bad times, thereby amplifying downturns under weak economic conditions (Morozumi and Veiga 2016; Afonso and Furceri 2010; Chu et al. 2018). There is, indeed, quite strong evidence that public investments have been the main victim of the fiscal consolidation efforts during the euro area debt crisis (Barbiero and Darvas 2014; EFB 2019). A third reason to endorse a golden rule is that, if focused on specific classes of public investment, it would be more effective in mobilising resources (Pekanov and Schratzenstaller 2020).

Recently, Darvas and Wolff (2021) proposed to introduce a Green Golden Rule, i.e. a rule that excludes a specific measure (or class) of capital expenditure from the computation of certain fiscal requirements (be it the expenditure benchmark or the budget deficit), to cope with the needs of the green transition and meet the EU's ambitious emissions reduction targets.[3] Following the same rationale, various scholars and policymakers have long been advocating for the introduction of a European social golden rule (see Zuleeg and Schneider 2015; Hemerijck et al. 2020). Yet even though the proposal for a qualified treatment for social investment under the EU fiscal framework has been circulating in the debate for a longer period, it was never operationalised. As we illustrated elsewhere (Corti et al. 2022), the reason is at least threefold.

First, current statistics are quite poor. As admitted by the members of the High-Level Task Force, the quality of—and access to—data on public investments is insufficient to carry out systematic comparative analyses and identify country-specific social needs. Second, to justify a qualified treatment, one should be able to measure returns of social investments. Yet, only a few empirical studies have systematically analysed the social returns of public social spending with findings somewhat contradictory (see for instance Hemerijck et al. 2016; Bakker and Van Vliet 2019). By contrast, the literature largely focuses on the potential impact of public social spending on GDP growth (economic outcome), *de facto* ignoring the potential social outcomes (see for instance Gemmell et al. 2016; Dissou et al. 2016; Barbiero and Cournède 2013; Fournier 2016; Fournier and Johansson 2016). Even in this case, however, findings are contradictory, with educational and healthcare expenditure indicated as the only "productive spending". Finally, as observed by Vesper (2007), for any investment to be eligible for qualified treatment, an exact definition of the relevant expenditure should be given. While sensible, this is not straightforward. Most literature focusing on the impact of

---

3   Based on the Commission Impact Assessment on 'Stepping up Europe's 2030 climate ambition. Investing in a climate-neutral future for the benefit of our people' (European Commission 2020), to achieve the 55% reduction target in GHG emission compared to the 1990s level by 2030, the average annual green public investment need amounts to €145.7 billion between 2021 and 2030 and €166.2 billion between 2031 and 2050.

social expenditure on GDP uses expenditure at the aggregate level. Yet, when we break down social expenditure by type of spending (capital and current), we observe that only a minor part of education expenditure is devoted to what is traditionally understood as public investment (infrastructure and R&D activities), while the largest part comprises current costs (staff salaries, contracted and purchased services, and other resources such as fuel, electricity, telecommunications and travel expenses).

With these caveats in mind, in the next section we provide a first operationalisation attempt of a European social golden rule. To this end, we apply—in an exploratory fashion—this operationalisation only on two types of social expenditure, i.e. education and healthcare. The choice is justified based on two criteria. First, existing literature on economic returns (i.e. GDP) of social spending converge on the idea that these spending voices are 'productive', therefore we might expect more consensus on a special treatment for this kind of spending. Second, contrary to other social protection spending, like pension, unemployment benefits and even housing, education and healthcare have both a component of current spending, and one of capital expenditure (investment *stricto sensu*). This allows us to measure the different implications of the selection of one specific type of expenditure.

13.3 A European Golden Rule for Social Investment

Different variants of the golden rule have been put forth (Feigl and Truger 2015; Darvas and Anderson 2020; Bogaert 2016; Giavazzi et al. 2021). All of these variants agree that such an exemption should be applied only to net public investment. The distinction between net and gross is indeed key to operationalise a qualified treatment. Net investment is the total amount of resources that the government spends on capital assets minus the cost of depreciation of the existing assets. The practical importance of the difference between net and gross investments is shown in the table below, which compares social public investment trends in France, Germany, Italy and Spain between 2016 and 2019. Gross investments in education and healthcare have been more or less stable in all four countries at around 0.3% and 0.4% of GDP, with only the exception of France at around 0.6% of GDP. Net investment was positive in Germany and France but negative in Spain and Italy over the entire period, which means both countries invested less than the minimum requested to maintain the existing stock of capital.

The application of a social golden rule on healthcare and educational spending thus changes quite significantly if we consider gross or net spending. In the first scenario, public expenditure in education and health gross fixed capital formation is exempted from government fiscal targets. In this case, the largest relative gain in all years would be France, with a 0.6 to 0.7 percentage point (pp) decrease in budget deficit. The possible gain for other economies would have been around a 0.3 pp drop in budget deficit in both Italy and Spain, and a 0.3 pp increase in budget surplus in Germany for most of the years. The second scenario assumes a golden rule applied

Table 13.1 Healthcare and education gross and net fixed capital formation (% GDP), selected countries.

		2015	2016	2017	2018	2019
DE	Gross social investment (% GDP)	0.3	0.3	0.3	0.3	0.4
	Net social investment (% GDP)	0.01	0.02	0.04	0.06	0.11
IT	Gross social investment (% GDP)	0.4	0.3	0.3	0.3	0.3
	Net social investment (% GDP)	-0.02	-0.07	-0.06	-0.07	-0.05
FR	Gross social investment (% GDP)	0.7	0.6	0.6	0.6	0.6
	Net social investment (% GDP)	0.05	0.01	0.02	0.03	0.07
ES	Gross social investment (% GDP)	0.3	0.3	0.3	0.3	0.3
	Net social investment (% GDP)	-0.06	-0.08	-0.04	-0.01	0.01

Source: own elaboration, based on AMECO and Eurostat.[4]

to net public social investment, namely exempting only actual additions made to pre-existing capital stock. The corresponding outcomes are shown to be small, up to only a 0.1 pp increase in budget loss in Italy and Spain, and a 0.1 pp improvement in budget balance in Germany and France. Interestingly, if a net social golden rule was in place in the case of Spain and Italy, this would have been an incentive to spend more to improve their budget balance. describes the hypothetical impact on the calculation of the budget balance that would have been achieved by applying the golden rule to social (healthcare and education) investment, under the two alternative scenarios illustrated above. It is important to point out that the calculations do not take into account the potential increase in investment that could have been driven if the fiscal rule was already in place.

In the first scenario, public expenditure in education and health gross fixed capital formation is exempted from government fiscal targets. In this case, the largest relative gain in all years would be France, with a 0.6 to 0.7 percentage point (pp) decrease in budget deficit. The possible gain for other economies would have been around a 0.3 pp drop in budget deficit in both Italy and Spain, and a 0.3 pp increase in budget surplus in Germany for most of the years. The second scenario assumes a golden rule

---

4   To calculate net investments, i.e. measuring capital consumption of public sector capital stock, we estimated the average lifespan of educational buildings to be around forty years, with a need for at least one major repair or renovation. The useful life of other educational facilities or equipment is expected to be between five and ten years. By contrast, the average useful service life of each investment category in healthcare amounts to twenty-three years in infrastructure, seventeen years in fixed machinery and equipment, and thirteen years in organisational structure. We applied such depreciation rates starting from 1995 and assumed that the depreciation of the investment asset spreads out equally over its lifetime, in a so-called 'straight-line' depreciation.

applied to net public social investment, namely exempting only actual additions made to pre-existing capital stock. The corresponding outcomes are shown to be small, up to only a 0.1 pp increase in budget loss in Italy and Spain, and a 0.1 pp improvement in budget balance in Germany and France. Interestingly, if a net social golden rule was in place in the case of Spain and Italy, this would have been an incentive to spend more to improve their budget balance.

Table 13.2 Estimated volume of investment allowed under a social golden rule.

		2015	2016	2017	2018	2019
DE	BB (% GDP)	1.0	1.2	1.3	1.9	1.5
	Option 1	1.3	1.5	1.6	2.2	1.9
	Option 2	1.01	1.22	1.34	1.96	1.61
IT	BB (% GDP)	-2.6	-2.4	-2.4	-2.2	-1.5
	Option 1	-2.2	-2.1	-2.1	-1.9	-1.2
	Option 2	-2.62	-2.47	-2.46	-2.27	-1.55
FR	BB (% GDP)	-3.6	-3.6	-3.0	-2.3	-3.1
	Option 1	-2.9	-3.0	-2.4	-1.7	-2.5
	Option 2	-3.55	-3.59	-2.98	-2.27	-3.03
ES	BB (% GDP)	-5.2	-4.3	-3.0	-2.5	-2.9
	Option 1	-4.9	-4.0	-2.7	-2.2	-2.6
	Option 2	-5.26	-4.38	-3.04	-2.51	-2.89

Source: authors' calculations.
Note: BB = Budget balance; Option 1: BB excluding gross social investment (% GDP); Option 2: BB excluding net social investment (% GDP).

As observed above, the introduction of a qualified treatment for social investment in healthcare and education would imply a minimum deviation from the historical values of member states' budget balances if we consider only net investments, i.e., only new additional investments. Even in the case of applying the golden rule to gross investments, the amounts involved would not be significantly high. Yet, the idea of an exemption of net gross fixed capital formation is to incentivise countries to invest in order to maintain the existing stock of capital and possibly increase it, so as to fill the infrastructural gap reported above. In terms of legal feasibility, elsewhere we discuss three main options (Corti et al. 2022). There, we recommend—in the short term—an extension of the discretionary approach used by the Commission in the interpretation of the SGP flexibilities to allow for an exemption of social investments, potentially linked to the RRF. In the long term, we envisage a Treaty on the Functioning of the European Union (TFEU) change through the introduction of an investment clause.

Even in this case, however, we recommend that such a qualified treatment should not be applied automatically, but should be accompanied by an adequate assessment from the Commission of the proposed measure's outcomes *vis-à-vis* the country-specific normative framework.

13.4 Amortisation of Public Investments

Another way to operationalise a special treatment of public investment would be to adapt public sector accounting and amortise the monetary cost of an investment over its useful life. Amortisation can take many forms. In practice, most often it is linear, implying that each year a constant proportion of the capital good is amortised. Under this approach, it is the annual amount of amortisation that would be counted as expenditure in the calculation of the fiscal aggregates relevant to the fiscal rules. There would thus be a difference between the cash deficit and the 'economic' one, which would contain only the amortised amount.

Amortisation is different from a golden rule based on net investment, according to which the value of the investment, in the example above for the railway, minus the depreciation of the existing stock of public capital, is exempted from the calculation of the relevant budget indicator and imputed all at once. With the amortisation there is no exemption from the rules. It is the calculation of the budget balance reported in the national accounts that is affected. Yet, for both approaches the calculation of the depreciation of capital investment is central.

Like the calculation of the net investment, adopting the amortisation approach requires careful analysis of the spending that governments classify as investment to isolate the part that creates new long-lived assets.[5] A key issue in this context is to distinguish between maintenance and the construction of entirely new infrastructure, and whether to extend the amortisation approach to pure maintenance spending and repairs. The distinction between the two may create an incentive to favour the building of new infrastructure over maintenance, although it is generally recognised that proper maintenance yields very high returns.

Contrary to the golden rule, the introduction of an amortisation for eligible public investment would not require a change in the current fiscal framework, but a revision of the national public financial management (PFM) systems. Currently, EU member states' PFM systems rely on cash-based, single-entry bookkeeping, which means government revenues and expenditures are recorded in a cash book by putting most of the emphasis on levels of public debt and cash balance (Núñez-Ferrer and Musmeci 2019). This is different to an accrual-based double-entry accounting system, like the one used by New Zealand. Under this approach, a transaction value is reported both on the credit and the debit accounts, ensuring equivalence between the amounts

---

5   Intangible assets are more difficult to amortise because it is harder to determine their useful economic life, yet accounting standards exist.

recorded. Such a reporting approach is traditionally suggested in order to better assess the sustainability of public debts (see Núñez-Ferrer and Musmeci 2019) but it would also allow the amortisation of investment expenses incurred by the government.

As illustrated in Corti et al. (2022), a baseline approach could free between 0.3% and 0.6% of GDP (compared to a single year reporting, however, the remaining value of the investment will appear in a future budget) for social investment. If applied to other categories of investments as well, as should be the case given that the change would imply a different reporting principle in public accounts, the impact would be much larger. Importantly, the change in principle should not deteriorate the quality of public finances. On the contrary, it may even improve it. A key requirement for the change to work is a full transparency of public accounts and high governance standards.

13.5 Conclusions

The interlinkages between the objectives of economic growth, environmental sustainability and social fairness have often been addressed in pairs. Notably, the literature has focused on the interaction between economic growth objectives and either green or social ones, while the focus on the socio-environmental nexus is far more recent. In this respect, the EU has played a key role not only in linking for the first time the three economic, green and social objectives together, but also explicitly addressing the connection between the environmental objectives and the need to maintain high social standards. The EGD, and even more strongly the RRF, were somehow pivotal to shifting political attention, as well as academic interest, to social and environmental objectives, alongside economic growth. Yet, with the EGD the EU initially framed the eco-social nexus following a compensatory logic, whereby social policies intervene to cushion the social consequences of the green transition on the most vulnerable citizens. By contrast, with the Recovery and Resilience Facility, a more comprehensive and integrated understanding of the interlinkages between social and green objectives seems to emerge.

To support the green transition building resilient, activating and inclusive welfare states alongside the post-pandemic recovery, the RRF provides financial support to the EU member states. Such support, however, is not enough to close either the green or the social investment gap by 2030. National governments need many more resources to support their welfare states and infrastructure gaps. This issue brings back the longstanding question of national public investment and how to make sure that they are stable over time and EU fiscal rules are not an impediment. The latter point is particularly important at the present juncture, given the current debate about the reform of the EU fiscal framework. While the political debate has often focused on how to support countries' budgetary efforts in the achievement of green objectives, proposals on how to fill the social infrastructure investment gap far less developed.

In this chapter, we explore the option of introducing a European golden rule to support social investment and illustrate a possible application on healthcare and education investments. The results suggest that such a rule would not only be desirable but also technically and legally feasible. If applied to net investments, it might also function as a disincentive for member states to cut down on social public investment during economic downturns.

In addition, and with a view to a more generalised approach, we consider the possibility of introducing the amortisation of public investment into governments' balance sheets, by revising the national public financial management systems. Following the principle applied to private investment, and giving governments the possibility to amortise investments over several years, instead of budgeting the full amount in one year, could generate a non-negligible fiscal space. It should be stressed that such an approach would not entail direct changes to EU fiscal rules (although they would be affected indirectly), but it would require a change in public accounting rules, as has already been done in other countries.

To conclude, the response to the COVID-19 pandemic and recent developments in energy markets are pushing for an acceleration of the green transition in Europe. The European Commission has taken the lead in setting the framework of the transition: it should be socially just. In this context, the European welfare states have resurfaced, playing a crucial role as guarantors of newly recognised public goods such as public health, social security, poverty relief, and education. Yet, to make the green transition socially just, it is not enough that social policies are deployed to compensate for the externalities of the green transition. An integrated approach, combining activating welfare states with clear environmental objective, is needed. Making sure that all member states are (fiscally) equipped to put in place resilient *activating* welfare states is thus a pre-condition for any post-pandemic strategy that aims to bring together economic growth, environmental sustainability, and social fairness.

References

Alfonso, A. and Furceri, D. (2010) "Government Size, Composition, Volatility and Economic Growth", *European Journal of Political Economy* 26 (4): 517–32, https://doi.org/10.1016/j.ejpoleco.2010.02.002.

Bakker, V. and van Vliet, O. (2019) "Social Investment, Employment Outcomes and Policy and Institutional Complementarities: A Comparative Analysis across 26 OECD Countries", *Department of Economics Research Memorandum* 2019.01, Leiden University, https://10.1017/S0047279421000386.

Barbiero, F. and Z. Darvas (2014) "In Sickness and in Health: Protecting and Supporting Public Investment in Europe", *Bruegel Policy Contribution 2014/02*, https://www.bruegel.org/sites/default/files/wp_attachments/pc_2014_02.pdf.

Barbiero, O. and B. Cournède (2013) "New Econometric Estimates of Long-Term Growth Effects of Different Areas of Public Spending", *OECD Economics Department Working Papers* 1100, December, https://dx.doi.org/10.1787/5k3txn15b59t-en.

Bogaert, H. (2016) "Improving the Stability and Growth Pact by Integrating a Proper Accounting of Public Investments: A New Attempt", *Federal Planning Bureau Working Paper* 1, https://www.plan.be/uploaded/documents/201601211007080.20151221_WP_EN_golden_rule.pdf.

Chu, T., J. Hölscher, and D. McCarthy (2018) "The Impact of Productive and Non-productive Government Expenditure on Economic Growth: An Empirical Analysis in High-income Versus Low- to Middle-income Economies", *Empirical Economics* 58: 2403–30, https://doi.org/10.1007/s00181-018-1616-3.

Corti, F., C. Alcidi, D. Gros, A. Liscai, and F. Shamsfakhr (2022) "A Qualified Treatment for Green and Social Investments within a Revised EU Fiscal Framework", *CEPS Research Report* 2022–02, May, https://papers.ssrn.com/sol3/papers.cfm?abstract_id=4135460.

Darvas, Z. and J. Anderson (2020) "New Life for an Old Framework: Redesigning the European Union's Expenditure and Golden Fiscal Rules", *Study Requested by the ECON committee*, European Parliament Research Service, October, https://www.bruegel.org/sites/default/files/wp-content/uploads/2020/10/IPOL_STU2020645733_EN.pdf.

Darvas, Z. and G. Wolff (2021) "A Green Fiscal Pact: Climate Investment in Times of Budget Consolidation", *Bruegel Policy Contribution* 18/2021, https://www.bruegel.org/sites/default/files/wp_attachments/PC-2021-18-0909.pdf.

Dissou, Y., S. Didic, and T. Yakautsava (2016) "Government Spending on Education, Human Capital Accumulation, and Growth", *Economic Modelling* 58: 9–21, https://doi.org/10.1016/j.econmod.2016.04.015.

European Commission (2019) "The European Green Deal", *Communication from the Commission*, COM(2019) 640 final, 11 December, https://ec.europa.eu/info/sites/default/files/european-green-deal-communication_en.pdf.

European Fiscal Board (2019) "Assessment of EU Fiscal Rules with a Focus on the Six and Two-pack Legislation", https://ec.europa.eu/info/publications/assessment-eu-fiscal-rules-focus-six-and-two-pack-legislation_en.

European Parliament and the Council of the European Union (2021) "Regulation (EU) 2021/241 Establishing the Recovery and Resilience Facility", 12 February, https://eur-lex.europa.eu/legal-content/EN/LSU/?uri=CELEX:32021R0241.

Feigl, G. and A. Truger (2015) "The Golden Rule of Public Investment. Protecting Fiscal Leeway and Public Infrastructure", *ETUI Policy Brief* 12, https://www.etui.org/sites/default/files/Policy%20Brief%202015.12%20Feigl%20Truger.pdf.

Fournier, J. (2016) "The Positive Effect of Public Investment on Potential Growth", *OECD Economics Department Working Papers* 1347, https://doi.org/10.1787/18151973.

Fournier, J. and Å. Johansson (2016), "The Effect of the Size and Mix of Public Spending on Growth and Inequality", *OECD Economics Department Working Papers* 1344, https://www.oecd.org/economy/the-effect-of-the-size-and-mix-of-public-spending-on-growth-and-inequality.htm.

Fransen, L., G. del Bufalo, and E. Reviglio (2018) "Boosting Investment in Social Infrastructure in Europe. Report of the High-Level Task Force on Investing in Social Infrastructure in Europe", *European Economy Discussion Papers* 074.

Gemmell, N., R. Kneller, and I. Sanz (2016) "Does the Composition of Government Expenditure Matter for Long-Run GDP Levels?", *Oxford Bulletin of Economics and Statistics* 78 (4): 522–47.

Giavazzi, F., V. Guerrieri, G. Lorenzoni, and C. Weymuller (2021) "Revising the European Fiscal Framework", https://www.governo.it/sites/governo.it/files/documenti/documenti/Notizie-allegati/Reform_SGP.pdf.

Hemerijck, A., R. Huguenot-Noel, F. Corti, and D. Rinaldi (2020) "Social Investment Now! Advancing Social Europe Through the EU Budget", *FEPS Report, https://www.researchgate. net/publication/350886633_SOCIAL_INVESTMENT_NOW_Advancing_Social_Europe_ through_the_EU_Budget.*

Hemerijck, A., B. Burgoon, A. Di Pietro, and S. Vydra (2016), "Assessing Social Investment Synergies (ASIS), A Project to Measure the Returns of Social Policies", *Report for DG EMPL*, European Commission, Brussels.

Laurent, E. (2015) "Social-Ecology: Exploring the Missing Link in Sustainable Development", *Documents de Travail de l'OFCE* 2015–07, https://hal-sciencespo.archives-ouvertes.fr/ hal-01136326/document.

Mandelli, M. (2021) "Conceptualizing Eco-social Policies: An Analytical Attempt", unpublished paper presented at the *ECPR Joint Sessions of Workshops 2021*, Session 'Climate Change and the Eco-Social Transformation of Society', virtual event, 27–28 May 2021.

Matthies, A. L. (2017) "The Conceptualisation of Ecosocial Transition", in A. L. Matthies and K. Närhi (eds), *The Ecosocial Transition of Societies: The Contribution of Social Work and Social Policy*, London, Routledge, pp. 17–35.

Morozumi, A. and F. Veiga (2016) "Public Spending and Growth: The Role of Government Accountability", *European Economic Review* 89 (C): 148–71, https://10.1016/j. euroecorev.2016.07.001.

Núñez Ferrer, J. and R. Musmeci (2019) "Beyond Public Debt The Hidden Rapid Erosion of EU Government Balance Sheets is a Financial Threat to Society", *CEPS Research Report* No 10, March, https://www.ceps.eu/publications/beyond-public-debt.

Pekanov, A. and M. Schratzenstaller (2020) "The Role of Fiscal Rules in Relation with the Green Economy", *EP Study*, September, https://www.europarl.europa.eu/RegData/etudes/ STUD/2020/614524/IPOL_STU(2020)614524_EN.pdf.

Reuter, W.H. (2020), "Benefits and Drawbacks of an "Expenditure Rule", As Well As of a "Golden Rule", in the EU Fiscal Framework. Euro Area Scrutiny', *Study Requested by the ECON Committee*, European Parliament Research Service, September, https://www.europarl. europa.eu/RegData/etudes/STUD/2020/645732/IPOL_STU(2020)645732_EN.pdf.

Sabato, S., M. Mandelli, and B. Vanhercke (2021) "The Socio-Ecological Dimension of the EU Recovery. From the European Green Deal to the Recovery and Resilience Facility", *Eurosocial Social Cohesion Learning Series*, Eurosocial Collection 24, https://www.researchgate.net/ publication/354751682_The_Socio-Ecological_Dimension_of_the_EU_Recovery_From_the_ European_Green_Deal_to_the_Recovery_and_Resilience_Facility.

Truger, A. (2016) "The Golden Rule of Public Investment—A Necessary and Sufficient Reform of the EU Fiscal Framework?", *IMK at the Hans Boeckler Foundation, Macroeconomic Policy Institute*, IMK Working Paper 168–2016, https://www.boeckler.de/pdf/p_imk_wp_168_2016.pdf.

Vesper, D. (2007) "Staatsverschuldung und öffentliche Investitionen. Studie im Auftrag der Hans-Böckler-Stiftung", *IMK Policy Brief*, November, http://hdl.handle.net/10419/107079.

Zimmermann, K. and P. Graziano (2020) "Mapping Different Worlds of Eco-Welfare States", *Sustainability*, 12 (5): 18–19, https://doi.org/10.3390/su12051819.

Zuleeg, F. and J. Schneider (2015) "What Role for Social Investment in the New Economic Governance of the Eurozone?", *EPC Policy Brief*.

Contributor Biographies

Cinzia Alcidi is Director of Research and Head of the Economic Policy Unit and the Jobs & Skills Unit at the Centre for European Policy Studies (CEPS) in Brussels. She is also Lecturer at the University of Ghent (Belgium). Her main research interests include macroeconomics, economic policies, labour markets and EU governance. Cinzia holds a PhD in International Economics from the Graduate Institute of International and Development Studies, Geneva (Switzerland).

Claudio Baccianti is Senior Associate at Agora Energiewende in Brussels. He works primarily on green fiscal policy, sustainable finance and the EU Green Deal. Previously, he was an Economist at a global macro hedge fund in London. Claudio started working on climate policy at the Centre for European Economic Research (ZEW) in 2011, where he specialised in developing modelling tools to assess the impacts of environmental and innovation policies. Between 2018 and 2019, he was a PhD candidate at the European Central Bank and he interned at the International Monetary Fund during the Summer of 2017. Claudio holds a PhD in Economics from Tilburg University and has a MSc in Economics and Econometrics from the University of Essex. He previously studied Economics at the University of Siena and the University of Florence.

Daniel Balsalobre-Lorente is Professor at the Department of Political Economy and Public Finance, Economics and Business Statistics and Economic Policy of the University of Castilla-La Mancha, Spain. His expertise is in public finances, energy economics, economic growth, environment, tourism and innovation processes. He has published numerous papers in international refereed journals including *Energy Economics, Technological Forecasting and Social Change, Journal of Cleaner Production, Sustainability, Environmental Science and Pollution Research, Resources Policy, Energy Policy, Energies,* and *Journal of Public Affairs*, among others. He has been an editor and reviewer of indexed journals and handbooks.

Giovanni Barbieri is a Research Fellow at Cranec (Centro di ricerche in analisi economica e sviluppo economico internazionale) at Università Cattolica del Sacro Cuore. He holds a PhD (2017) in Institutions and Policies. He previously worked as Adjunct Professor of History of International and Commercial Institutions at the University of Palermo (DEMS, Italy) and Project Researcher on the Kone Foundation Project "Regional Challenges to Multilateralism", based at Tampere University,

Finland. His main expertise is in international political economy (IPE), in particular the problem of uneven deveolopment and the new challenges posed by developing countries to the current global governance scheme.

Nicoletta Batini is the Lead Evaluator of the International Monetary Fund's Independent Evaluation Office. Prior to the IMF, she was Advisor to the Bank of England's Monetary Policy Committee, Professor of Economics at the University of Surrey, and Director of the International Economics and Policy Office of Italy's Department of the Treasury. She holds a PhD in international finance (SSSUPS Anna) and a PhD in Monetary Economics (University of Oxford). Currently, her research focuses on the economics of energy and land and sea use transitions for climate mitigation. Her new book, *The Economics of Sustainable Food: Smart Policies for People and the Planet*, was published in June 2021 by Island Press and the IMF.

Andrea Brasili is a Senior Economist at the EIB (Luxembourg) where his research interests are both micro (firm level) data analysis and macroeconomic developments, in particular those related to fiscal policy. He received his PhD in Public Economics from the University of Pavia (Italy). Before joining the EIB, he worked in the private sector (in Italian banks and asset management companies) as a research economist, whilst still collaborating with academia.

Floriana Cerniglia is a Full Professor of Economics at Università Cattolica del Sacro Cuore (Milan) and Director of CRANEC (Centro di ricerche in analisi economica e sviluppo economico internazionale) She is the Co-Editor-in-Chief of *EconomiaPolitica, Journal of Analytical and Institutional Economics*. She received her PhD from the University of Warwick (UK) and her research interests lie in public economics and macroeconomic policies. She has published in leading international journals and she has coordinated and participated in a number of peer-reviewed research projects.

Francesco Corti is an Advisor to the Belgian Minister of Social Affairs and Health of Belgium, an Associate Research Fellow at CEPS, and Adjunct Professor at the University of Milan, where he teaches economic and social governance of the EU. He is an expert in European social and employment policies, EU budget, EMU governance and social investment. Francesco is also external expert at the European Court of Auditors, Eurofound. Francesco holds a PhD in Political Science from the University of Milan.

Claudio De Vincenti is Professor of Economics at the University of Rome La Sapienza and Senior Fellow at the LUISS School of European Political Economy. His main fields of research are: competition and market regulation, macroeconomic theory, economic policy and public economics. He was the Director of the PhD Programme in Economics of the University La Sapienza and is currently a Member of the Scientific Council of the LUISS School of European Political Economy and of the Scientific Council of Fondazione ASTRID. He is the author of several books on macroeconomic theory, regulation theory and practice, economic policy, and has published a number of articles in Italian and international journals. Over the years he has held institutional appointments in the Italian Government and currently he is the Chairman of the Aeroporti di Roma company.

Mario Di Serio is a Research Fellow at the University of Salerno. He has been a consultant for the Cohesion Policies Department of the Presidency of the Italian Council of Ministers since 2021. He worked as an economic consultant for the Italian Ministry of Economics and Finance from 2017 to 2021. In 2018 he obtained a PhD in Economics from the University of Salerno, with a thesis on the non-linear effects of fiscal policies on EA and US economies. His research focuses mainly on fiscal policy, monetary policy and macroeconometrics.

Lorenzo Ferrari is Lecturer in Microeconomics and Public Economics at the Department of Economics and Finance of LUISS Guido Carli. Moreover, he is currently the manager of the CESARE Laboratory for Experimental Economics, where he is responsible for the organisation and implementation of experiments on economic behaviour. Lorenzo was previously a Post-doctoral Research Fellow at, and still collaborates with, the School of European Political Economy of Luiss Guido Carli. The main focus of his research project was issues related to public investment in the European Union and Italy. In recent years he has taught as Adjunct Professor at LUISS, John Cabot University, and the University of Rome Tor Vergata, where he obtained his PhD in Economics, Law, and Institutions. His research interests are public policy and finance, experimental economics, and political economy.

Matteo Fragetta is an Associate Professor of Macroeconomics at the University of Salerno. Previously, he has been Visiting Scholar at the Cass Business School (with Professor Lucio Sarno) and at the University of Leicester. His research focuses on fiscal and monetary policy from an empirical point of view and on the role played by active and passive policy on labour outcome. He holds a PhD in the Economics of the Public Sector from the University of Salerno.

Zaihan Gao is Lecturer of Economics and Finance of the Built Environment at the Bartlett School of Sustainable Construction at University College London. Zaihan holds a doctorate in finance from Durham University and has published several papers in top journals (including *Transportation Research* and *Finance Research Letters*) in finance, management, sustainable and transport economics. Zaihan is also the principal investigator of a collaborative research and enterprise project between Shenzhen Green-Tech Institute of Applied Environmental Technology Co. Ltd and UCL, focusing on the future-proof emission reduction credit standard.

Miguel Gil Tertre is the Chief Economist at the Directorate General for Energy of the European Commission. He leads the team responsible for modelling the impact and ensuring the economic coherence of policy proposals in the field of energy. His previous responsibilities include the negotiation of the Recovery and Resilience Plans for Poland, Czechia, Hungary and Slovakia and the coordination of the European Semester. As a member of the Cabinet of Vice President Katainen, he was responsible for the design and coordination of the investment plan for Europe (known as the 'Juncker' Plan). He was assistant to the Director General in charge of Economic and Financial Affairs during the euro crisis (2011–2014). Prior to joining the Commission, he worked for ten years on network industries regulation. Miguel Gil Tertre has an MBA from the Instituto de Empresa Business School and two degrees in economics from the Paris IX-Dauphine and Autonomous University of Madrid (special graduation award).

Giuseppe Francesco Gori is a researcher at IRPET (Istituto Regionale Programmazione Economica della Toscana), where he works on public economics. His most recent activities have focused on the analysis of the efficiency profiles of public spending with particular attention to the public procurement market and the impact evaluation of public investments. His recent work has focused on public spending and contract reforms, and he has authored numerous research reports and contributions to the debate, including: G. F. Gori, P. Lattarulo, and M. Mariani (2017) "Understanding the procurement performance of local governments: A duration analysis of public works", *Environment and Planning C: Politics and Space* 35 (5), 809; and Giuseppe Francesco Gori, Lucio Landi, and Patrizia Lattarulo (2020) "The procurement of public works in light of recent reforms", *UPB working notes* 2/2020.

Daniel Gros is Member of the Board and Distinguished Fellow at CEPS, where he has been Director from 2000 to 2020. Prior to joining CEPS, Daniel worked at the IMF and at the European Commission. His main areas of expertise are the European monetary union, macroeconomic policy, public finance, banking, and financial markets. Daniel holds a PhD in Economics from the University of Chicago.

Meriem Hamdi-Cherif is an environmental economic researcher. After sixteen years spent at CIRED in the Imaclim Energy-Economy Modeling team, she joined the ThreeME team of the Environment Division at OFCE (Observatoire Français des Conjonctures Économiques). She studies the interactions between energy, economy and the environment; the choice of climate policy instruments and the articulation between domestic policies and international agreements. Her PhD focused on analysing the costs and opportunities for China to transition to a low-carbon economy in an adverse overall economic context.

Lucía Ibáñez-Luzon is a PhD candidate in Economics at UCLM, and a regulation and energy markets specialist at EDP Comercial. She has broad expertise in energy economics and the environment, and she has been working in the energy and environment field since 2014 within the public and private sectors and at both national and international levels. Her email is lucia.iba@opendeusto.es.

Atanas Kolev is Principal Advisor at the Economics Department of the EIB. He has worked on a wide range of topics related to investment and investment financing at the firm-, sector-, and economy-wide levels. He has been an organiser and contributor to the annual economics conference of the EIB on topics like economic and social cohesion, investment in the energy sector, adaptation to climate change, public investment, and infrastructure investment. Atanas Kolev is currently a coordinator, reviewer, and economics editor for the EIB Annual Investment Report. He holds an Economics PhD from Universitat Autònoma de Barcelona.

Patrizia Lattarulo is Head of Research Unit on Public Economy and Territorial Policies at IRPET (Regional Institute for Economic Planning of Tuscany at Villa la Quiete alle Montalve). She works on federalism and public services, decentralised taxation, investment and infrastructure.

Klaas Lenaerts is a Research Analyst at Bruegel. He holds a Master's in Economics from KU Leuven and in European Economic Studies from the College of Europe. Additionally, he spent one semester at Uppsala University. Before joining Bruegel he worked as a trainee on EU enlargement discussions at the Belgian Permanent Representation, and at the European Securities and Markets Authority in Paris, where he contributed to the work of the Risk Analysis and Economics Department on sustainable finance.

Xi Liang is currently Professor of Sustainable Construction and Project Management at the Bartlett School of Sustainable Construction at University College London. Xi is a Standing Committee Member for China's Climate Investment and Finance Association (CIFA) and Deputy Director for China's Carbon Capture, Utilization and Storage (CCUS) Committee, within the Chinese Society for Environmental Sciences. He is also the core advisory member in the drafting of China's Climate Investment and Finance Policy Document and in the development of regional pilots. Xi is also a key project member for various climate finance projects in China, including standard development, policy formulation and municipal climate finance pilots, and has delivered training on climate finance to municipal government officials. Xi has been appointed as the International Lead of the Asian Development Bank's CCS Centre of Excellence (Guangdong) Project, PI of the World Bank Network Carbon Market (China), and PI of multiple UK Foreign and Commonwealth Government Office (FCO) Strategic Programme Fund projects.

Alessandro Liscai is an Associate Research Assistant at CEPS (Brussels) and a Research Assistant at Astrid Foundation (Rome). He holds a BSc in Economics and Management from Luiss University (Rome), an MSc in Economics from Nova School of Business and Economics (Lisbon) and an MA in European Economic Governance from Luiss School of European Political Economy (Rome).

Paul Malliet is a Senior Economist at the French Economic Observatory (OFCE), working on macroeconomic modelling of climate and energy transition policies. He is part of the team working on the development of the THREEME model (Multisector Macroeconomic Model for the Evaluation of Environmental and Energy policy) in collaboration with the French Environmental Agency (ADEME). Its latest research includes carbon accounting from a consumption-based perspective, redistributive impacts of the climate and energy policies and economic impacts and assessment of the economic impact of a low-carbon economy transition.

Adolfo Maza is Full Professor at the University of Cantabria. Professor Maza received his PhD in Economics in 2002. Later on, he completed a postdoctoral role at the University of Berkeley. His main areas of research include regional economics, economic integration and globalisation, the labour market, migration, and energy economics. He has published more than seventy papers in various international scientific journals, most of them included in the Journal Citation Report (JCR) database. He has also participated in many international congresses and meetings. He was awarded the "Young Researchers Prize" by the Spanish Regional Science Association. He is the Coordinator in Spain of the Erasmus Mundus Joint Master in Economics of Globalisation and European Integration (EGEI). Finally, he has acted as a reviewer for numerous scientific journals, as well as for international funding agencies such as the National Science Foundation (USA), the Austrian Science Fund, and the Czech Science Foundation.

Valentina Meliciani is Full Professor of Applied Economics at the University LUISS Guido Carli, where she is also Director of the School of European Political Economy and Coordinator of the PhD in Management. She has a Master's in International Economics from Sussex University, a PhD from SPRU (Sussex University) and a doctorate from the University of Rome Tor Vergata. She has held the positions of Full Professor of Economic Policy at the University of Teramo, Visiting Fellow at SPRU (Sussex University), Visiting Scholar at the University of Minnesota and Visiting Professor at the London School of Economics. She has published in international refereed journals in the fields of industrial economics, international economics, regional economics and economics of innovation. She has participated in EU-funded research projects on the social and economic changes created by the new information-based economy.

Giovanni Melina is a Senior Economist in the African Department of the IMF. Previously, he worked for several years in the IMF's Research Department, as an Associate Professor of Macroeconomics at City University London, and as a Research Fellow at the University of Surrey. His research focuses on understanding the sources and propagation of macroeconomic shocks, on the design of monetary and fiscal stabilisation policies, and the link between macroeconomic policy and growth in developing countries. Recently, his research has also focused on green investments, the effects of climate change on the macroeconomic outcomes of disaster-prone countries and related policies. He holds a PhD in Economics from Birkbeck, University of London.

Mathieu Plane is a Deputy Director of the Analysis and Forecasting Department at OFCE, the research centre in economics at Sciences Po in Paris. He is in charge of economic forecasts for the French economy and works on economic policy issues. He has written several articles in scientific journals and has participated in several reports for public institutions. He teaches at Sciences Po, Paris and at the University of Paris Panthéon-Sorbonne. In 2013–2014, he was economic advisor to the Ministers of the Economy, Industry, and Digital Sector. He speaks and writes regularly in the media. He has recently published, in collaboration with other authors from the OFCE, *Budget 2019: Purchasing Power but Deficit, Saving(s) Growth: Economic Outlook for the French Economy 2019–2021*, and *French Economy 2020* .

Debora Revoltella has been Director of the Economics Department of the European Investment Bank since April 2011. The department comprises thirty economists and provides economic analysis and studies to support the bank in defining its policies and strategies. Before joining the EIB, Debora worked for many years at CESEE, was head of the research department in COMIT, and later worked as Chief Economist for CESEE in UniCredit. Debora holds a PhD in Economics and has also worked as Adjunct Professor at Bocconi University. She is a member of the Steering Committees of the Vienna Initiative and CompNet, an alternate member of the Board of the Joint Vienna Institute, and a member of the boards of SUERF and the Euro 50 Group.

Frederic Reynès holds a PhD in economics (Sciences Po Paris) and is a specialist in macroeconomic modelling and quantitative analysis methods. His main expertise and research interests are in applied macroeconomics, energy and environmental issues (in particular fiscal policies and the oil market), and the labour market. He has solid experience in implementing research and studies for national and international institutions (UNDP, AFD, ADEME, COR, European Commission, Eurostat, FAO). He is currently director of the NEO (Netherlands Economic Observatory), and is also an associate researcher at OFCE (Observatoire Français des Conjonctures Economiques), where he is in charge of the Environment Unit. In the framework of a research collaboration with ADEME, he supervises the development of the ThreeME model (Multi-sector Macroeconomic Model for the Evaluation of Environmental and Energy Policy).

Katja Rietzler is Head Unit of Fiscal Policy at the Macroeconomic Policy Institute (IMK), part of the Hans-Böckler Foundation. She holds a PhD from the Freie Universität, Berlin. Among other topics, her research focuses on fiscal issues of the municipalities, the German tax system, public investment needs, and fiscal rules. In addition, she is responsible for the IMK's macroeconometric model. As an expert she regularly participates in parliamentary hearings on issues such as tax legislation, annual budgets, or the debt brake and its implementation.

Francesco Saraceno is Deputy Department Director at OFCE, the research centre in economics at Sciences Po in Paris. He holds PhDs in Economics from Columbia University and the Sapienza University of Rome. His research focuses on the relationship between inequality, macroeconomic performance, and European macroeconomic policies. From 2000–2002 he was a member of the Council of Economic Advisors for the Italian Prime Minister's Office. He teaches international and European macroeconomics at Sciences Po, where he manages the Economics concentration of the Master's in European Affairs, and in Rome (Luiss). He is Academic Director of the Sciences Po-Northwestern European Affairs Program. He is a member of the Scientific Board for the LUISS School of European Political Economy and formerly of the Confindustria's Scientific Committee. He advises the International Labour Organization (ILO) on macroeconomic policies for employment and participates in IMF training programmes on fiscal policy.

Bert Saveyn is the Team Leader of the Modelling team in the Chief Economist unit of DG ENER. Before joining DG ENER, he worked for the Impact Assessment and Better Regulation unit of the Secretariat General of the European Commission; and was Team Leader in the Economics of Energy, Climate Change and Transport unit of the Joint Research Centre in Sevilla. He holds a PhD in economics and a Master in environmental engineering from the KU Leuven.

Jochen Schanz is Senior Economist at the European Investment Bank. After a PhD in game theory at the European University Institute, he worked at Lehman Brothers, the Bank of England, and the Bank for International Settlements on monetary and financial stability. At the European Investment Bank, he focuses on public investment and human capital.

Simone Tagliapietra is a Researcher at the Faculty of Political and Social Sciences of the Catholic University of the Sacred Heart in Milan. He is also a Senior Fellow at Bruegel and an Adjunct Professor of Global Energy and Climate Policy at the Johns Hopkins University—SAIS Europe in Bologna. He has published in leading scientific and policy journals such as *Nature, Science* and *Foreign Affairs,* and he is the author of *Global Energy Fundamentals* (Cambridge University Press, 2020). His columns and policy work are published and cited in leading international media, such as *BBC, CNN, The New York Times, The Financial Times,* and *The Wall Street Journal.* He is Member of the Board of Directors of the Clean Air Task Force in Boston. He holds a PhD in Institutions and Policies from the Catholic University of the Sacred Heart in Milan.

Alexandre Tourbah is an economist who graduated from Sciences Po and École des Ponts, specialising in the economic impact assessment of resource uses. After his first role at the French Water Circle (Centre Français de l'Eau), Alexandre has now joined the OFCE to work specifically on the assessment of infrastructure requirements in the context of a low-carbon transition.

José Villaverde is Full Professor of Economics (University of Cantabria). He received his PhD in Economics from the University of País Vasco. He has been Visiting Professor at many universities in Denmark, England, Taiwan, China, United States, Belgium, Chile, Poland, Czech Republic, Ecuador and Argentina. The scope of his current research interests encompasses international and regional economics, economic integration, and globalisation and the labour market. He has authored several books and published more than 150 papers in refereed journals. He has also participated in many international congresses and meetings. He has acted as a consultant for the World Bank and the European Commission. He has also served as a reviewer for numerous scientific journals in the field of Economics.

Anthony Waldron is a specialist in biodiversity finance and economics, based at the Cambridge Conservation Initiative in Cambridge University. He was lead author on the global economic analysis for the CBD 30x30 target and is Director of the biodiversity economics consultancy WACC. He led on the creation of the global database of conservation spending and published the first analysis of the effectiveness of that spending worldwide, in the journal *Nature*. Before Cambridge, he also worked at Oxford University, the National University of Singapore, UESC Brazil, and as Conservation Director of Fundacion Maquipucuna in South America.

Andrew Watt is Head Unit of European Economic Policy at the Macroeconomic Policy Institute (IMK), part of the Hans-Böckler Foundation. He holds a PhD from the University of Hamburg. His main research areas are European economic and employment policy and comparative political economy, with a particular interest in the interaction between wage-setting and macroeconomic policy. Recent work has focused on reform of the economic governance of the euro area, emphasising the need to coordinate monetary, fiscal, and wage policy in order to achieve balanced growth and favourable employment outcomes. He has served as advisor to numerous European and national institutions, including the European Commission, the European Economic and Social Committee, and Eurofound.

Guntram Wolff is a political economist working on the European economy and governance, climate change and geoeconomics. He is the director and CEO of the German Council on Foreign Relations. From 2013–2022, he was the director of Bruegel. He is also a part time professor at the Free University Brussels. His work has been published in academic journals such as *Nature, Science, Nature Communications, Energy Policy*, and the *European Journal of Political Economy* and policy outlets such as *Foreign Affairs* and *The Financial Times*.

List of Illustrations

List of Tables

About the Team

Alessandra Tosi was the managing editor for this book.

Melissa Purkiss and Sarah Harris performed the copy-editing and proofreading.

Jeevanjot Nagpal designed the cover. The cover was produced in InDesign using the Fontin font.

Luca Baffa typeset the book in InDesign and produced the paperback and hardback editions. The text font is Tex Gyre Pagella; the heading font is Californian FB.

Luca produced the EPUB, AZW3, PDF, HTML, and XML editions — the conversion is performed with open source software such as pandoc (https://pandoc.org/) created by John MacFarlane and other tools freely available on our GitHub page (https://github.com/OpenBookPublishers).

This book need not end here...

Share

All our books — including the one you have just read — are free to access online so that students, researchers and members of the public who can't afford a printed edition will have access to the same ideas. This title will be accessed online by hundreds of readers each month across the globe: why not share the link so that someone you know is one of them?

This book and additional content is available at:

https://doi.org/10.11647/OBP.0328

Donate

Open Book Publishers is an award-winning, scholar-led, not-for-profit press making knowledge freely available one book at a time. We don't charge authors to publish with us: instead, our work is supported by our library members and by donations from people who believe that research shouldn't be locked behind paywalls.

Why not join them in freeing knowledge by supporting us: https://www.openbookpublishers.com/support-us

Follow @OpenBookPublish

Read more at the Open Book Publishers **BLOG**

You may also be interested in:

Transforming Conservation
A Practical Guide to Evidence and Decision Making
William J. Sutherland (ed.)

https://doi.org/10.11647/OBP.0321

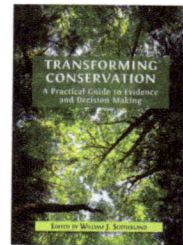

Politics and the Environment in Eastern Europe
Eszter Krasznai Kovacs (ed.)

https://doi.org/10.11647/OBP.0244

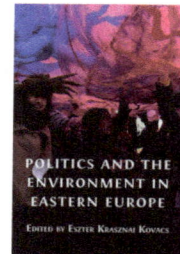

Negotiating Climate Change in Crisis
Steffen Böhm and Sian Sullivan (eds.)

https://doi.org/10.11647/OBP.0265

www.ingramcontent.com/pod-product-compliance
Lightning Source LLC
Chambersburg PA
CBHW050236220326

41598CB00044B/7416